Moral
Personhood

SUNY Series in Ethical Theory
Robert B. Loudon, editor

Moral
Personhood

*An Essay in the Philosophy
of Moral Psychology*

G. E. Scott

State University of New York Press

Published by
State University of New York Press, Albany

©1990 State University of New York

For information, address State University of New York Press,
State University Plaza, Albany, N.Y., 12246

Library of Congress Cataloging-in-Publication Data

Scott, G. E., 1931-
    Moral personhood : an essay in the philosophy of moral psychology
/ G.E. Scott.
        p.   cm. — (SUNY series in ethical theory)
    Includes bibliographical references.
    ISBN 0-7914-0321-1. — ISBN 0-7914-0322-X (pbk.)
    1. Ethics.   2. Self (Philosophy)   I. Title.   II. Series.
BJ1031.S37   1990   89-39221
170—dc20   CIP

10   9   8   7   6   5   4   3   2   1

To D.C.D.—
whose writings roused me from several sorts of slumber

CONTENTS

PREFACE

In our efforts to get our thinking clear in moral matters, some concepts in particular have seemed to cause more difficulty than others whenever anyone—not excluding those of us who are professional philosophers—has tried to deal with some of the issues involved. This has meant that some discussions of certain moral issues have been at cross purposes through no fault of the discussants: for at times the protagonists have not really been arguing *with* each other at all, for the reason that they have not been employing the same concepts. This unfortunate state of affairs has been highly visible in many public abortion debates, where there has been and continues to be obvious disagreement about the meaning and proper application of 'human' or 'person'. Convincing the discussants that such is the case, however, is seldom an easy matter and is sometimes not even possible. While it has been one of the traditional jobs of philosophers to deal with precisely this sort of problem, it is true, alas, that they also are as prone as anyone else to arguing past, rather than with, each other in this way—especially if they are grinding certain axes, which frequently they are.

If there is any one concept that is central to the whole enterprise of moral thinking, it is very likely that of moral personhood. It is surprising, indeed, that while philosophers have lavished an enormous amount of attention upon the notion of personal *identity*, relatively little has been given to the notion of what constitutes a *moral* person. In fact, in many books on ethical matters there is not even an entry in the index for "person," much less a discussion of what it is to be a person in a sense appropriate to the subject of ethics. I suppose it has just been assumed that we all know what persons are, since we—you, my dear reader, and I—are persons, after all! It is quite likely that many of us should not have thought it necessary even to raise certain kinds of questions about the nature of persons if not for some of the remarkable developments in medical technology in the last few years.[1]

It is ironic indeed that the technology that has made possible the rescue of persons once thought irretrievably lost to death—and so given a new lease on life (whatever its quality)—has at the same time produced new forms of personal bondage. For it has become routine for paramedical personnel to perform what only a short time ago would have been looked upon as miracles as they, arriving upon the scene of some awful mishap, restore a clinically dead individual to life. But these techniques, and the refinements of them made possible in many modern medical centers, are not necessarily respecters of persons: the order to resuscitate may be a blind order, and may be carried out as part of a mechanical routine. No matter that the individuals being resuscitated may not *want* to be resuscitated: they may awaken once again in the very straightjacket of pain and immobility thought escaped from for good with the coming of death.[2]

It is not that those who issue these orders, or that those who carry them out, necessarily *intend* to place anyone in a straightjacket. Their general intention, of course—presumably via Hippocrates (who happily for him was born more than two millenia too soon to have enjoyed the technology now current)—is to liberate those upon whom their orders are executed, to make possible life, and life more abundant.[3] And, it perhaps goes without saying, to escape the very real bogeyman of malpractice suits (that marvelous American growth industry and lucrative contribution to the practice of law which is now having serious effects upon the availability of medical care in certain specialties such as obstetrics)—whether or not the patient upon whom they are lavishing their expensive attention is, with his or her family, pushed into penury.

Now I, by putting the matter in this way, am undoubtedly exercising a certain degree of dramatic license. It is not true that *all* of those experiencing very steep medical expenses find themselves facing bankruptcy. But there are certain assumptions being made in the course of such practices in medical matters, assumptions of a variety of sorts, but many of them involving notions connected with that of moral personhood, and many of them just as difficult to unearth and to expose to careful scrutiny as that of moral personhood itself. One of my purposes in this essay is to bring to light a number of these assumptions, and to examine them very critically indeed. My aim is not just to illuminate these assumptions and the concepts upon which they depend, but by so doing to help to create a way in which our practice might be modified in light of our clearer concepts. By our practice, I understand not just medical matters, but matters involving legislation, jurisprudence, and moral philosophy as well, and ultimately, as is sometimes portentously said, the very fabric of our society. And connected with these areas is a wide array of other matters involving morality and the quality of our lives as individuals and as members of an assortment of communities.

Our generally accepted right (in the United States) as individuals to the refusal of medical treatment, for example, collides directly with the socially and legally imposed duty placed upon certain parties to render aid. Unfortunately, in practice this right has been at times rather capriciously recognized, for it is a right the exercise of which may require, in a manner significantly different from some other rights, the special assistance of other persons when the individual concerned, for a variety of reasons, is unable to exercise it for him/herself. The collision has worked sometimes more to the detriment of the individual than to the aid-giving parties, and the needed legal remedies are slow in coming. Also slow in arriving, of course, are the changed perceptions of a large segment of our society that may be not only the necessary precursors of legal change, but perceptions themselves providing the only environment in which law itself can reliably function.

So far as my own perceptions are concerned, if I might refer to some actual cases that had the greatest initial effect in removing the scales from my eyes, it would be just two: those of Joan Robinson and John Storar. Joan Robinson (as reported in "The Story of Joan Robinson," a documentary film first shown on Public Television during the 1970s) elected, with the assistance of her husband, not to commit suicide ("euthanize" herself) but to proceed with recommended medical treatment for her terminal cancer. As a condition of doing this she proposed that a cinematic record be made of the course her life was to take during her last months, as a service to others. The impact upon the viewer of this unsettling documentary is considerably heightened by the fact that as funds ran low it was necessary to switch from color to black and white film at about the time that her life became more and more confined to a hospital environment, and her existence became increasingly constricted by the improvisational nature of the medical treatment provided. "Quality of life" as referring to a concept forming a part of the notions connected with the notion of moral personhood thus became graphically apparent to me.

John Storar, at the time the legal resolution of his case was commented upon in an editorial in the *New York Times*,[4] was a fifty-two-year-old individual with the apparent mental development of an eighteen-month-old child, who also was suffering from a form of terminal cancer. The New York Court of Appeals (ruling after Mr. Storar's death) overturned the ruling of a lower court which (on petition from Mr. Storar's mother) had allowed that blood transfusions be withheld from Mr. Storar (resulting, presumably, in his death). The (nonunanimous) ruling of the appeals court (according to the editorial writer) was based in part on the ground that even if Mr. Storar were competent he would be in no position to make a judgment with regard to his own fate: he was entitled, in effect, to the protection afforded children. This case brought home to me the obscurities present in ideas we employ every day— and in courts of law: what a child is, what mothering is (or parenting), what "competence" entails, etc. How these obscurities are related to being a moral person (or *not* being one), as indicated by the uneasiness many of us feel about the outcomes of such legal deliberations, is an area clearly calling for careful examination. The cases of J. Robinson and J. Storar by no means exemplify all of the notions I intend to examine in the course of this study. I shall be describing other actual and possible cases as I proceed.

Probably the greatest single problem I have encountered in trying to get my own thinking in order has been that of finding a perspicuous scheme or framework for assembling the notions and concepts that seem to be required for sorting out the nature of moral personhood. A conceptual scheme, as those familiar with the philosophic enterprise well know, seldom lends itself to any straightforward simple ordering. And if one shares the belief (as do I) held by a number of philosophers that there is no such thing as *the* correct conceptual scheme, the task of finding an optimum one is part of an unending process of refinement. One of the many difficulties besetting any attempt to come up with a conceptual scheme adequate to the task of capturing the nature of moral personhood is that the scheme must in a fairly straightforward manner "correspond to reality" in something like the way in which a theory in experimental science corresponds to reality: it cannot be merely an imaginative exercise of the essentially unfinishable sort found in some works of fiction, nor can it be the promulgation of a dogma; it also must be amenable to revision as our knowledge develops. Furthermore, it must have the feature of universalizability; in spite of apparent differences among persons in ordinary ways of speaking, there must be common features as well. The nature of morality, it is quite generally agreed, requires this. I shall have more to say about such matters below, when the time comes to set about the task of actually setting up the conceptual framework and sketching in the nature of moral personhood.

The need for an adequate account of the nature of moral personhood has clearly become more and more pressing during the time since I began my serious deliberations (*circa* 1981).

ITEM: In the Spring of 1983, Robert Veatch (Professor of Medical Ethics at the Kennedy Institute of Ethics), in a presentation at a conference at the East Carolina Medical School, depicted in a vivid fictional scenario a practice that has already become common: the shuttling, from one hospital (usually profit-making) to another (usually non-profit-making) of patients unable to pay for their own treatment. Veatch described the possible need for what he (jokingly) called a "medivan"—a vehicle so fully equipped that it could provide full emergency room treatment for the longer and longer trips that would be required to make it from one hospital to another until one could be found that would take in the indigent patient.[5] The "future crisis" in medical care was a main theme of the conference: the arrival of the crisis was projected for around 1993.

ITEM: The public debate touched off by Daniel Callahan's *Setting Limits*.[6] Callahan (a philosopher who is Director of the Hastings Center) in his book makes policy proposals that would have the outlay of federal funds for the health care of older citizens turn heavily upon some features of the nature of persons, especially as this nature is reflected in the *chronological age* of a person, an age which, Callahan argues, can be mapped against the "natural lifespan" of human individuals. By his proposal, certain types of costly treatment would be withheld from individuals near the end of their natural lifespans. No such individual, however, would be denied the wherewithal for a "tolerable death," one made free from unnecessary pain and anxiety by the use of appropriate drugs.

ITEM: Norman Daniels (a philosopher at Tufts University) has also entered this fray with his *Am I My Parents' Keeper?: An Essay on Justice Between the Young and the Old*.[7] He, among other things, offers the proposal that each citizen be allocated from the public coffers a lifetime sum of money for health care: for those who were prudent—and lucky—there would in their old age still be funds left in their pots—money to "burn" on expensive treatment. Those who had used up their stipends presumably would still be allotted monies for Callahan's "tolerable death."

Such reminders of the finiteness of our medical and economic resources have never been welcome. But they have become part of the facts of life with which we must deal, and have given added urgency to the business of getting as clear as possible about what it is that is constitutive of moral persons. Without such clarity, some aspects of our policy debates are almost certainly guaranteed to be at cross purposes.

ACKNOWLEDGMENTS

The original impetus to move ahead on this project came from Dick Wasserstrom, during his visit to Warren Wilson College in the spring of 1982, and I remain most grateful to him for that and for his continuing interest in the years since. Maynard Adams and George Graham have encouraged me to persist, as have others of those who have read all or parts of the manuscript at various stages. These folks have included: Dallas High, Russell Perkins, Lora Scott, Sam Scoville, Sally vander Straeten, Ron Wilson, and Anne Wray. I have also had rewarding conversation and/or correspondence with Annette Baier, Dan Dennett, Fred Feldman, Harry Frankfurt, Arnold Levison, and Bill Lycan. During an NEH Summer Seminar 1989 with Maynard Adams at Chapel Hill, North Carolina, I benefited from conversations with all of my colleagues, and especially from comments made by Charles Crittenden, Deryl Howard, James Kelly, and James Peterman. A former student, Chris Chandek, generously undertook the unenviable task of a very close reading of the MS, and furnished me with a sheaf of comments at the very last stages of revision.

It is customary to acknowledge the patience of the many students and colleagues who have had to put up with one's developing ideas over a period of years; I add also those who participated in a Humanities Division Seminar in 1981, the people who attended a Faculty Lecture in November of 1985 on the subject, and the wonderful group (including some M.D.'s) who subjected themselves to a short course on moral personhood for Elderhostel the summer of 1986, all at Warren Wilson.

A sabbatical leave from Warren Wilson in 1984-85 made possible the production of a good first draft. A Mellon-funded James Still Fellowship under the auspices of Alice Brown and the Appalachian College Program at the University of Kentucky in the summer of 1987 afforded time and thinking room for further research and refinements, as well as the opportunity to try out some of my ideas on some of the other Fellows.

Finally, acknowledgment must be made of the patient support of my wife and children, in spite of my solitary stints at the computer in my attic office. I am indebted as well to the anonymous readers and copy editor, and to Carola Sautter and Marilyn Semerad, Editor and Production Editor, respectively, at SUNY Press.

Marshall, N.C.   G.E.S.
October 1989

1

Square One

A brief word as to what is to take place in this chapter is in order. In section 1, I describe, to begin with, some apparently uncomplicated *beliefs* that I shall entertain (as is sometimes said, "for the sake of argument") with regard to certain actual and possible past, present, and future states (or conditions) of myself. I do this in lieu of amassing a set of case histories, both for the sake of simplifying the presentation of the sorts of problems I take to be crucial, and also as a way of conveying the perhaps sentimental—but hopefully uncloying—notion that these matters, in a very fundamental sense of the expression, are of *personal* concern. Then I supply some *moral opinions*, again, of an apparently uncomplicated sort, that I think it is possible to hold with respect to these beliefs. In section 2, I direct attention to certain notions and concepts that are present in or connected, either explicitly or implicitly, with these beliefs and opinions, notions and concepts most of which have been under scrutiny by philosophers. This scrutiny in some cases has provided illumination for the darker reaches of some of the issues under examination. Then, in section 3, I outline the strategy I propose to employ in the actual investigations which are to follow. My aim in the remainder of the entire essay, of course, is to try to show, by providing a sketch for a theory of moral personhood, how certain beliefs and opinions, of which those in section 1 are to be taken as representative, are both possible and plausible, or else might best be rejected or at least modified in some way. The end result will be to shed at least some light upon the nature of moral persons and how it is that they ought to be dealt with in our daily lives.

1. Actual and Possible Human States, Beliefs, and Opinions

I believe, as I write this, that I am a moral person, that is, someone possessing the capacities for acting morally or immorally, for making judgments about the similar actions of others, and that I am myself deserving of the treatment ordinarily accorded moral persons. Moreover, I believe that I have been such a person for many years, and that, with the exception of presently unanticipated events that could make it otherwise, I shall continue to be so for an indefinite (albeit finite) future. But I also believe that for the whole of the time since my birth I may *not* have been a moral person in the sense in which I now am (and have been for many years) one: in other words, there was a time in my life when it is possible that I was in some sense not a moral person at all. Whether during that time, or a part of that time, I was not in some sense a person either, is a possibility that I think needs to be examined. And with regard to my future, there is a possibility also needing examination: namely, that I might cease to be in some sense a moral person, or a person, and yet (in some sense) remain "alive."

Given the knowledge that I have of the culture in which I live, I know that there were people who thought they were treating me morally during the time in my past that I believe it is possible that I was in some sense not a moral person; and even if it is possible that I was during part of that time in some sense not a person, there were people who thought they were treating me as a person. And similarly, I know that if I should cease to be in some sense a moral person and should remain in some sense alive (and this I do believe to be a possibility), there would very likely be some people who would try to deal with me as they think they should deal with moral persons; and if I should cease to be a person altogether, while remaining in some sense alive (and this I also believe to be a possibility), there would very likely be those who would think they were treating me as a person.

I also believe, what is contrary to fact, that if I had been born with certain defects such that I never should have developed beyond the mental age of, say, an eighteen-month-old child, there might have been those who would have thought they were treating me morally, and would have thought they were dealing with me as they would have dealt with (normal) persons.[1] By putting it in this manner I mean to make allowance for the possibility that it might *not* have been the case that there would have been those who would have thought they were treating me in the ways I have described. On the assumption that I had been born that way, and in addition, had lived for a number of years—say, to the age of fifty-two—and then had suffered an accident or a disease that had further reduced my mental age or left me in an irreversible coma, I believe that there might (or might not) have been those who would have thought they, in their dealings with me, were treating me morally, and would have thought they were dealing with me as they would have dealt with any other (normal) person.

Keeping the sense of "I" stipulated in the previous paragraph, I believe as well that it is possible that I might have been born an anencephalic individual, and that there might have been those who would have thought, in their relationships with me, that they were treating me morally, and those who might have thought they were dealing with me as a person. (Again, this allows for the possibility that there might *not* have been those who would have treated me in these ways.) And, paralleling the previous possible state of myself, if I had continued to live for a certain time but had then, through accident or disease, been reduced to some lesser state, it is possible that there might (or might not) have been those who would have thought they were treating me morally or as a person or as both. I believe that the sort of individual I have described myself as being in these two states could *never* have become, in fact, either a moral person or a person in the sense in which I am now both of these things.

I believe, in addition, that it is perhaps in some sense possible to say that I might never have been born,[2] in the sense of my not having lived through birth: in other words, that I might have been aborted (intentionally or accidentally) at any stage of development.[3] Whether there might have been those who would have thought they were treating me morally or as a person or both (or those who would have treated me as neither) is more problematic, especially at the earlier biological stages of my development, given the divergence of beliefs present in my culture with respect to such matters.[4]

In addition to describing states of myself, past and future, that I believe to be possible, I need to include, for the sake of completeness, two such states that I believe *not* to be possible. a. I believe that it is not possible that *I* existed, *as a person* (*or otherwise*), prior to the fertilization of a certain egg by a certain sperm (this, I think, is entailed by the hypothesis that persons are a certain kind of material or physical objects, about which I shall have more to say in the investigations to follow). While there may indeed have been a gleam in my father's eye (and my mother's, too, it perhaps needs to be insisted in these feminist days), gleams and persons (or even human individuals) are far from being identical.[5]

b. I must also admit to believing that it is not possible that *I* shall continue to exist *as a person* after my death. Again, this is connected with the hypothesis just referred to, and does not rule out the possibility that I might continue to have a kind of existence in the memories of other persons for a time, in the genes of my descendants, or in an even more tenuous way in artifacts of my own contriving. I know that there are those who believe in what they refer to as the transmigration of souls; I do not find this belief coherent, but this need not rule out as a (possible) possibility that some part of myself (whatever it might be) might persist in some form so as to make work for those who (like Ian Stevenson 1975) collect stories told by or about folks who claim to have memories and personality features not their own, features which could, via the transmigration hypothesis, turn out to be mine. So far as I now know, while such memories and personality features may be a source of pleasure or displeasure to me now, or in whatever future I have remaining as a person, how they could be a source of either to me after I am no more I do not know. There is rich and relatively unexplored empirical territory here, undoubtedly, for aficionados of personal identity problems.

I also believe, in addition to the *beliefs* I have already enumerated, that with regard to certain possible past and future states of myself such as those I have described, I am entitled to the following *moral opinions*:

a. Vis-à-vis the possible situations I have depicted in connection with the variations on what might have been the case with regard to my past history: Of each situation I feel that I am entitled to say of those who might not have treated me as either a moral person or as a person, that *on the assumption that I was not then, and never could have become,* a moral person or a person (which I view as a possibility), they would have done nothing immoral. However (on this same assumption), those who might have treated me morally or as a person or both would have done nothing moral (or immoral): they would have been simply mistaken, but need not have deserved to receive any blame because of that. Actually, given the lack of knowledge and the climate of opinion surrounding the subject of child development in the years during which *I* could have been in such a position, they might even have deserved some faint praise for, in effect, at least temporarily withholding judgment as to my status at an early stage of my development.

b. Apropos the possible future states of myself: It would now be morally permissible for me, if I were to receive on good report the information that I had acquired Alzheimer's disease, or any other similarly progressive, destructive, and incurable major neurological disorder, to make suitable arrangements for bringing about my demise at a time prior to the time it is possible that I would cease in a significant way to be a moral person; and if that demise should be not coincidental with my ceasing to be a person, that that also be arranged; and if *that* demise should not be coincidental with my ceasing to be alive, that that also be arranged. Further, I think that there are certain kinds of circumstances which, if present, could render the making of such arrangements morally *obligatory* and not just morally permissible: for example, if the cost of keeping me alive were to be borne by my family alone, and this cost far exceeded anything they could muster short of undue deprivation or bankruptcy.[6] However, if they had unlimited resources, they might very well wish to keep me alive as long as they pleased, out of some sort of "respect for the subhuman in human life" (Rolston 1982), or merely as a sort of hobby or small indulgence, so long as they did not run into any legal or social problems— for example, where having me present for parties, complete with feeding and hydration tubes, ventilator, etc., might put a damper on the festivities, given current social practices.

With other modifications in circumstances, it would follow that if I were not in a position to make these arrangements for myself, the moral responsibility for making them would then pass to other persons: I would have to trust them to do for me (if they would, could, and without undue hardship to themselves) what I could not do for myself. In the case that the onset of the neurological disorder were so rapid (perhaps through an accident producing severe brain damage) that I should have no opportunity to make the arrangements just described, then my belief is that again the moral responsibility for making these arrangements would have to be shifted to other persons, whether or not they would assume it.

There are circumstances and circumstances, of course, and if it should turn out that I had no family or friends who would be adversely affected by my continuing to be kept alive after I had ceased to be either a moral person or a person or both, and especially if there should be some morally good purpose to be served by so doing (say, using my sound organs for transplants), then it need not be morally required to bring about my immediate demise. For even if I had specified that I were not to be kept alive, I do not see that this would be an overriding consideration, especially if there were an advantage to keeping me alive that either I had not foreseen or could not have foreseen. Perhaps television producer-writer Norman Lear (or someone of his ilk) would donate a large sum of money to medical research in exchange for using "me" in a new television situation comedy [sick] series, life-support apparatus and all.

Now I also believe that there could be possible future states of myself which, while not afflicted with features so absolutely destructive of moral personhood (or personhood) as the conditions I have just described, might still merit that similar arrangements be made. What I have in mind here could range from a life of constant and unrelievable pain (or pain relievable only by such massive doses of drugs that nothing like a normal conscious existence would be possible) to a life of (pain-free) physical disability so restrictive as to be psychologically devastating. And, as before, the possible moral roles to be played by other persons would depend in part upon my own ability to make the arrangements I believed to be morally permitted or demanded (and be subject to the same considerations as regards the continuation of my life in spite of my wish to the contrary). And it certainly seems possible that I, because of terrible things that had already happened to me in the past, might arrive at similar conclusions with regard to the prolongation of a life I might have come to perceive as so unbearable as to be no longer worth enduring.

I believe, again given the knowledge I have of the culture in which I live, that the making of the arrangements I have just been describing would encounter a variety of problems of both a legal and a social nature, especially as they connect with the institution of medical care. The existence of such problems would of course have to be taken into account, and as a result certain aspects of such arrangements might be made very difficult indeed. But legal and social matters do change over time, and the causes of this change are due, among other things, to the coming into existence of patterns of thought that have not previously existed or at least have not been widely recognized or entertained, sometimes due to their very complexity. It is a rather well established view among philosophers that what is *thought to be moral* at a particular place and time need not correspond to what *is moral*; and with societal changes from what is thought to be moral to what is moral, it follows that there will also be changes in our expectations and finally in our laws, however slow these changes may be in making their appearance.[7]

2. Relevant Concepts

The relatively small number of apparently simple beliefs and opinions I attributed to myself in section 1 above I do not believe are necessarily mine alone; but I also do not believe that all of them by any means are beliefs and opinions that are entirely self-explanatory or self-justifying or likely to be adopted (or even acknowledged as plausible) at face value by every reader. What I do in the course of this essay is to try to show, by assembling a few theoretical points, how and why it is that *some* of these beliefs and opinions (and others like them) are both possible and plausible, and in so doing perhaps begin to persuade some readers of their merit, and possibly even to bring them to see that a few, at least, of these beliefs and opinions might be numbered among those they have already held, perhaps without their having been fully aware of it.

My primary focus, naturally, is upon the notions of morality and personhood, notions figuring rather prominently in and making possible the beliefs and opinions expressed in section 1. For better or for worse, these notions and a number of connected ones have been dealt with in a variety of ways by philosophers for many years, and so I shall attempt to illuminate some of the more troublesome reaches of these notions (and their connections with others) by making use of the results of philosophical investigations of my own and of other philosophers in as judicious a manner as possible. By this I mean that I shall try to avoid employing as an explanation, or for the purposes of clarification, a philosophical view that might appear to be more obscure than the view for which it is proposed as explanation or clarification—and this itself can be a potentially bothersome matter, asking as it clearly does for judgment calls on my part.

My rationale for the choice of the possible human states I have depicted is simply that it is, in my opinion, in such states that most of the really troublesome issues surrounding the concept of moral personhood and its applicability show up, and I apologize to the reader who may have found them, or certain aspects of my description of them, to be in any way offensive.[8]

As a part of the investigation of the nature and applicability of the concepts to be encountered in connection with the use of "moral" and "person," I shall need to examine with some care a possibility assumed by my talk in section 1., viz., that these concepts need not necessarily coincide with one another: a particular individual might, while having the features characteristic of a person, not possess the features of a *moral* person. Sometimes the distinction is put in the form of speaking of "moral persons" as opposed to speaking of "metaphysical persons." This is a possibility denied by some of those who have thought about the matter.[9] There appears to be more unanimity as regards the claim that in order for an individual to be a moral *agent* s/he must possess the relevant features of a person; or, in other words, that being a person is a necessary, if not a sufficient, condition for being a moral agent; so that the concepts, while not identical, do overlap.[10] As might be expected, there is disagreement among philosophers as to what constitutes the best way of characterizing the meaning of "moral"; so again, I shall take this as an indication that considerable care needs to be exercised, so as not to beg too many (or the wrong sorts of) substantive questions. Since moral beliefs and opinions are, after all, just a species of beliefs and opinions, one of the tasks that must be undertaken is that of finding a proper location in the scheme of things for them; and this, as we shall see, curiously enough seems to lead straight back to talk of persons.

Implicit in the possible human states or conditions described in section 1. are other notions as well. For example, to speak of certain states of affairs, such as my having not been born, or of my acquiring in the future a major irreversible neurological disorder, is to indulge in the making of what philosophers have come to call *counterfactual* claims, i.e., claims describing states of affairs which are contrary to the way the facts now are, or to speak of *possible worlds* (a "possible world" is a way things might have been or might turn out to be, as opposed to the way things have been and are now in the actual world). There is a sense, too, in which talk of making a moral decision (or any decision, for that matter) entails the existence of a possible world, or of several possible worlds, such that the carrying out of the decision brings into existence an actual world that had not previously existed. As it has turned out, there seems to be some consensus among philosophers that counterfactual talk and talk of possible worlds sustain important connections with one another.[11] Such talk of possible worlds in its turn entails talk of the identity and reidentification of individuals across such worlds, a concept described in the next paragraph.

Probably the primary source of uneasiness on the part of some readers with regard to the way I employed "I" and "my" in section 1. can be traced to some of the matters that philosophers have discussed for many years under the general heading of "the logic of identity": for the "I" that I employ when I speak of my presently being a moral person and the "I" that I employ when I say that *I* might, while remaining alive, be neither a person nor moral, seem not necessarily to refer to exactly the same thing in any "strict sense" of identity. And there is a similar problem afflicting my attempt to refer to *myself* as I was at the age of eighteen months, although perhaps not so severe a problem as that which results when I speak of *my* not having been born. The literature in this area is vast, and again the problem of picking out results that are both relevant to the present task and yet still have some measure of consensus about them is a difficult one. One thing at least does seem clear, however, and that is that unless the persons who are said to have chosen to do certain things remain the *same* (identical) persons (in some relevant sense) over time, they could not be held responsible, morally or otherwise, for their choices. Thus there can be no denying the importance for morality of getting as clear as possible about what goes into making a moral person the same person over time, however morality itself is defined, so long as one thinks it important that persons be among the sort of things that can be held responsible for the choices they make.

Among the other concepts requiring attention, in order to have as complete a picture as possible of the nature of moral personhood, is one I have only touched upon in passing: the *concept of law* and related notions, such as rights, responsibility, and punishment. Again, there has been considerable disputation in the fields of political philosophy, philosophy of law, and jurisprudence as to the proper approach to be taken to putting together all of the notions needed to capture the essence of this concept, and to show how it is (or ought) to be connected with the concept of morality. I think that it is necessary to have some sort of a working sketch of a theory of law here, and shall try to show as well how it might be possible to establish points of contact with law as it exists in practice.

While not mentioned in so many words, the notion of *quality of life* must surely play a role in the sorts of possible human states I have described.

This is a notion which, to my knowledge, has not been subjected to any very extended philosophical examination.[12] And, as far as I know, no attempt at all has been made to try to discover the nature of what one might refer to as *the quality of life of persons, or in particular, of moral persons.* There is a sense of "quality of life" that might be associated with the ancient query of Socrates with regard to "the sort of life worth living"—and in this sense, a great deal of effort has certainly been expended over the intervening centuries to describe The Good Life.

"Quality of life" of course has figured in a number of political presentations in the United States, beginning at least with the days of Lyndon Johnson, and has come to mean, for the most part, the quality of economic life. Such a notion does not appear to begin to touch some of the types of considerations entering into the kinds of possible human states or conditions of interest to us here, since obviously no amount of money could alter the nature of the individuals in some of the depicted conditions. Saying this need not be taken, of course, as ruling out the possible utility of expenditures to support research the result of which could be to alleviate or in some way to prevent conditions such as those I have described, if this were thought to be *morally* desirable. There enters here (as well as with the concepts of law and punishment), in an important way, I believe, the notion of the right to privacy.

Another concept also has been exemplified in some of the possible human states I have described, and it is a concept rather inescapable for *human* persons, whether they are aware of it or simply instantiate it: the *concept of death.* Unlike the notion of quality of life, the concept of death has received relatively extended treatments by three philosophers in recent years: Robert Veatch 1976, Douglas Walton 1979, and Jay Rosenberg 1983 (there was also the provocative short piece of Thomas Nagel's, "Death," which appeared in the first and second editions of Rachels 1979). But one of the areas not yet wholly free of obscurity has to do with the significance of the death of persons, or of moral persons, as opposed to the death of patients or of certain individual members of the species, *homo sapiens.* The medical profession by 1968 began seriously to come to terms with some of the troubles that have long afflicted the definition of "medical" death;[13] but in so doing, it has for the most part so far tended to steer clear of the complications involved in making the (nonmedical) decision that the prolongation of the lives of certain individuals (or the heroic resuscitation of same), at great expenditure of human time, energy, and/or money, may not be *morally* justifiable. It has not been just a matter, by any means, of there being only conceptual or semantical confusions and unclarities as regards the term *death,* of course: for both the legal system and the social and political scenes which form the background for the operation of our entire institution of health care enter the picture and contribute to the problems (and must be the source of solutions), such, for example, as those surrounding the treatment of the terminally ill and of defective neonates.

Still another notion implicit in some of the possible human conditions I have described is the very complex and troublesome notion of the *development* (or the lack of it) of those who become (or fail to become) moral persons. Since the only genuinely moral persons with whom we are familiar apparently require a relatively extended period of time to make their appearance, we certainly would like to know as much as possible about what is involved (and in as much empirical detail as possible) in their getting to be the sorts of things that they are. We have a very strong societal interest, certainly, in attempting to find out the best ways for insuring, as part of our general educational system, that as many genuine moral individuals make their appearance as is at all possible.

The well-known and extensive, "stage-based" psychological studies of moral development by Lawrence Kohlberg (1981, 1983) and his associates (themselves founded upon work of Piaget), in the opinion of some observers (such as Annette Baier 1985, Carol Gilligan 1982, and Gareth Matthews 1988), appear to leave something to be desired; and this is due, in part, certainly, to the difficulty we encounter in drawing an adequate picture of the very moral person—Kohlberg's "sixth stage" individual—whose development it is that we seek to track. The flip side of moral development—moral decline—is one to which much less attention has been paid. Its relevance to our considerations here is, I think, clear enough.

3. Investigative Strategy

My strategy for carrying out my suggestion in section 2 that at least some of the beliefs and opinions I described myself as holding in section 1 are both *possible* and *plausible* will take the following form: it will require that I start with some quite general considerations and then work down to the particular matters of concern expressible by and about the human individuals we come to characterize as moral or persons, both, or neither. So I begin by describing in chapter 2 the nature and locus of *beliefs* and *opinions* in the physical or material world, via the hypothesis that persons, moral or otherwise, as the prime carriers of beliefs and opinions, are material (biophysical) in nature. Then I show, by the introduction of the notion of *intentionality*, that they are, as *intentional systems* (à la Daniel Dennett), capable of performing in a variety of ways, the explanation of which cannot be "reduced" to (or derived from) the sorts of causal explanations commonly employed in some of the existing physical sciences. In other words, intentional "effects" will require intentional "causes," and an understanding of intentional performances will require intentional "explanations."

One of the primary features of such "persons," a feature causing both great satisfaction and sometimes enormous distress, is what I shall refer to as the *malleability* of their intentionality, that is, the way in which their beliefs, opinions, and systems of beliefs and opinions, as individuals and as groups, both over historical time and at particular times, are so widely various as to be subject to almost no constraints.[14] Chapter 3 is devoted to an examination of this notion of malleability.

The presence of the feature of malleability requires, among other things, that considerable pains be taken to determine how it is that methods might be devised for appropriately sorting, in some objective manner, these highly variable (and sometimes conflicting) beliefs, opinions, and systems of beliefs and opinions. Experimental science, for example, has provided a means for doing this for some beliefs and opinions about *non*intentional objects, perhaps via the sort of scientific "realism" described in Hilary Putnam 1978. In spite of its apparent desirability, however, there are certainly problems afflicting the attempt to devise a "realism" capable of sorting "real" from "fictional" intentional objects[15]. But clearly, this, or something like it, must be done if we are to be able to come up with one of our desired goals, that of an accurate picture of the person as a material, intentional, malleable being; in this connection, the "hypothesis of intentional selection" is introduced in the last section of chapter 3.

It is only with such an appropriately constrained account of persons that we can, with any degree of confidence, mark the theoretical (and empirical) boundaries of *moral* persons—where what is "moral" will have an appropriately delineated special status in the domain of intentional objects (as argued for in chapter 4), a domain not only so generously populated with all of the hopes, dreams, delusions, fancies and fantasies, etc., the human species has fallen heir to as to be not only surfeited, but apparently free from any problem of overpopulation—in order to show how these boundaries lie with respect to the *biological* conceptions, births, and deaths of human individuals. The enterprise I am describing here might usefully be termed a kind of investigation in the philosophy of moral "science," or moral psychology, a discipline which naturally would have intimate connections with cognitive science (for a definition of this field, see below, chapter 3. "Malleable Persons," section 2. *A Model for Malleability: the Computer*.) and a common source in our so-called folk or commonsense psychology (about which, too, more will be forthcoming).

Some, at least, of the elements of a philosophy of moral psychology are finally assembled in the first section of chapter 5, in terms of the person and moral person "schemata" outlined there. This is the heart of the argument of the entire essay, and is that to which chapters 2, 3, and 4 are directed, and that upon which depend the discussions of the topics developed in the remaining chapters.

With such an account in hand, it then becomes possible to begin to work out suitable ways of describing such related matters as the right to privacy, the "quality of life" and the identity over time of moral persons. And, in turn, to deal in a meaningful and useful manner with such concerns as the nature of law and the way in which it impinges upon our medical and moral practice, and to provide a perspective for viewing the nature of moral development as a special case of intentional development.[16] Such an account of intentional beings who not only develop over time but who may decline, either gradually by way of normal aging, or with sometimes frightening swiftness by way of accident or disease, may require that we devise a special way of describing the variety of possible worlds they are capable not only of conceiving but of bringing into existence by their intentional activities.[17]

In the final chapter I return to the actual and possible states of myself depicted, and to the beliefs and moral opinions expressed about these states in the first section of this chapter. I bring to bear upon these beliefs and opinions the full weight of the theory developed in the intervening chapters, theory that allows us as well to delineate more clearly the varieties of the states or conditions in which human individuals may actually be found.

2

Material Persons

In section 1 of this chapter I introduce the hypothesis that persons are material objects, and say something about the way in which contemporary or 'new-type' materialism represents a rather remarkable change from some of the earlier versions of this rather ancient view. Perhaps the principal difference between the new and most versions of the old materialism is that it is now possible to speak of material objects in what is called an "unreduced" sense, which simply means that one need not today, in the name of materialism, require that everything (including minds) be constructed in some relatively simple-minded way out of (or "reduced to") rather gross material bits and pieces in the manner that was found offensive to idealists and spiritualists in the days, say, of someone like William James, for whom some form of Hobbesian materialism seems to have been the villain.

There can be no denying, of course, that such a way of thinking goes against habits of thought ingrained in our language itself, and thus it should be no surprise that the discourse devised to facilitate thinking in this new way has an unfamiliar ring, whether one is talking about the "functional isomorphism" of Hilary Putnam 1975, the "anomalous monism" of Donald Davidson 1970, or perhaps the "homuncular functionalism" of Daniel Dennett 1978, 1987 or William Lycan 1987 (the reader's patience will be rewarded shortly with definitions of these strange terms). Compatible with and even essential for these ways of speaking, as will be shown in section 2, is the notion of intentionality. This notion, especially in the work of Dennett, has turned out to be a far richer one than one might have been led to expect if one had been familiar with only the uses and early interpretations of it found in the writings of philosophers such as Franz Brentano and Edmund Husserl.

13

For, as it has happened, this notion of intentionality has provided what appears to be one of the keys needed to unlock some philosophical puzzles of quite long standing, first and foremost among them being the so-called mind-body problem. While there are still plenty of puzzles remaining to be solved, it is no longer necessary to beat one's head against this particular wall—one now can simply walk away from it. Thus it is that section 2, which comprises the bulk of this chapter, is devoted to an exposition of some of the concepts that have come to be viewed as central to philosophical talk of intentionality, such as the concept of an intentional system and the concept of the intentional circle, as well as some related ones.

Philosophers did not, by any means, themselves fabricate all of this newer way of speaking from scratch, since some of it certainly has its basis in what has come to be called "folk" psychology or the varieties of ways of explaining human behavior that antedated psychology's appearance as a science (cf. n. 27). This folk psychology has received one form of development in the hands of those who today do cognitive psychology and cognitive science (for an explanation of these terms, see below, chap. 3, sec. 2, *Embodied Turing Machines; Hardware, Software, and Computer Science*). What some recent philosophers have done and are doing—and what this essay might be viewed as a contribution to—is to work toward a refinement and subsequent redrawing of the features of some parts of our conceptual framework as it impinges upon important segments of our intentional lives previously only dimly seen. This chapter will provide much of the necessary vocabulary, as well as some of the conceptual structures, needed to begin to supply some of the considerations which, when taken together, will allow us to see what it is that we might best mean when we speak of *moral persons*, by first of all seeing what it means to speak of *persons as material higher order intentional systems*.

1. Material Objects: 'New-Type' Materialism

One of the hypotheses I shall find myself exploring in the course of these deliberations is that—whatever else they may be—persons are to be best located in a certain group of physical or material things. Given the ordinary connotations of the terms *physical* and *material*, both in the history of philosophy and without, which require that they be viewed as standing in opposition to "spiritual" or "immaterial," and which usually carry in their train mind-body dualism, it would undoubtedly be desirable to reword the hypothesis, if there were better words available. I am not sure, however, whether saying something like "a person is a certain type of spatio-temporal object" would do much better, because "spatio-temporal" is also subject to similar readings. If my arm were twisted, I would have to say that I would subscribe to *some* form of "mind-body identity" of the materialist sort—but as the word *materialist* has come to be employed in the writings of the philosophers referred to in the previous section.[1]

To be a materialist in this sense is not, as in earlier years, necessarily to commit oneself to the view that some sort of fairly straightforward "reduction" of mental stuff to physical stuff is required. Nor is it even necessary to worry overly much about what the actual "stuff" is out of which minds are in some sense fabricated, so long as there is a demonstrable functional isomorphism between the objects designated as minds.[2] Minds, in a *functional* sense, *are* what they *do*, whatever their embodiment might be, as a heart-lung machine (made of totally different materials) performs the same functions as the organs it replaces during certain types of surgery. A pair or a set of minds that can do the same things are functionally isomorphic with each other, whatever their construction or constituents. Contemporary materialists need not subscribe to such positions as that, for example, statements about mental events must be translatable into statements mentioning only physical events in some heavy-handed sense of "physical event," or that descriptions of mental events must be rephrased in terms of observable behavior, again in some rather gross (Skinnerian) sense of "observable behavior." Nor is it necessary to commit oneself to some rigorous and debilitating "mechanistic determinism," of the sort traditionally supposed to be in opposition to free will.[3]

What I shall do next, in order further on to be able to offer something in the way of considerations that would count towards a confirmation of the hypothesis that persons are material objects, is to supply more information about the foregoing matters and some others of the issues involved in trying to explain the sort of materialism being referred to here, and in this way to be able to show how it may be said to escape most of the shortcomings of the more traditional forms of materialism. I should point out before I proceed that I also am in the position of arguing, not necessarily for the falsity of, but at least for the irrelevancy in this context of, some traditional claims about the "spiritual" nature of persons.

There need be nothing amiss in claiming that persons have a spiritual aspect—perhaps an immaterial soul, or that they, in some sense, are (in the sense of being identical with) souls, or even of saying that this spiritual aspect is in some way their "essential" nature—provided that one does not suppose that in so doing one has thereby given an *explanation* in the sort of functional terms required here of what a person is. To propose the spiritual aspect account of persons as an explanation of the features of persons that are of interest in the present context is most likely to make a move which simply encapsulates, in the form of a sort of homunculus, the very aspects of persons I would like to uncover.[4] One all too easily falls into talk of "spiritual persons" who in some way lie behind the scenes and who, by possessing the characteristics of interest to us, thus account for the behavior of ordinary persons.

Or it might be that one seeks, by using the term *soul* to fasten upon some "essential" feature of persons, to much the same effect. Aristotle actually did something like this, by assigning "souls" of varying sorts to what he perceived to be essentially different types of living beings (viz., vegetative, sensitive, rational, with these categories selected on the basis of a kind of functional analysis), so that each kind of living thing had its own appropriate "soul."[5] Only centuries later were Christian theologians concerned to assign immortality to the tokens of the Aristotelian type, rational soul. It is not at all clear that theologians have ever entirely succeeded in working through—much less solving—the puzzles (puzzles already affecting Plato's thinking) afflicting the nature of immortal souls, or of personal immortality.[6]

If one were interested in employing some notion of the spiritual, or of souls, in formulating or defending a religious belief system, that is of course a different but quite familiar enterprise, and one equipped with its own peculiar problems. The present enterprise has problems enough of its own without having to include those in the theologians' thicket as well. It is possible, however, that some of the results of my work here might be of use in sorting out some features of the theologians' problems.

Materialism, AKA "physicalism" in one of its earlier twentieth-century forms, took its shape in the hands of some of the proponents of logical positivism under the rubric of "the unity of science." One of its fundamental notions was that physics was to be taken as the paradigm science, and that all other sciences, if restructured in the right way, could be shown to be reducible to physics, or translatable into the "language" or "vocabulary" of physics. Since it was assumed that much of the vocabulary of physics could be itself reduced to descriptions of spatio-temporal objects, it seemed to be plausible that any other (genuine) science might also be translated into the same "physicalist" vocabulary.[7]

As it turned out, one of the factors contributing to the decline of interest in the unity of science movement was the eventual recognition (sometimes belated, as Putnam admitted for his own case with respect to some of his own earlier positions,[8] for example, on a certain form of "Turing machine reductionism")[9] that the concept of reducibility[10] itself is subject to misunderstanding and to misuse: there could be an alteration in the content and significance of the subject matter being reduced to the extent that after the reduction had been made one no longer retained the very features of the unreduced subject matter that had made it of interest in the first place.[11] In other words, it has come to be seen that not all subject matters can be reduced in the manner originally thought to be necessitated by some versions of the unified science thesis, which seemed to require that all explanations of the behavior of material objects be physical explanations of a specified narrow sort.

Happily, one can now argue, as a 'new-type' materialist, that even if beings with mental lives (psychological beings) are some sort of material/ physical object, there can be legitimate nonphysical, nonbehavioristic (that is, *intentionalistic*) explanations—of which more is to follow shortly—of their behavior. I make no attempt here to chronicle the details of the changes in the thinking of philosophers about these matters,[12] but shall, in keeping with my earlier promise, describe what, in my opinion, is the primary area where such a reductive failure is relevant to my present enterprise: this is the area of intentionality.

2. Intentionality as a Feature of Material Objects

By 'intentionality' I shall understand a generic term[13] referring to the feature of some—but by no means all—human beings we have in mind when we say of them that they are capable of having or experiencing such mental things as beliefs, desires, understandings, volitions, expectations, and intentions, to mention only a few of the members of this family. *An intention* in this sense, unlike the dictionary sense of an "intentional action" as one done on purpose, can be a way of indicating that the particular mental things in question may point (at least ostensibly) to something beyond themselves, a "something" that can also be referred to as an "intentional object." Intentional objects may be wholly or in part fictional, or may be said to be connected, in a manner requiring considerable explanatory ingenuity (as we shall see in this chapter in connection with natural kinds, and then in chapters 4 and 5 with intentional kinds and moral realism), with a reality outside of themselves. For example, one may believe (hope, desire) that there are such things as leprechauns, or that a water hole is to be found nearby while one is in the desert; or that the stairs one is climbing will not collapse under one's feet. In this context the leprechauns, the water hole in the desert, and the stairs not collapsing are all intentional objects—the leprechauns presumably don't really exist, the water hole may exist, and the collapsing stairs need not exist.

If there proves to be reason, as well there might, to attribute some form of intentionality to nonhuman animals, we shall, following Dennett 1978, refer to the animal counterpart of the human's capacity for intentions and belief store as an "intentional whatnot." Of the matters related to intentionality that have been under recent examination in this area, I shall now discuss two: the so-called circle of intentions and the notion, due to Dennett, of an "intentional system." I begin with the notion of an intentional system.[14]

Intentional Systems: First Order

Dennett, in depicting what he calls an "intentional system," offers three defining characteristics: (1) it must be a thing we can describe as rational, (2) it must be a thing to which we can apply intentional predicates, and (3) it must be a thing toward which we can take an intentional stance. He makes it quite clear that the "thing" we are referring to is not necessarily a human individual: as a matter of fact it does not even need to be a living thing—a chess-playing computer could count as an instance of an intentional system.

To say of such a system that it is rational, as Dennett understands the term in this context, is to say of it only that it appears to follow some rather basic rules of logic (this is not to say that it must in some genuine sense *understand* these logical rules). For example, the behavior of a chess-playing computer might be observed to conform to the following logical pattern, given certain specifiable configurations of pieces on the board: *If the king is not moved to a certain square, then it will not be in check. The king is not moved to that square. Therefore, it is not placed in check.*

We would say of such a computer that it is rational. If it were to move the king into check we certainly would have some serious doubts about its rationality in the sense defined (i.e., chess-playing-program-rationality). To say of such a computer that intentional predicates may be applied to it is to say things of the following sorts: it *believes* that moving the king to a certain square would result in checkmate; or, it *understands* what the consequence of the move would be; or, it *intends* or *desires* not to make a move that would result in checkmate. To take the intentional stance toward such a computer would be simply to make predictions about its future behavior couched in such intentional terms, and possibly to have these predictions borne out by its subsequent behavior. If, as a matter of fact, such predictions were not confirmed, one might then be forced to take up either of two other stances, which Dennett calls the "design stance" and the "physical stance."

By taking up the design stance, one would most likely raise questions about the nature of the chess-playing program itself and investigate whether the programmer had inadvertently left some bugs in it. If an examination of the program showed that it was not at fault, then one, by taking the physical stance, would make inquiry into the functioning of the hardware, e.g., looking for a failed fuse, IC chip, etc. In any case, the appropriateness of assuming a particular stance would be determined by the success or failure of the predictions made in accordance with taking the stance.

Attention needs to be called to the fact that Dennett is at great pains in his description of intentional systems to show that it is not at all necessary, in order to say of a thing that it is an intentional system, that one know that it in some sense actually "has" intentions. In other words, an intentional system need not have what Haugeland 1981 has called "original intentionality,"[15] or the sort of intentionality we do in fact attribute to certain sorts of human beings when we say of them that they have beliefs, desires, intentions, etc.

Now, a valuable result of Dennett's way of employing the notion of an intentional system is that it shows how we may avoid the sort of reduction I described earlier as being of the wrong sort: the attempt always to reduce all explanations of the behavior of material objects to physical explanations. As a matter of fact, an intentional explanation of the moves of a chess-playing computer might not only be highly useful, but a physical explanation might turn out to be, if actually possible, at least hopelessly impractical in terms of the amount of time it would take to describe the (realtime) functioning of the electrical networks involved. And, as Dennett has argued, even more hopeless would be an attempt to predict its future moves on the basis of a sort of Skinnerian analysis of the observed present and past behavior of the computer. (I shall say more shortly about the problems with Skinnerian analysis in connection with the circle of intentions.) Thus intentional explanations of the behavior of systems to which we would very likely hesitate to assign original intentionality may still be valuable, in the sense of being both practical and efficient in terms of the predictions they may allow us to make, in comparison to either design or physical explanations.

For systems about which we might not hesitate quite so much in assigning intentionality, such as nonhuman mammals, there seems to be a degree of naturalness at work when we, for example, say that the beagle there in the field *believes* there is a rabbit in the hole at which he is furiously barking. And in general it certainly makes good sense to predict the future behavior of beagles on the basis of what appear to be their beliefs and expectations with regard to the actions of rabbits. For if we should see a rabbit traverse the field and then observe the beagle, after crossing the rabbit's trail, go off in a direction perpendicular to the trail and continue in that direction indefinitely, we might suppose that such irrational (for beagles) behavior is due to some factor that might call for our taking up a stance other than the intentional one towards such a beagle.

There are complications of sorts, of course, even with beagles, with regard to how we ought to answer the question whether they really have intentionality. One might be inclined to say that following rabbit scent is "hardwired" (that is, genetically programmed) into beagles, and as a result one need not attribute (rabbit-) beliefs to them. However, for beagle behavior of the sort induced by some form of Skinnerian operant conditioning (cf. n. 19) there might be more of a temptation to attribute a nonbehavioristic form of intentionality—unless, of course, one *were* a behaviorist, in which case one would, as a point of received doctrine, at least try to resist the temptation.

I am not sure how much hangs upon resolving the issue whether such animals do or do not have original intentionality (although I shall say something in this connection when I discuss (in chapters 4 and 5) the nature of morality and the claim that animals have moral rights). For, as with the chess-playing computer, intentional explanations may here, too, have certain advantages over physical, or even design, explanations. For invertebrates such as insects it is generally easy enough to see that their behavior is more likely to be explained by reference to their being hardwired, or in another way of putting it, to their failure to respond to operant conditioning (see also the notion of "skinnerian creature," n. 19).

With the intentional systems about which we may hesitate the least in assigning intentionality, namely, humans, there are more complications, and these complications will have to be dealt with before I can claim to have come even close to having pinned down the nature of moral personhood. But for the moment, it should be noticed that here, too, it is true that taking the intentional stance toward a particular human individual need not always produce good results in terms of enabling us to predict the future behavior of that individual. In fact, as for chess-playing computers and beagles, so too for some humans, apparent irrational behavior may call for the assumption of a stance other than the intentional one. The design stance, now in terms of, say, certain inherited features, might be required in order to explain behavior which would be inexplicable in terms of the intentional stance: for example, the responses of a colorblind individual to certain visual stimuli (an individual who might perfectly well *intend* to give what are supposed to be the acceptable responses). Or the physical stance might be required in order to account for the behavior of someone whose performance appears to be markedly irrational, as when it turns out that the individual is suffering from seizures of some sort.

It is of course possible that the apparently irrational behavior of an individual might have an intentional basis. For, as we well know, given the malleability (a fuller story on this is to follow) that is characteristic of human beings with respect to their beliefs and belief systems (and, if Frankfurt 1982 is right, their capacities for caring), we need not be surprised at the performance of a religious or political fanatic. Indeed, the behavior of fanatics is predictable only by taking up a suitable intentional stance (at least so far as I am now aware, no one has succeeded in uncovering any design or physical features that are uniquely characteristic of fanatics. Perhaps one day this will be possible. And then there will be a new moral problem with which to deal, with regard to what we ought to do with such individuals *before* they proceed to do the things they can be predicted with high probability to be capable of doing!).

It should be clear at this point that the account so far given of the nature of intentional systems is quite inadequate as a description of persons, and of moral persons in particular. Dennett has said much more about the nature of persons as special kinds of intentional systems, and I shall return to his views on this subject in what is to follow, in connection with a discussion of higher order intentional systems. But I turn now to the business of explaining the meaning of what I have referred to as the "intentional circle."

The Intentional Circle

The so-called intentional circle makes its appearance when one attempts to supply a strictly behavioristic account of intentionality. For certain purposes—as B. F. Skinner, the paradigm behaviorist, argued in particular, "scientific" purposes—it might appear desirable to be able to dispense with the supposition that there are such things as beliefs, desires, intentions, etc. which in some way exist as nonphysical unobservable mental objects or events, in favor of a description of the physically observable behavior of the individual who is said to have the intentional features in question. In other words, if one could give the right sort of account of the observable physical behavior of the individual when he/she is said to have the intentions under scrutiny, then the intentions might be said to have been *reduced* to the behavior. In that case, one need no longer suppose that the intentions have any mode of existence apart from the observed behavior.

There is certainly an admirable ontological simplicity in so arguing, and Skinner, of course, thought that this was the only possible way to go if one wanted a genuinely scientific account of intentionality.[16] For example, suppose that one wanted to be able to say, in terms of his behavior, whether a man has a certain belief. One might try either asking him (assuming that language is a kind of behavior) or simply watching to see what he does. To get an idea of what is involved, suppose that one wished to determine, say, whether some hypothetical male individual named Smedley believes that a tire on his car needs replacing. Our asking him this assumes that he *understands* our language, and if he understands the language that he then *desires* to respond truthfully to our query, and that if he desires to respond truthfully he does not suffer from akrasia, or weakness of will—and so on, *invariably employing some intentional qualification or another.*

If we pursue the other approach, that is, simply "watching" what he does, his nonverbal behavior, we face similar difficulties. Suppose we observe that he goes to a service station and while he is there a tire on his car is replaced. This by itself is no conclusive proof that he has the belief that the tire needs replacing. For all we know, he may have a service contract calling for the replacement of one tire after the odometer in his car registers a certain number of miles whether or not he believes that it needs replacing. Or it may be that the tire was replaced because the mechanic had discovered a break in its sidewall (and Smedley, given his naïveté about tires, may not have believed him and believed instead that he was being ripped off by an avaricious mechanic). In other words, the behavior we observe is consistent with a variety of intentions on Smedley's part, and I have by no means begun to exhaust the possibilities. What we seem to be faced with is the apparent fact that we cannot determine that a particular piece of behavior corresponds to *just one* particular intentional object without *asking* (in some way) the individual concerned whether this is so. But as soon as we so ask, we are again launched into the kind of series of intentionally qualified claims with which we started.

The upshot of these observations, it has been claimed, is that there seems to be no way to get out of the circle of intentions. Behaviorists, of course, had hoped to do precisely this by reducing intentional objects, capacity, or whatnots to observed behavior, and in so doing had tried to indulge in exactly the sort of reduction I have characterized as illegitimate: only now it was an attempt to supply a behavioral—rather than a physical—explanation of something apparently calling for an intentional explanation. Thus we seem to be left with the need to say that intentional explanations are irreducible—unless, of course, they fail, and one then is forced to other sorts of explanations altogether, such as are required by taking up the design or the physical stances.[17]

But the irreducibility of intentionality by no means entails that intentional explanations cannot be successfully employed in making predictions about the future behavior of intentional systems. Admittedly, there are constraints upon the nature of the predictions, constraints not present in the usual sorts of physical predictions (and I shall shortly say more about this in discussing Donald Davidson's 1970 "anomalous monism"). But an interesting consequence is that it is possible to say that it is not just in the domain of physical events that one may speak of causes.

For one may make quite good sense in claiming that beliefs, desires, etc. may themselves be causes of intentional actions, of genuine actions as opposed to "mere behavior."[18] Intentional explanations may thus serve, in a way physical explanations could not, to enable us to predict the future intentional actions of intentional systems. This is not to say, it is to be remembered, that such physical explanations are impossible in principle—since the intentional is assumed, *ex hypothesi*, to be in some sense a species of the physical—but only that for certain purposes there is a definite advantage to be had in employing unreduced intentional explanations. To make this observation more plausible, I shall next turn to a description of *higher order* intentions, intentions of the type required in order to be in a position to show how talk of persons is possible. And eventually, of course, of moral persons. It will be seen that the phenomena associated with the intentional circle presuppose, after all, the existence of such higher order intentional systems.

Intentional Systems: Higher Order

Again following Dennett 1976, one may have a pair of intentional systems of the type recently characterized, of which it would be possible to say that a relation of "reciprocity" holds between them: The first intentional system, call it A, might be in the position of having a belief about the second intentional system B to the effect that A believes that B has a certain belief, desire, or whatever. And B also could believe that A has a certain belief, desire, or whatever. Such a state of affairs is common enough between human beings, we suppose, but an important point to notice is that its possibility rests upon the assumption of intentional systems: the existence of intentional systems is a necessary (although not a sufficient) condition of the possibility of reciprocity.

Reciprocity, because it requires belief about belief, etc., describes a kind of second (or higher) order intentionality. Since simply being an intentional system is not sufficient for reciprocity, it will thus be inappropriate to attribute beliefs about beliefs to what we may now call a first order intentional system. To use one of our previous examples: while we may find it advantageous to take an intentional stance toward a computer in order to be able to make certain predictions about its performance, it is not necessary that we also speak of it as actually having beliefs or beliefs about beliefs. We do, in fact, come close to this when we are working with a computer program that has been designed, say, to correct input errors of our own making, as when we might say of the program that it 'believes' that we, in miswriting x for y, had intended to write y. But we need not do this in order to utilize the program, any more than we need say that a pay telephone 'believes' that we intend to make a call when we drop a coin in the slot when we wish to use the phone. Whether we ought to attribute second order intentionality to non-human animals is perhaps more problematic. But, as Dennett has argued, it seems to be possible in most cases to get around doing so by the expedient of saying that the animal in question may simply be functioning in such a way as to treat other intentional systems as first order intentional systems of a sort no more complicated than that of the kind Dennett has designated "skinnerian creatures."[19]

Given a suitable pair of higher order intentional systems, the stage is set for the possibility of a special kind of higher order performances: reciprocity, as the capacity for higher order intentionality, is itself a necessary (although not a sufficient) condition for the possibility of verbal communication. For then it can happen that the following state of affairs occurs: Where A and B are now assumed to have the capacity for reciprocity, A may *say* something x to B with the intention of B's understanding by x that A really means something else y. What is going on here is that not only is A attributing a certain belief to B, but that A believes (hopes, expects) that B has a certain belief (understanding) about A's intention (meaning in using x), and this could not be the case *unless verbal communication has taken place*.[20] And again, while we can see that such states of affairs as this are common enough between some (but by no means all) human beings, it is difficult even to take seriously the suggestion that we might make similar attributions to certain computer programs (this in spite of some Artificial Intelligence hype apparently to the contrary). With nonhuman animals things fare no better—it is difficult enough, for example, to teach a dog to fetch a stick by shouting "fetch!" without hopelessly confusing matters by trying to have the dog understand that by your saying "fetch!" you really intended "heel!"[21] In spite of possessing many virtues, man's best friend, by lacking verbal communication, must, among other things, forever lack the virtue of laughing at one's jokes, or the capacity to learn to bring one's slippers only on prime-numbered days of the month! The accession to power made possible by the capacity for verbal communication carries with it, ironically, a feature that will dog our efforts at a later stage to pin down the nature of persons, and of moral persons. But more of this later.

Once again, continuing Dennett's line of reasoning, with the capacity for verbal communication as a necessary condition, it is possible to describe the capacity usually associated with human beings, namely, their capacity for consciousness and self-consciousness. But since the capacity for verbal communication *is* a necessary condition for consciousness, we are faced with problems in the presence of those who may never have had it, or those who may once have had it but no longer do so. The attribution of consciousness in the absence of any way of confirming the attribution via verbal communication pushes us close to saying that we are then talking about a mere (i.e., first order) intentional being: we might *desire*, certainly, to attribute the capacity for consciousness to certain individuals, for a variety of reasons (e.g., if one has a comatose relative), but this desire by no means by itself is enough to guarantee that consciousness (or the capacity for it) is indeed present.[22]

Consciousness—and especially self-consciousness—when present together with the necessary conditions making it possible, also makes it possible for individuals having it to be capable of (verbally) communicating with themselves: such self-conscious individuals possess the capacity to conduct a kind of internal discourse with, or examination of, themselves (i.e., to "dialogue" with their own beliefs, desires, intentions, etc.) in an intentional sense. This means that they can have and articulate beliefs about their own beliefs, desires about their own desires, and so on.

Individuals capable not only of self-communication but of controlling their own desires, or of changing their desires at will, are said (à la Harry Frankfurt 1971) to have second order volitions; and such individuals may be said to be *free* in an important sense that is necessary for our being able to attribute to them genuine responsibility. Such individuals thus have one of the features, it can be argued, that is essential to their being persons. Not all human beings, by any means, are capable of changing their desires at their own volition; many are no different from nonhuman animals who simply have desires of the first order kind, which they may follow or not—they are not at liberty to alter the desires that they in fact have by substituting others in their places, or even of framing to themselves the possibility of doing so (assuming they lack this sort of self-awareness). I, for example, as a non-heroin-addict, may have the desire to know what it is like to have the desire for heroin that the addict has, without yielding to that desire; the addict is not free in this sense.

Our account of Dennett's argument is now almost complete. A person, he wants to say, is the sort of thing which all of the capacities we have described, linked as they are as necessary conditions each of the next, beginning with the capacity for being a first order intentional system, through the capacities for second and higher order intentions and verbal communication, and ending with the capacity for consciousness and self-consciousness, conjointly make possible. But, curiously enough, he stops short of saying that all of these conditions, while individually necessary, add up to being a sufficient condition for personhood. The reason he gives for this state of affairs is that the concept of a person is "inescapably normative," and this is due to the fact that "there is no objectively satisfiable sufficient condition for an entity's *really* having beliefs" (285). The only avenue we have for determining what are, in fact, an individual's beliefs is by way of verbal communication. And this is a part of the intentional circle, it will be recalled, according to which there can be no reduction of beliefs to behavior: so an individual's *telling* us that he/she has a certain belief is all we can have to go on in the final analysis; it is impossible for anyone to have direct access to the beliefs of another. We make the normative assumption that an individual's avowals of his beliefs will accurately capture them. Whence the problem I shall refer to in what follows as that of the veridicality of belief.[23]

According to Dennett, what is true of persons is true of moral persons as well. Although he does not himself supply anything explicitly in the way of a moral theory, one of his assumptions seems to be connected with the familiar Kantian one to the effect that moral persons are those who are capable of following a rule, or of making the judgment that a particular action of theirs falls under a certain rule or is of a certain kind. If this were not the case, it would be impossible to hold them responsible for their actions. Obviously, only an individual who is a person, that is, in Dennett's sense, one who is self-conscious, could do this. For Dennett the concept of a person thus defined is an essentially normative one, and the concept of a moral person, which has for its possibility the concept of a person as a necessary condition, is also essentially normative. Furthermore, as he puts it, the two concepts simply occupy different positions on the same continuum (I shall refer to this in what follows as Dennett's "continuum hypothesis"). This normative feature of persons leads Dennett to say:

> Our assumption that an entity is a person is shaken precisely in those cases where it matters: when wrong has been done and the question of responsibility arises. For in these cases the grounds for saying that the person is culpable (the evidence that he did wrong, was aware he was doing wrong, and did wrong of his own free will) are in themselves grounds for doubting that it is a person we are dealing with at all. And if it is asked what could *settle* our doubts, the answer is: nothing. When such problems arise we cannot even tell in our own cases if we are persons.[24]

It is on this not entirely optimistic note that Dennett ends, in the 1976 article, his deliberations upon the nature of persons and of moral persons. He does, however, throw out an additional idea in another paper, where he suggests that "it is of the essence of personhood that a person can change his mind"(Dennett 1978 309).[25] He argues that "changing one's mind" is to be characterized as changing one's opinions, but not one's beliefs, where he defines an opinion as a belief to which one has assented (304). It is difficult to be sure how much significance is to be attached to this way of talking about a distinction between beliefs and opinions, since in yet another essay he suggests that beliefs are themselves, in fact, to be understood as being "essentially" the sorts of things that he says have been "*endorsed* (by commission or omission) by the agent on the basis of . . . [their] conformity with the rest of his beliefs" (252). It is not clear exactly how mind changes, however they ought to be described in terms of beliefs and opinions, should be fitted into the set of necessary conditions for personhood he has provided—perhaps somewhere in the capacity for being conscious and self-conscious—or why he wants to say that it is essential to personhood—unless he intends mind changes to be one of the things, like one's first order desires, that may be under one's control.

It should be noted that Dennett's account is a functionalist one in the following sense: intentional systems, of whatever order, may presumably be realized in a variety of ways. It is not necessary that humans be the only higher order intentional systems. There are, it is to be conjectured, any number of levels of *non*intentional features at work behind the intentional scenes, including the features responsible for accounting for what it is like to have the first-person "feel" of colors, sounds, etc., as well as the elusive first-person "feel" of what it is to be conscious and self-conscious generally (cf. Lycan 1987, especially chap. 4).

It would be appropriate at this point to summarize the aspects of Dennett's approach that seem to call for more attention if we are to be able to have in our hands anything like an adequate picture of *moral* personhood, on the assumption that his account of *personhood* represents at least a good first approximation of what is needed:

1. With the exception of a somewhat enigmatic reference to Rawls's theory of justice (as developed in Rawls 1971), in which Dennett argues that "our grounds for considering an entity a person include our ability to view him as abiding by the principles of justice" (282), where he says that Rawls "intends" to argue that justice is not the result of *human* interaction but of *personal* interaction—and, as such, is connected with morality—Dennett himself does not introduce anything in the way of either an explicit moral theory or a theory of justice. The reason I say that this is enigmatic is that Dennett introduces what he takes to be a notion implicit in Rawls's account into his own description of the conditions of personhood prior to the point at which he has in place all of the conditions he considers to be necessary for personhood; and these conditions, in the way he sets them up, must be in place before one is able to talk about moral personhood. In fact, according to his own argument, Dennett suggests that the possibility of holding a (higher order) intentional system *responsible* for its actions must await the presence of the necessary condition of personhood we have referred to as having to do with the capacity for consciousness, and in particular the sort of self-consciousness allowing such a system to judge that its actions fall under a certain rule or concept. Dennett suggests that all of the conditions preceding this one "may play a role in ethics"(281), but does not really elaborate upon how this is to be done. Clearly something more is needed in the way of an account both of moral theory and of the manner in which it is to deal with higher order intentions and, especially, the capacity for verbal communication. So this will be another of the things to which I shall have to devote more attention in the investigations to follow, in particular in chapter 4, "Moral Theory."

2. Dennett says nothing, really, about two elements, apparently indispensable to a theory of moral personhood, elements that will figure very much in the discussion to follow: namely, the process by which certain human individuals get to be moral persons, and the manner in which some moral persons cease to be moral persons (either slowly or very abruptly). These elements, I shall argue (in chap. 5), must be a part of what I shall be describing as a *person schema*, or the sort of intentional template or conceptual framework to be found in those natural (or better, it will proposed, *intentional*) kinds which

actually develop into persons. Elaborating this description presupposes, of course, a suitable adaptation of talk of "natural kinds" (most discussions of which have up until this time been devoted to other sorts of things entirely) to the case of persons, and even to moral persons. Some of this development will take place in the section to follow, and the rest further on.

3. Connected with 2, it will be necessary to set up a way of making sense of the notions of intentional causation and intentional explanation, neither of which is really developed in Dennett's account in the detailed manner they require. Again, much of this will take place in the section to follow.

4. A proper accounting of the problems to be met with in mind changing, apparently unresolved in Dennett, as we recently noticed, needs working out, especially in view of the feature of persons I am referring to as their malleability. This is a feature creating a problem of its own of a rather serious kind, and one unnoticed in Dennett's discussion. And it is connected as well with such matters as the interesting claim made by Herbert Morris 1968 that persons who have violated moral or legal rules have a right to punishment rather than to treatment, on the ground that (the proper sort of) punishment would leave intact whatever mechanisms are responsible for the intentional aspects of a person, while any form of treatment would alter some of these mechanisms. I shall discuss these matters in chapter 5. Related to this also is the notion of Dennett's I have referred to as his "continuum hypothesis," which is his claim that persons and moral persons occupy two points on the same continuum, an hypothesis about which I shall have reason to raise questions.

Intentional Causation, Intentional Explanation, Natural Kinds, and Anomalous Monism

Several times in the foregoing discussion I have made reference to intentional causes and intentional explanations, and to connections between these notions and the possibility of moral personhood, with the promise that more about these notions would be forthcoming. So I shall at this point take the opportunity to make a beginning at fulfilling that promise.

In keeping with the hypothesis that human persons, whatever else they might be, are at least material or physical objects of some sort, it could be expected that there would be connected with them, or to start with, at least with their bodies or nonintentional features, causal relationships of the familiar sort known to experimental science. For example, it is quite well established that there are causal connections between a variety of environmental conditions and things that occur in living human bodies, and vice versa. To mention only one of these connections, think of the manner in which oxygen and carbon dioxide are involved, with living human bodies requiring the first for metabolism to occur, and giving off the second as a metabolic product.

Thus to understand, or to give an explanation of, the process of metabolism in living human bodies, requires reference to at least these substances, one a chemical element and the other a chemical compound, which play fundamental causal roles in the life process.

With such an explanation in hand, it then becomes possible to make a variety of predictions, or to describe certain projectible features, features which are true of the behavior of such bodies under a variety of conditions. One way of expressing such matters is to use the lingo of counterfactuals or of possible worlds: one might say, for example, of a certain living human body that is presently seated before a computer in my study, that if it—contrary to fact, or counterfactually—were placed ten feet under water with no provision made for a supply of oxygen to its lungs, metabolism in that body would cease after a specified length of time, and it would be a dead human body. Or alternatively, that there is a possible world in which that living human body would not long remain alive. We feel rather comfortable with the claim that what is being predicted here would take place, given the actual occurrence of the conditions which are presently contrary to fact (or which hold only in a possible world and do not hold in the actual world), and we would be inclined to be rather impatient with anyone who professed to believe otherwise.

Suppose, for example, that there were those who did believe otherwise, and who were in fact adherents of a religious group whose members, instead of testing the strength of their "faith in the Lord" by way of handling poisonous snakes or drinking a solution of strychnine, chose to accomplish this goal by temporally extended complete immersion of themselves in water. The fact that there are no living members who have tested their faith in this manner need not deter the rest, of course, from following in the footsteps of their dear departed brethren. The fact that this is a small—and constantly decreasing in size —religious group would be an indicator to most of the rest of us that their avowed belief in the possibility of human bodies remaining alive for extended periods of time under water is an objectively false belief. And, moreover, we would think that the demonstrated fact that they are willing to die for their belief does nothing to change this (nor does the fact that in the United States they presumably have the constitutional right to do what they do in the name of religion).

But now we do have examples that illustrate some of the notions to which we have been referring. The process of metabolism in living human bodies, and its relationship to oxygen and carbon dioxide, would be described as a nonintentional matter involving *nonintentional causes*; the explanation of metabolism as a process dependent upon the properties of these compounds would be a *nonintentional explanation*. Now the only plausible—and relatively simple, given our present ability to understand the neurobiochemistry of human beings—explanation (at least pending the discovery of some hitherto unrecognized Freudian aqueous complex, caused, perhaps, by a prenatal fixation upon the fluid life!) for the behavior of our aqueous believers is an *intentional explanation.* While it is certainly true that the county coroner would list drowning as the cause of death—and this is a straightforward nonintentional causal matter—the explanation for *these* drowning victims being underwater must be attributed to an *intentional cause*: namely *their belief* that the Lord would sustain their lives while under water if their faith were sufficiently strong, or at the least the belief that they would lose face in the eyes of their brethren if they chose not to take the plunge. This, notice, is a higher order belief, requiring as it does a reference to the beliefs of other higher order intentional systems: hence we have a higher order intentional cause. It needs to be remembered, certainly, that the intentional explanation, and the associated intentional cause, because of the assumption of the materialist hypothesis, are both in principle connected in some way to a nonintentional explanation and to nonintentional causes. But we are so far from being able to make such connections that we are quite well-off operating with the unreduced intentional cause and explanation as we have described them.[26]

There are, however, some rather formidable problems that must be faced in connection with the employment of such unreduced intentional causes and explanations.[27] These problems have been concealed so far by my rendition of the examples chosen here, but they have been alluded to above, in the discussion of Dennett's views on the nature of belief. Before I proceed to an account of some of these problems, however, I want to bring into the picture one additional piece of philosopher's paraphenalia, in order both to focus more sharply the discussion and to make more evident how pressing is the need for dealing with these problems; and, as it turns out, to pose yet another problem to be handled as regards the nature of moral persons. This piece of paraphenalia is known as the concept of *natural kinds.*

It is a familiar enough observation in philosophy that the construction of categories of things can be done quite arbitrarily: one can, with (almost) no limit define classes of things as one pleases.[28] And this arbitrariness could lead one to espouse some form of self-stultifying subjectivism or relativism. Thus it is no surprise that philosophers since the time of Plato (who apparently was quite concerned to combat such a tendency toward subjectivism or relativism as he saw them exemplified in the deliverances of his rivals, the sophists) have sought to come up with a way of picking out some features of reality that could be viewed as "really there," no matter what one's subjective viewpoint might be. In recent years, several philosophers (Rogers Albritton, Saul Kripke, Hilary Putnam, and W. V. Quine, among others) have proposed ways of doing this in terms of "natural kinds" as categories of things that are in a suitable sense "really there" in the physical world, independently of the contrivances of human beings. I shall describe the way Putnam 1970, 1973 has proposed that this be done, since his approach will figure in the discussions of persons and personal identity to follow. I shall place in brackets the manner in which Saul Kripke's notion of a "rigid designator" might be employed in this connection.

Putnam's version of natural kinds stipulates (roughly) that the only natural (as opposed to conventional) kinds are the groupings of individuals or substances made in accordance with the most adequate true scientific theory. This means, among other things, that the surface appearances (i.e., those perceptible to those with human senses) of these individuals or substances need have little or nothing to do with making the classification. For the basis of the classification, which has to be in conformity with scientific (i.e., in some sense "natural" as opposed to conventional) law, may refer to features of the individuals or substances that are in some sense hidden in their "deep" structure. One of the examples most frequently employed has been that of 'water', as a natural kind term, understood, of course, in the sense of H_2O, which together with the related physical theory and/or the relevant natural laws, picks out in a unique way [Kripke: rigidly designates] a certain kind of "stuff," independently of any description (subjective or otherwise) of its surface (i.e., humanly perceivable) appearances.

Another way of saying what is wanted, perhaps, is that a thing is an instance of a natural kind if there is a description of it possible that will be invariant with regard to the nature, location, construction, etc., of its observer(s). One of the hopes of Putnam (and others) has been that our present scientific way of designating water (i.e., H_2O) captures precisely such a sufficient condition. But, presumably, there is no need to require that it be a necessary condition as well, for it is certainly possible for there to be other ways of referring to the stuff we designate as H_2O, ways which would also be sufficient (such, for example, as future versions of our own scientific theory which might turn out to be unrecognizable as such by us) to pick it out as a natural kind.

Some of the connections between talk of natural kinds and our talk of intentional causes and explanations, in terms of my examples, to start with, are as follows. Oxygen (i.e., O_2) and carbon dioxide (i.e., CO_2), are, of course natural kinds, and via the appropriate natural laws, are related (causally) to metabolism, which is a *natural process*. Thus to supply a nonintentional explanation of metabolism in terms of natural kinds and processes is to supply a genuinely scientific explanation, because of the definition of 'natural'. To supply an intentional explanation of the behavior of our religious friends, in terms of the intentional cause (that is, their belief in aqueous testing of the strength of their faith in their Lord) of their performances, it is apparently not necessary to refer explicitly to any natural kinds or processes.

So such an intentional explanation, whatever else might be said of it, is not a genuinely scientific explanation, in spite of the fact that we might have a relatively high degree of confidence in predicting the future behavior of the living members of the sect. To put it in another way, we would say that the thing—the particular belief—referred to by the expression 'belief in aqueous testing of the strength of one's faith in the Lord,' for which a kind term could always be devised (such as 'aqueous belief'), does not represent an instance of a natural kind, for the reason that no intentional object is a natural kind, nor is any intentional term a natural kind term, in the sense intended by Putnam. [In Kripkean lingo, 'aqueous belief' would not be a rigid designator, for the reason that no belief (or other intentional) term could be.] That particular intentional objects, of whatever sort, are not and cannot be instances of natural kinds is due, for one reason, to the fact that they are not individuals or substances, in the sense in which this term is intended to pick out certain naturally occurring material objects or substances, such as water and other chemical compounds.

So if one proposes, as we have seen Dennett doing, that persons are to be viewed as a certain sort of higher order intentional system, it would appear that there is no chance whatsoever of describing them as instances of a natural kind, and consequently, no chance of having *scientific* explanations of their actions *as persons*. Scientific explanations with respect to them could be had only by adopting either a design or a physical stance towards them, and this would mean, of course, that they would not be being viewed as persons. Now couple this outcome with Dennett's apparent pessimism with regard to determining in a conclusive way such things even as that one is oneself a person, because of the difficulty of having any objective way of showing that anyone (including oneself) *really has* any belief (much less a whole set of beliefs), because of the problem of the veridicality of belief, in spite of the capacity for verbal communication, and it begins to look as if the prospects for really adequate intentional explanations, and for uncovering genuine intentional causes, do not appear very favorable.

Thus with no scientific explanation possible, and the possibility of only an inadequate intentional explanation, one apparently has a double reason for being pessimistic about the chances of arriving at an understanding of intentional systems (i.e., those with original intentionality) as such, or of persons qua persons, even on the assumption that they are indeed such systems. A measure of relief from such pessimism (or, I suppose, some might read it as a further *confirmation* of such pessimism!) can be gleaned from a doctrine advanced by Donald Davidson 1970 ("Mental Events") which he called "anomalous monism," an account of which I shall now supply.

Davidson's anomalous monism was originally devised (at least in part) in order to supply a solution to certain problems raised by an identification of the mental with the physical, and thus as a contribution to formulating a version of the sort of materialism I referred to at the beginning of this chapter. The "monism" being described is precisely a type of materialism, and is expressed by the claim that all events, including mental (i.e., intentional) events, are physical (material). But by saying that it is an *anomalous* monism, Davidson wishes to enter a caveat to the effect that while mental events are physical, it is not the case that they can always be given explanations in terms of the sorts of laws (nomoi) ordinarily employed in the explanations of other physical events. For example, the (nonintentional) causal (or other natural) laws to which one might appeal in giving an explanation for a certain non-mental physical event could not be appealed to in giving an explanation for mental (physical) events. Thus, to speak as I have been doing of intentional causes, and of explanations based upon such causes is, according to Davidson, to employ the word *cause* in a special sense. In other words, the drowning of one of our aqueous believers, which I said was *caused* by a certain belief, should actually be viewed as an anomalous event if one understands that "cause" and "causal law" are being reserved exclusively for descriptions of nonmental physical events. To speak of drowning as the cause of death of a certain individual would by no means be anomalous, but would be simply an application of a standard use of a causal relation of a law-like sort. Indeed, an essential part of Davidson's thesis is that saying that mental events are physical entails that they are dependent upon physical events in a variety of ways: viz., particular mental events can be the causes of, or the effects of, physical events. Otherwise our aqueous believers would not be able, by taking the plunge, to put their beliefs into action, nor would they have been able to acquire their belief from others in the first place.

But again, the anomalous feature of such mental or intentional events as decisions based upon beliefs is reflected in the observation that there can be no strict psychophysical laws or strict law-like links between them and the nonmental events of which they are the causes or effects. The primary reason for this state of affairs is one that is by now familiar enough to the reader: there can be, according to Davidson, no "reduction" of the mental or the intentional to the physical in terms of a behavioristic account of physically observable objects. In other words, the intentional circle is in effect, and no kind of genuine "translation" of mental or intentional vocabulary into a strictly physical vocabulary is possible.

The only avenue available to us for determining that *specific* (contentful) mental events are even occurring is via verbal communication: we do not, after all, know that the cause of our aqueous believer's taking the plunge is the decision to act in accordance with a certain belief unless s/he *tells* us.[29] For what we *observe* would be no different if s/he had decided (for whatever reason) to commit suicide by drowning in this particular manner. And there are, in fact, many nonintentional kinds of things possible, which if they happened to an individual, would produce observable outcomes of exactly the same sort.

Now Davidson apparently has seen no cause for alarm or pessimism as a result of adopting the doctrine of anomalous monism. Indeed, he rather has viewed the adoption of the doctrine as an honest and straightforward admission that the science of psychology, insofar as it is understood to be concerned with mental or intentional events and capabilities, must of necessity operate under constraints different from those to be discovered in sciences whose subject matter is to be found in the domain of the nonintentional. Furthermore, he has thought, apparently, that the doctrine makes it possible to show that those who may have believed that the advance of science (i.e., science of the nonintentional) somehow has made inroads of a destructive sort in the area of mental autonomy, have been laboring under a kind of illusion. Saying this need in no way be understood either as belittling the stature of psychology as a science or as detracting from the undeniably successful efforts of the sciences of the nonintentional.

Davidson's belief, with regard to those philosophers who (following Wittgenstein) for many years argued that there was no role to be played by the concept of cause in connection with explanations of intentional behavior, might be expressed by the suggestion that they suffered from having a cramped notion of cause.[30] The doctrine of anomalous monism, by making clear just what the proper nature of mental or intentional events might be, and by showing what some of the constraints to be placed upon explanations of mental or intentional events are, at the same time makes it possible, by preserving mental/intentional autonomy, to argue for moral autonomy, on the assumption that the moral is nothing else than a species of the mental/intentional.

Davidson has himself said little about the details of the linkages between morality, intentionality, and moral personhood, so one of the things I view myself as doing in some of the investigations still to follow is simply to draw out some ideas which I take to be implicit in his work.[31] Davidson (1970, 116) has said, in a tantalizing way, about persons: "To the extent that we fail to discover a coherent and plausible pattern in the attitudes and actions of others we simply forgo the chance of treating them as persons." Left unanswered are the questions, What, exactly is "a coherent and plausible pattern in the attitudes and actions" of an individual? and What would constitute such a pattern in the moral attitudes and actions of another (person)? It becomes possible, I shall propose, to describe such patterns once one has in hand the moral person schema sketched below (chap. 5, sec.1). But an understanding of that schema requires explanations of the notions of malleability and intentional selection, tasks to which we turn in the next chapter, and of the notion of morality, to which initial attention is given in the chapter that follows it.

3

Malleable Persons

In what is to follow immediately here, I shall sketch first what I understand by the notion of malleability, both as a feature of human individuals and as a feature of the species. Then I shall, by making use of some results from the domain of Computer Science, suggest some ways in which a certain type of computer might serve as a kind of model for the sort of malleability of interest here. The reader who is unfamiliar with talk of Turing machines or computer jargon, or who, for whatever reason, is intimidated by such talk, might do well to skip directly to the section on *Insights from Computer Science*. Finally, I shall attempt an explanation, via some speculations with regard to the possible manner in which certain kinds of mechanisms might have developed in the human species over evolutionary time, by way of what I call "the hypothesis of Intentional Selection," of the malleability which seems to be a necessary feature of persons.

1. Malleability

In order further to help get our thinking in order on the subject of persons, it will be instructive to pursue the following query: what sort of a thing must a person be if it is to be possible that he/she/it be capable of such things as: granting (informed) consent, having a right to x, being an agent, being responsible, etc., in moral and legal contexts; or, *in general* of being *malleable* to the extent of being able to take on and to affirm, or to subscribe to, widely divergent and sometimes conflicting beliefs and belief systems of varying types and orders such as those found in ideologies, religions, and cultures.[1] In a manner of speaking, the notion of malleability might be looked

upon as a generalization of the sort of view expressed many years ago by
Margaret Mead in connection with her anthropological investigations, which
suggested the cultural variability of sex roles:

> We are forced to conclude that human nature is almost unbelievably malleable,
> responding accurately and contrastingly to contrasting cultural conditions. . . .
> Standardized personality differences between the sexes are of this order, cultural
> creations to which each generation, male and female, is trained to conform.[2]

More recently, Richard Dawkins (in his *The Selfish Gene*, Oxford University Press, 1976) getting at the same sort of thing, only in terms of a capacity to simulate, has put it in the form of a biological mystery:

> The evolution of the capacity to simulate seems to have culminated in subjective
> consciousness. Why this should have happened is, to me, the most profound
> mystery facing modern biology.

But malleability also means being capable *in particular* of showing variability in believing things that are of direct interest to us in the present investigations. Such, for example, as believing in J. Reiman's right to privacy (Reiman
1976) as a right to the existence of a social practice, or of being reluctant to
formulate laws which could place such a right in jeopardy (Gavison 1980); or
of believing (or not believing) that the right to privacy is itself reducible to
other rights, legal and/or moral.[3] I have omitted to point out that the beliefs/
belief systems just referred to are relatively sophisticated—because they deal
with higher order intentions— when compared to the sorts of beliefs, intentions, etc. one might hold with regard to happenings in the physical world
involving one's dealings with things that are pretty clearly not intentional
systems, or if intentional systems, those other than the sort characteristically
found in normal adult human individuals. Perhaps some of the beliefs/systems
referring to the nonintentional world are not quite so prone to the wide variations afflicting those involving higher order intentions, at least if one accepts
the belief-sorting mechanisms of the experimental sciences. Granted, it would
be just as unrealistic to say that *all* human individuals are capable of operating
with—in the sense of being self-consciously articulate about—a wide range of
higher order intentions as to say that they could operate in a sophisticated
way with scientific concepts. But this is a capability the presence of which
would mark a sufficient condition for personhood, or at least for a certain
fundamental sort of moral personhood—and a necessary condition for the
existence of possible moral worlds (this is a point I return to below, chap. 6,
sec. 1).

As I see it, malleability is a property describing a function characteristic not only of the species, *homo sapiens* (and, I shall argue, of what I shall refer to as a "person schema" in chapter 5) but of human individuals, where it may manifest itself in terms of such characteristics as intelligence, foresight, and the capacity for sympathetic understanding of other similar individuals. What I intend to refer to here by using the term *malleability* is to something about the nature of the mind insofar as it might be a component of a (moral) person, *whatever the physical realization of such a person might happen to be.* If some version of functionalism is right, of course, minds and their intentional capacities might be realized in locations other than the brains of human beings.[4] What I would like to be able to describe is the structure of the mind that is found in these realizations, the structure that makes it possible for some such realizations to be called "persons". Something about this structure must account for the presence in it of what we have referred to as the feature of intentionality: the capacities for having differing orders of beliefs, desires, intentions, expectations, etc.—the whole range, in fact, of the things that characterize higher order intentional systems—as well as the immense variety of actual beliefs, intentions, etc., the mental referents or instantiations of the things to which I have alluded as intentional objects.

In short, what I want is a functionalist account of persons as those minds with the property of higher order intentionality having a certain type of physical embodiment.[5] And it may well be the case, as a matter of fact, that what I shall be forced to settle for may come up short on some kinds of detail. I shall very likely have to be content with an explanation at the level of what Haugeland (1981, 256) has termed an "intentional black box" account of the mind: as when the mind is supplied with intentional input and intentional output emerges, but what it is that happens "inside" the mind (whether the "mechanism" is reduced or unreduced) in the interim remains a mystery. What I mean by this is that the manner in which intentions, beliefs, etc., are encoded, or represented, in the mind is left unresolved. In *some sense*, it must be true that most human individuals are genetically programmed to be potential persons, although the details of this programming are presently unknown. This need not prevent us from trying to describe the (unreduced) features of persons: such a description will be forthcoming in chapter 5, sec. 1, in terms of what I there refer to as a "person schema."

It would also be of interest to be able to have an explanation for the fact that beliefs are found to occupy positions in systems, systems which, while to some degree consistent with themselves, may turn out not to be consistent with other belief systems.[6] What I understand here by "consistent" need not, of course, be the strict sense of formal logical consistency familiar to philosophers and logicians. But rather a notion that might more appropriately be called "belief consistency," or a form of *intentional consistency*, to indicate that the holder(s) of the belief system is(are) in the position of *believing* it to be consistent (whether or not it is in fact logically consistent: the locution, intentional object, may be used to refer to such "believed-to-be-consistent" things, things which could, of course, include fictional elements). This allows, certainly, for the possibility that a pair of belief systems believed to be inconsistent with each other could turn out to be in actuality mutually consistent from a logical point of view.

Historically, probably some of the most socially troublesome belief systems involving intentional consistency have been found in the area of religion. This is due to the fact that one of the beliefs typically found in some religious belief systems is the belief that only that system can be the "true" system, and only adherents to that system can be "true" believers.[7] The presence among scientists of those who subscribe to rather fundamentalist religious belief systems has always fascinated me, and might be cited as further evidence for the malleability of persons, if such evidence were needed.[8]

Unlike those religious belief systems where the adherents of systems believed to be inconsistent with each other may actually kill each other in the name of religion, the *scientific belief system* settles for the more humane practice of the killing off only of the results of research that does not meet the standards of the scientific institution (this does not rule out the possibility that particular scientists might have too much of themselves personally tied up in the results of their research, and that its demise might be causally connected (in both an intentional and a physical sense) with their demises). It is perhaps unnecessary to remind ourselves of the fact that political ideologies may also function in the same way, and that (to use a well-known historical example) not all scientists and intellectuals followed the lead of Albert Einstein and others in fleeing Nazi Germany: evidence again of the malleability of persons in their capacity to hold remarkably varied beliefs and belief systems.

It is possible that religious belief systems have played a part in the development, over time, of the intentional features of those human beings we shall have reason to characterize as persons. This is a theme to which I shall return shortly in this chapter in the section to follow, Malleability and Evolution: Intentional Selection.

2. A Model for Malleability: the Computer

Embodied Turing Machines: Hardware, Software, and Computer Science

A useful model for the demonstrated malleability of persons may be found by reflecting upon the nature of a certain type of suitably programmable computer. By a "suitably programmable" computer I mean a computer of a design sufficiently sophisticated that it can (with the help of the right sort of programmer) be programmed to do anything that any computer (within specified limits) can do. This, to those familiar with Turing machines, might be described as an actual embodiment of one kind of universal Turing machine.[9] Thus one and the same such computer demonstrates a high degree of malleability: it can be a word processor, a calculator, a manipulator of spread sheets, or whatever it might be that an as yet undesigned program might allow it to be. Until a program is loaded into it, however, it is not any of these things in particular—one might say that it is a "potential" word processor, etc. The right sort of such a computer could, of course, be several of these things at the same time (when it is running TULIP 345, or CONCERTO, for example) without there being any sort of internal conflict (subject to the design of the computer's central processing unit, its memory capacity, whether it has time-sharing capability, etc.).

It is fast becoming commonplace to say that human beings also are "programmed" over the course of time to become the sorts of individuals they eventually turn out to be. Thus they, like the computer I have just described, also are potentially a wide variety of things. But, as with many commonplace observations, there are upon closer examination some troublesome features of the computer model, features that are a continuing source of disputation among those who engage in inquiry in this area.

Those who work in Artificial Intelligence (AI), cognitive psychology (which together with linguistics are sometimes called "cognitive science"), and philosophy of mind have produced no small budget of problems, many of them connected with the applicability of computer models to the mind. I shall make no attempt to canvass all of the loci of disputation, by any means.[10] But one of the unavoidable features of work in this domain has turned out to be the very rapidity with which developments have taken place in both hardware and software, and this has undoubtedly contributed to some of the sorts of confusion—and the delusions—that are observable in some discussions of both achievements and of prospects, especially in AI. There has also been a tendency on the part of some of those involved in the writing of AI programs to be misled by their own vocabulary into thinking that the computers programmed with their programs have rather extraordinary capacities.[11]

Putting aside the hype, however, there is not only some truth to the claim that a certain kind of computer is potentially a whole range of distinct things, but there do exist explanations of the nature of the structures, in terms both of hardware and software, that make this claim possible. There was at one point, certainly, a temptation to ease rather too quickly into transferring computer talk to our attempts to understand the human mind. A number of philosophers, for example, yielded to the temptation and rushed rather hastily to the conclusion that the human mind could be "reduced to" certain sorts of Turing machines, a view sometimes labeled "Turing machine functionalism."[12] Subsequent investigation, as well as actual developments in computer design, have shown that this was at least an oversimplification, if not something worse, for it is not true without qualification even of what I have been referring to as a current generation suitably programmable computer. Turing himself, although a programmer as well as a theoretician, could not have foreseen, among other things, the development of several layers, or levels, of programming languages, and the enormous increase in memory capacity making possible the stored program, artifacts resulting from the empirical nature of computer science.[13] This development not only made life easier for programmers—and may (so we are told) be on the verge of eliminating the jobs of certain kinds of programmers by programs that do programming—but has contributed as well to the need to revise our model of what a "suitably programmable" computer is.[14] And, in turn, the manner in which we might employ computer models in examining the nature of human minds.[15]

The so-called higher level programming languages, like the various dialects of BASIC and PASCAL familiar to students in the 1980s, greatly simplified the business of programming, since it is no longer necessary—at least for certain purposes—to do what is now called "machine language programming," or what in earlier days *was* programming, i.e., employing the ones and zeroes now frequently viewed as rather tedious and theoretical (someone still must write machine language [the code the machine actually operates by] and assemblers [the code of a higher level sort that clumps together frequently used stretches of machine code], but these tasks have been made much easier by some of the developments in computers themselves which, along with new generations of software, can be enlisted to perform much of the drudgework).

Insights from Computer Science

But it is some of the insights made possible by such advances that are most worth remarking: one can use a computer in certain ways today without having to know anything at all about what is going on at the machine language (or assembly language) level in the computer. The simplest of actions, like pressing a key to get a certain character displayed on the computer's monitor, have underlying them and making them possible a quite complex series of things happening out of sight of the operator in the form not only of hardware but of software as well. (And, with a term itself taken over from the design of electronic circuits, "biofeedback" allows those of us who have trained ourselves in the right sort of way to make things happen in our own bodies, the details of which we need have no knowledge. For example, relaxation techniques allow changes to be made voluntarily in what have traditionally been referred to as the autonomic systems of the body, in which very complex neuro-biochemical processes take place.) Part of the insight is that while what we see happening can look familiar enough to us, what is going on unseen several layers down would be hopelessly unfamiliar and intimidating except to those trained to operate at those lower levels—whether in computers or human neurophysiology.[16]

Another part of this insight is that there is a high degree of uniformity in the nature of the combination of hardware and software making all of this possible: the physical computer I have referred to as "suitably programmable" and potentially so many different sorts of things may be produced by many different manufacturers under many names. (One of the stated goals to be met in the designing of the "right" sort of programming language has been that it be "transportable," or usable on a variety of computers independently of the hardware configuration; the attainment of this goal would mean that there would be a similar kind of universality in software as well as hardware—within the practical constraints, of course, of the competitive nature of the industry.) The *functional* similarities are such that, for a simple example, one may expect that what one does with the keyboard of one computer is going to correspond closely enough to what one does with another that ordinarily no insurmountable problems are produced by moving from one computer keyboard to another.

Still another insight, and perhaps one of the most important, is the sort we have seen referred to in terms of taking up the "intentional stance" toward a thing (chap. 2, sec. 2 above). It has become fairly routine to take up the intentional stance toward certain programmed computers, such as those programmed to play chess, as when we ask, Will it *choose* to sacrifice its bishop? Or when we find ourselves asking such questions as, Has the computer *recognized* the extra memory with which we have equipped it? Our predictions of what such computers are going to be doing with future input are much more easily dealt with by assuming, via the intentional stance, that they "know" (or do not "know") what move to make, or whether there is sufficient memory to perform a certain task, than by taking up either a design (perhaps the computer recognizes the extra memory but its program does not call up and display on the monitor a message to that effect—this would require actually looking at the program) or a physical stance. It may be granted, certainly, that we, before the appearance of such computers, did indeed take up such a stance toward objects such as plants (as well as animals). But the computer case has somehow impressed upon us the importance of the stance for the purposes of a quite legitimate kind of understanding and prediction.

The power of such insights when brought to bear upon the nature of the human mind has yet to be fully probed. It will become commonplace, no doubt, to speak of the human brain as hardware (or "wetware"), having essentially the same structure in all (normal) members of the species (wherever they happen to be "manufactured"). Or, as it might better be expressed, there is at least a strong functional isomorphism between the brains of all members of the species. Putting it in this way allows for certain (functionally inessential) variations in the anatomical structures of individual brains (and in the observed apparent shifting of functions from one area to another in damaged brains) or, for example, the visually observable differences between male and female brains. It is far from clear at present how this wetware functions in detail, and not at all clear how many layers of "programming languages" there might be built into it (cf. Hofstadter 1979; Fodor 1983). But a persuasive case has been made for the claim that the capacity to learn a language is in some way built into (hardwired or "wetwired" into) the brain (cf. N. Chomsky 1975). *So, like the suitably programmable computer that is potentially so many different things, human beings, because of their brain structure, are suitably programmed to be, potentially, users of many different languages* (assuming, of course, that there are no genetic defects or irreparable accidental destructive changes in the structure of their brains). There is apparently a known limitation of a temporal sort: an individual deprived of the opportunity for language acquisition at a certain developmental age seems not to be able to make up the deprivation, as in the famous case in India of Ramu the "wolf" boy (and many others). This too, perhaps, is wetwired.

There seems, however, to be a difference between having a certain sort of capacity for language and having a capacity for beliefs, or at least between some ways of using language and *understanding* language (cf. Searle 1980). I shall be saying more about this, since part of the business of probing the insight about the commonality of wetwiring in all members of the human species has to consist of discovering whether it can be useful in guiding us to see why it is that human beings have the higher-order intentional capacity for beliefs (and for having belief systems) that seems to be required for personhood. (It might be noted that one of the stumbling blocks in AI research has concerned the problem of programming a computer to operate with a system of beliefs, in a higher order way, as opposed to operating with a system of data structures. And there is the associated unsolved puzzle about the manner in which the coding or representing (and retrieval) of beliefs, first but especially higher order, occurs in the human brain. Cf. Dreyfus 1979, Fodor 1985.)

That the manner in which a particular human being is able to employ language might be decisive for personhood can easily be seen in such cases as the one referred to by Dennett: the woman who because of brain damage "could no longer comprehend any language at all, but who parroted back everything that was spoken to her exactly—except for grammatical errors, which she always corrected!"[17] This case resembles those of the so-called idiot savants, the calculating prodigies and the otherwise mentally retarded musical 'geniuses' who can almost instantly play back on musical instruments quite complex musical compositions they have heard, sometimes for the first time. Ascertaining that such individuals possess beliefs or subscribe to certain belief systems would be impossible in the absence of any other present or past evidence of linguistic competence or capacity to communicate beliefs, and one might thus with good reason be inclined to say that there is no longer, if there ever was, a *person* (in the full sense of the term yet to be delineated) *there*.[18]

Now, whatever the details of the belief structures might be, it seems not implausible to suggest that there is a resemblance of sorts between the malleability of persons, with respect to the beliefs and belief systems that they can hold, and the way in which a suitably programmed computer is potentially a variety of things: that is, a type of functional isomorphism. And, as unsettling as it may be at first glance, there seems to be little apparent limitation upon the types of beliefs or belief systems to which an individual person may subscribe. Granted, once some beliefs are accepted, there seem to be limitations placed upon the sorts of beliefs subsequently accepted (a Spinozistic observation), especially if one wishes to use the term *rational* as applied to the person holding the belief system; and given certain belief systems, upon the acceptance of other belief systems. We tend in practice to place a variety of constraints upon the possible concatenations of beliefs, and in so doing decide that certain individuals are simply mad. And one sense of irrationality is precisely that which we ascribe to an individual who is in the position of apparently subscribing to beliefs or belief systems of a mutually destructive sort in a logical sense.[19]

Admittedly there are obvious differences between suitably programmable current-generation computers and human individuals: when we say of a child that s/he has potentially a certain sort of character (which itself presupposes one kind of belief system or perhaps a collection of belief systems), we are using the word *potentially* in a rather different manner from the use made of it with respect to a computer when we say of it that it is a potential word processor or whatever (at least until there exist computers capable of the kind of learning presupposed by the acquisition of character in human individuals). The difference in the type of potentiality has something to do with the fact that computers apparently lack and are incapable of acquiring original intentionality; but what it is, exactly, that allows some human beings at least to appear to have it remains something of a mystery. But still there seem to be no innate limitations upon the content of the actual initial beliefs acquired by an individual (unless one wishes to count as innate in some sense the beliefs an individual acquires by being reared in a certain culture, since these beliefs may be among the most difficult to alter. Such, for example, are the beliefs and reactions most individuals have to those with obvious disfigurement). It is also true, however, that the wildest sorts of beliefs, especially beliefs about the physical world, may be summarily rejected on the basis of what we (normally) believe via a sort of commonsense realism about our causal interactions with that world. The belief (together with its associated belief system) that I can fly off a cliff just by flapping my arms is a belief that may very soon be laid to rest (along with my body), unless it is replaced by a more propitious belief or belief system!

3. Malleability and Evolution: Intentional Selection

Malleability, as the unlimited capacity for beliefs and systems of beliefs to be found in certain sorts of human beings—those, in fact, we (for reasons not all of which have yet made their appearance) are most inclined to describe as persons—clearly invites speculation of the sort in which I have been indulging with regard to its nature, via its resemblance to certain features of what I have referred to as suitably programmable computers. Even more interesting is the possibility, since human beings—unlike computers—are among the sorts of creatures having undergone evolution over thousands of years, that this capacity is no accident; or at least, if at one point in the evolutionary process it was an accident, it was one worth preserving (by natural selection) in the genetic code of the species. What I shall next do is offer some specific speculations: first of all, as to why this capacity was not allowed to shrivel away in the course of evolutionary time, and secondly, how it seems to have contained within itself an extraordinary further capacity for intentional self-correction and enhancement which I shall, for want of a better term, call "intentional selection."

The capacity for (consciously) holding and endorsing beliefs and belief systems is typically at least a second order capacity, since it requires that the individuals having it be in the position of sorting through their beliefs and electing to keep certain ones while rejecting others. And it requires as well the higher order capacity of self-awareness or self-consciousness making it possible for these individuals to be aware that the beliefs or belief systems in question are *theirs*. Dennett 1984, 37 ff. has speculated, with regard to the capacity for consciousness, that it made its appearance in the evolutionary process because of a need felt by the individuals involved to be able, before taking certain actions having a (nonintentional) causal effect upon either themselves or their environments, to see—in their mind's eyes, so to speak—the sorts of things that might happen before they actually took place. This was especially true, naturally, of things that might be said to involve danger to these individuals. So self-consciousness, by making it possible for the individuals having it to see in advance the results of certain possible courses of actions, not only tended to reduce wear and tear upon them (as well as lengthening their life spans), but would have become self-selecting, and the process of natural selection would have ensured its continuation; those with it would have had a higher rate of survival than those without it.

But consciousness without content, to vary a famous Kantian dictum, would not only have been blind but ineffectual as well, in the physical world out of which it evolved. The content, in this case, was, of course, the beliefs and systems of beliefs I have been referring to. There is little doubt that in the course of evolutionary time there were many, many human individuals who met their deaths by carrying out the very course of action at which I poked fun a few paragraphs ago: they found themselves not only in possession of the system of beliefs in accordance with which one might flap one's arms and fly, but they put this system into practice, with or without especially fabricated wing-attachments. I can say this with confidence, knowing how many individuals have done this in *recorded* history!

Now it seems reasonable to speculate that those biological individuals who were unduly limited with respect to the number of different beliefs and/or belief systems they were capable of keeping in mind and sorting would have had a lower survival rate, because they would not have been capable, in advance of putting a belief system into practice, of viewing it as a part of, or as connected with, some other belief system entailing their own possible destruction. Presumably, in nonhuman animals, at least the ones to which we are tempted to attribute beliefs, there likely would also be some kind of 'belief-system whatnot' (vis-à-vis intentional whatnot) at work, whether or not it is fully conscious. Thus one might want to argue that natural selection favored consciousness and rejected those without it; but consciousness, while certainly a necessary condition, could not have been sufficient by itself without malleability. The class of deceased would-be human flyers undoubtedly includes a large percentage of those with a highly developed capacity for consciousness and self-consciousness but with limited malleability. Since human flight is, as a matter of fact, the sort of thing that does involve experimentation, the class of would-be flyers must also include some of those with well-developed capacities for both consciousness *and* malleability. Purely intentional trials of beliefs and belief systems must, of necessity, yield to nonintentional trials where there can be no substitute for empirical inquiry; in science, after all, the gedankenexperiment must give way to the actual experiment.

Now these speculations invite another: what, in the course of evolutionary time, were the actual mechanisms, in terms of beliefs and belief systems, involved in the selection process? One tempting line of thinking is to suppose that the systems of beliefs we have come to label "religious" were either one such mechanism or a component of one, and a part of what I shall describe as the process by means of which one kind of *intentional selection* was to make its appearance. By "intentional selection" I understand a form of nonnatural selection patterned after the account given earlier of the notions of intentional causation and intentional explanation (see above, chapter 2, section 2). Natural selection, as understood in the theory of evolution, with its multiple mechanisms, entails a variety of types of nonintentional causation, and is itself one of the components of a nonintentional explanation for the actual forms in which living things appear today, in terms of such things as their morphology and speciation. Thus it is not surprising that one of the fundamental instances of the concept of natural kinds is that of a suitably defined biological species, although a proper account of such natural kinds is much more complex than that of the natural kinds earlier alluded to, such as H_2O, CO_2, etc.[20]

Now religious belief systems, which placed upon their adherents certain belief requirements, instituted just such a form of intentional selection. Those individuals who elected (or were programmed) to hold the belief system survived in a twofold sense: as physical individuals and as intentional creatures; those who did not do so were either ejected from the society—a form of ritual "murder" sometimes known as "shunning" or excommunication, thus suffering an intentional demise—or were actually killed. The talk in some religions of conversion experiences and spiritual rebirth is, of course, itself intentional in nature, as is the nonreligious "conversion," say, of a Democrat into a Republican. And while it could happen that religiously required beliefs coincided with beliefs about the physical world that would ensure the continued (physical) life of the individual subscribing to the beliefs—as is possible with some dietary beliefs—this was by no means necessarily the case, for some dietary rules had (and continue to have) only a religious (i.e., intentional) and not any scientific or physical basis. But viewed from a wide enough evolutionary perspective, such belief systems may themselves be seen as a naturally occurring experiment in malleability: *for the first time we had socially organized belief systems sustaining no necessary (nonintentional) connection with the physical world, but sustaining instead an intentional connection between the physical world and an intentionally fabricated world.* The appearance of temples, oracles, and other such paraphenalia, together with the shamans, witch doctors, priests, and rituals that went with them, have been a continuing testimony to the belief in, and the attempt to establish, such a connection. Whether this experiment has borne valuable fruit it is perhaps too early to say, for at least one of its features has turned out to be counter-productive in terms of the hypothetical evolutionary picture I have been sketching: the survival of many religious belief systems has been due in part, at least, to the fact that they placed upon their adherents the requirement that they impose severe limitations upon their individual capacities for malleability. This has resulted, of course, in an apparently endless sequence of religious persecutions, conflicts, and wars, precisely because those involved have placed intentional limitations upon their beliefs, limitations usually having no discernible basis in the physical world.

Genocide, the slaying of infidels or unbelievers, and some other kinds of mass killings are, of course, manifestations of intentionally fabricated and imposed belief systems admitting of limited or no malleability, whether of religious or political origin, and are usually implemented in a quite rational manner: only higher order intentional systems such as persons, horrifyingly enough, are capable of planning and of trying to carry out such mass exterminations of human individuals. This is due to the fact that the characteristics taken to identify members of the group to be eliminated ordinarily require higher order intentional objects to define them, such as being "an enemy of the people," an "infidel," or a "witch." All it has required, frequently, is that those in the class of desirables *believe* that a certain individual is a member of the class of undesirables for there to be sufficient reason to eliminate that individual. (Man's best friend, whatever his shortcomings, is at least *intentionally incapable* of genocide or witch-burning!)

While it might be conceded that it is still too early to evaluate the religious experiment in what I am calling intentional selection, it appears that there are quite definitely favorable results in two other areas: investigations in mathematico-logical matters, and those in experimental science. For in both of these areas the capacity for malleability, via intentional selection, has evolved ways of sorting beliefs and belief systems quite unlike those found in religious belief systems. Whether or not a mathematical structure has certain properties is something about which it seems possible for human individuals to reach agreement in a manner markedly different from the ways in which agreement is reached in a religious belief system regarding some religious structure. For example, whether a certain (relatively small) number is prime is a matter that can be determined to the satisfaction of anyone who possesses a minimal knowledge of numbers and a certain facility in applying this knowledge. However, whether a certain human action is in accordance with a religious doctrine is a much more troublesome issue, made even more troublesome by the usual requirement that one must first of all subscribe to the relevant doctrine before one can be in a position even to venture a judgment on the case in question. And, of course, whether one is in the proper sense a "true believer" can be established only by those who already are. Whether one is really a mathematician is not determined by expressions of belief, but by the actual production of proofs; and proofs are the sorts of things that can be produced by individuals whatever their religious views might be.

One of the really astounding facts about the way in which things have developed in the area of mathematics and logic is that there have appeared self-referential ways of operating: for example, it has turned out to be possible to *prove* that certain kinds of *proofs* are not possible, and to prove this to the satisfaction of most mathematicians! So in this area the business of sorting beliefs into those which are acceptable and those which are not has proceeded in a way distinctively different from the way things have gone in the sorting of religious beliefs;[21] and this in spite of the fact that the objects under scrutiny are not necessarily those which can be shown to be capable of sustaining (nonintentional) causal relationships. But it is clear that without the capacity for malleability, it would not be possible for new developments in the area to take place, for new discoveries and new belief systems to make their appearance. The significant thing is that here the capacity for malleability has itself evolved a particular higher order capacity for self-constraint.

Where it *is* a matter of dealing with beliefs about objects which do sustain nonintentional causal relationships with one another, experimental science has developed techniques for belief sorting that in many cases leave very little to be desired. Thus whether or not one is justified in believing that certain kinds of physical objects will perform in a certain way under specified circumstances is a matter that can be settled to the satisfaction of anyone with only the most minimal knowledge of the objects and relationships concerned. Indeed, the refusal to believe that certain configurations of physical objects will produce certain causal outcomes, as in the case of our aqueous believers (chap. 2, sec. 2), is frequently (and it is felt with good reason) taken as grounds for raising questions about the sanity of the individuals concerned. But again, the significant thing is that the capacity for malleability is not only indispensable, but that it has itself evolved by a kind of intentional selection not only the higher order capacity for self-constraint already mentioned in the area of mathematics and logic, but a whole collection of ways of placing constraints upon itself: all of those ways which we, sometimes for want of a better label, lump together and call "scientific method," and whose net result is probably the most powerful belief-sorting mechanism yet to make its appearance in our world.[22]

Another way of describing this state of affairs is to say that experimental science has succeeded in developing techniques for distinguishing between

(1) beliefs that have corresponding to them things that are in some sense "really there" in the physical world as nonintentional objects (in some way independent of our particular ways, as human beings, of being aware of them), and (2) beliefs whose objects are in some sense fabricated by us, as "mere" intentional objects, and are there in the physical world only in the way in which our minds and their intentional components and their particular contents are there in that world. For example, to describe Ronald Reagan as a token of the (biological) type, *homo sapiens*, would be to refer to a certain nonintentional object that is, in a scientific sense, really there in the physical world. To refer to him, however, as President of the United States, or as former professional movie actor, would be to refer to certain intentional objects having existence only as particular contents of the minds of those capable of having higher order intentions. Or, to employ the vocabulary already developed (chap. 2, sec. 2), where '*homo sapiens*' is a natural kind term (Kripkean lingo: rigid designator), 'President of the United States' and 'former professional movie actor' are not.[23]

Speaking in this way might also be looked upon as adopting a view currently known as scientific realism, and in so doing as rejecting views which are sometimes called scientific "constructivism," "conventionalism," or "instrumentalism" (historically, conventionalism and instrumentalism have been usually associated with logical positivism or empiricism, which for many years was the predominant approach in philosophy of science, and constructivism with neo-Kantian views of the nature of science such as those developed in Hanson 1958 and Kuhn 1970). Scientific constructivism has proposed, roughly, that the objects of scientific investigation are in some manner properly to be described as having been "constructed" out of a variety of "materials" all of them to be found in our particular way of apprehending, as human beings, what we call, in our scientific theories, "the physical world." In other words, according to scientific constructivism, there is no need to speak of objects that are in any sense "really there" in the physical world independent of our awareness of them via our scientific theories: for what is "really there" is necessarily theory-dependent.

The proponents of scientific realism have generally endorsed the celebrated observation of Hilary Putnam (for example, in Putnam 1978), according to which the thesis of scientific constructivism makes the success of science a miracle, for it offers no way of capturing even the minimal notion of a scientific theory's being approximately true, and thus making it possible to speak of the development of a theory over time resulting in a closer approximation to the truth. I shall make no attempt here to sort out the issues in this conflict between scientific realists and those in opposition to them— it is a conflict that will (as is typical of such philosophical disputes) undoubtedly continue for some years to come—but shall refer the reader to J. Leplin 1984 for a representative sampling of the debate. Whatever the outcome of the debate, it would appear to be quite safe to say that experimental science is, as a matter of fact, not only successful (for whatever reason or for no reason!), but I repeat, one of the most successful ways yet developed for sorting beliefs of certain kinds. If Richard Boyd 1983 is right, such scientific knowledge has required what he calls a "causal epistemology" where the emphasis has been placed not upon the *production* of beliefs but upon belief *regulation*, and this would appear to be another of the mechanisms developed in the process of what I have called intentional selection.

The material and/or physical basis for intentional selection is itself part of the hypothesis that persons are material/physical. Human individuals with a certain sort of developed capacity for intentional selection (i.e., persons, in the full sense for which we shall argue below, chap. 5, sec. 1) exhibit what we have come to call "intelligence."[24]

Conspicuous by their absence from the discussion so far are the views which taken together form the belief system(s) of morality; and, of course, a full account of the higher order intentional systems apparently required to support them. Again, as a matter of history, it is probably true enough to say that one of the origins of what might be called (in analogy with an accepted usage in discussions of Law) "positive morality" lay in religious belief systems. But if the observations I have recently made about the problems to be met with generally in religious belief systems vis-à-vis sorting beliefs are sound, religious accounts of morality would quite likely have inherited these problems, and, so far at least, have not developed suitable self-constraints upon such sorting. By "suitable self-constraints" I understand those which would not be restricted in any way to a particular religious belief system. There are certainly religiously idiosyncratic ways of sorting beliefs: e.g., in the Catholic religion, various members of the church hierarchy are in a position to do this, with the buck presumably stopping at the Pope. It would clearly be highly desirable to be able to devise for moral beliefs something like the sorting techniques developed in logic, mathematics, and the experimental sciences for mathematico-logical beliefs and empirical beliefs. *With malleability as a given, as well as the apparent irreducibly intentional nature of moral beliefs, it is imperative that suitable constraints be forthcoming, constraints in terms of which it would be possible to say that certain moral beliefs, as well as certain beliefs about the nature of morality, should be accepted and certain others rejected.*

So here we have another item for our agenda, an item connected, it now can be seen, with some of the items I earlier have uncovered in the course of my deliberations on the material nature of persons. One approach showing some promise for solving the sorting problem for moral beliefs is the doctrine of "moral realism" under development by Richard Boyd 1983, a doctrine patterned after the scientific realism I have lately described, and similarly designed to cope with moral conventionalism and relativism. To these matters I shall shortly turn in the next chapter.

4

Moral Theory

In this chapter I assemble the remaining considerations, which taken together with those already produced in chapters 2 and 3, will allow me in the next chapter to construct a schema (template, or conceptual framework) for depicting a moral person. To this point in the essay I have neglected to give any sort of explicit description of morality and moral theory. This, of course, must be done if we are to be able to proceed with our main task. In the first section of this chapter I propose that we adopt an intentionalistic reading of our ordinary moral language and the "folk" psychology built into it. After making some remarks about moral theory and its connections with intentionality, I describe some fundamental problems with which any proper moral theory must be prepared to deal. I then provide a sketch for one sort of moral realism (that proposed by Richard Boyd 1983 on the model of scientific realism), and proceed to suggest a way of giving an intentional reading for this realism. This reading requires, among other things, the notions of intentional kinds, intentional causation, and intentional explanation, paralleling the notions of natural kinds, nonintentional causation, and nonintentional explanation found in science.

1. Intentionality and Our Ordinary Moral Language

What I shall do in this section is suggest how our ordinary ("folk") moral language might, in a rather natural way, be recast in terms of the account of intentionality so far developed. In the usual course of human events, we speak (as I did in chapter 1) of such things as someone's being morally responsible, having done something deserving of moral praise or censure (and possibly meriting reward or punishment), having a moral obligation or a moral duty, having fulfilled a moral obligation or duty, having moral rights, having exercised moral rights, having violated moral rights, having defended moral rights, etc.; of someone's being morally trustworthy (untrustworthy), reliable (unreliable), strong (weak), etc., or of an individual's being morally consistent (inconsistent) or even amoral.

We also employ similar expressions in connection with *particular human actions*, as when we say of them that they (with appropriate modifications of tense) are (objectively) morally right (moral) or wrong (immoral), morally justifiable or unjustifiable, morally appropriate or inappropriate, etc. We may also wish to say of a certain *kind of action* (or of a particular action taken as an instance of a kind), that it is morally right or wrong, etc., in a *tenseless* way: i.e., that it would be morally right or wrong, etc., whatever the time of its occurrence, such as, for example, murder, which is ordinarily considered to be by definition immoral, irrespective of the time of its occurrence.

On occasion we may apply moral terminology to the *reasoning* that might be brought to support (or to reject) a course of action, as when we say that so and so employed morally sound (unsound), valid (invalid) reasoning to support his/her decision to do (or not to do) such and so. We also, at times, may decide that it is necessary to describe even an individual who is capable of performing moral actions, as having done something falling outside of the realm of morality entirely— or an action that fails to be classifiable within the realm of morality, or a piece of reasoning—as *non*moral. For example, Smedley, in tying his shoelace at a certain point in time (in specifiable circumstances), may be said to be nonmoral, or his action then of shoelace tying may be said to be nonmoral, or his reasoning in support of tying his shoelace then, might be said to be nonmoral. This is not to rule out, of course, the possibility that Smedley, in tying his shoelace in different circumstances, might be doing something for which he could be held morally responsible, or that he might be doing it for morally sound (or unsound) reasons. This is a reminder, on the assumption under which I am operating here—that moral entities are a species of intentional objects—of the irreducibility of the intentional to observable behavior (Skinnerian) or, in other words, of one particular location in which the intentional circle (see above, chap. 2. "Material Persons," 2. Intentionality as a Feature of Material Objects: The Intentional Circle) puts in an appearance, about which I shall shortly have more to say.

Taking the foregoing sketch as representative of some of our ordinary ways of using moral language, it remains only to point out how these uses might be recast in terms of the language of intentionality. To start with talk of an individual's being morally responsible: to say, in intentional terms, of an individual that he/she is morally responsible is to make use of higher order intentionality, or of Dennett's concept of reciprocity. For example, to say that A is morally responsible to B for performing a certain action x means that A believes that B (assuming B has the requisite developed capacity) has a definite expectation with respect to certain of A's possible voluntary actions, viz., x, and also that B believes that A believes this, and that anyone suitably aware of the matter would believe the same way about the relationship between A and B and the action x. An *expectation* on the part of B in this context may be thought of as representing the belief that someone else A (i.e., an appropriate higher order intentional system) can be trusted to choose to perform a certain type of action or actions (of which x is an instance), on behalf of B, actions B would ordinarily perform in B's own behalf, if physically possible. (Incidentally, this entails that A has the developed capacity, which is a (higher order) cognitive one, for recognizing not only types, but instances of types, of actions.)

It can thus be seen that the capacity for having an expectation in this sense requires that an individual have in normal working order most of the intentional capacities found in Dennett's account. (Such expectations are in real life more infrequently fulfilled in moral contexts than in some nonintentional contexts: see the comments at the end of this section.) Now if A's performing of x should require that A do something taking special effort or pains beyond any normal expectation, we might believe it appropriate to give moral praise to A for fulfilling his/her responsibility to B; however, if A could easily perform x, but does not choose to do so (and A's failure to choose to do so is not defeasible), we might believe it appropriate to censure A for failing to choose to do what he/she easily could have done.[1] We might also say of A's performing of x that it represented the carrying out or the fulfilling of a moral obligation or duty to B, which means that B has a definite expectation that A perform a certain action, and that B believes that A believes that this is the case, etc.: so again, the language of moral obligation or duty is shown to refer to certain higher order intentions.

To say of B that s/he has a moral right, entitlement, or claim might mean in intentional terms that B has (or is capable of having) an expectation that not only A, but *any* morally responsible individual who is in a position to do so, will voluntarily perform a definite action in B's behalf, which means that B believes that not only A but every morally responsible individual is capable of believing that B appropriately has this expectation. One way of saying of A that s/he is moral *simpliciter*, is to say that A in particular also shares the belief that is held by any morally responsible individual. (There are qualifications in order, of course, with regard to children, what might be referred to as partial or former persons, animals, as well as certain nonperson entities such as organizations, states, etc.) B, in believing in the manner I have just described, could be said to be presumptively exercising a moral right; if it should happen that A is the only one in a position to perform the action that is required by B's expectation (and the doing of which would fulfill it), and A (knowing this) easily could but fails to do this, we could say that A would be responsible for having violated B's right. If someone else C should be in the position of being the only one able to perform the action required by B's expectation, could easily do so but does not (and C's failure to do so is not defeasible), and A in effect comes to B's assistance by reminding C of his/her moral responsibility (and C then fulfills that responsibility), then we might say of A that s/he has defended B's moral right. (While a discussion of the semantics for 'moral' is initiated near the end of this chapter, I am postponing a final discussion until chapter 5; but it might be noted here that the ascription of moral rights in the intentional terms suggested presupposes higher order intentional systems. Thus what one can say about the "rights" of nonhuman animals would on the present argument turn upon their potential or actual roles as higher order intentional systems.)

To say of A that s/he is morally trustworthy means precisely that A is the sort of individual who will almost all of the time, if at all possible, choose to perform the sorts of actions that I have said were required by such expectations as those of B in the cases above—and, of course, that A would choose to perform such actions for not only B but for anyone having the same expectations whose situation is similarly related to B's. To say that A is not only morally trustworthy but is also morally strong would be to say that A can be relied upon to choose to perform actions of the sort I have described as required by the expectations of anyone in the position of B, even when this means that A must perform in adverse circumstances; i.e., A's being morally strong means that A would in fact be deserving of moral praise in the sense earlier characterized. An account of moral weakness goes in a similar way, and is linked with the earlier description of moral censure (more will be said about moral *defects*, such as akrasia and servility, once we have in hand a semantics for moral terms: see below, chap. 5, sec. 2). An individual who is morally consistent (reliable) resembles the morally trustworthy individual; a morally inconsistent (unreliable) one would be one who is untrustworthy, in the sense of sometimes doing the responsible thing but sometimes not.

To say of an individual A that s/he is amoral would be, in intentional terms, to say that such an individual, for whatever reason—being a dog, a child, a psychopath/sociopath, mentally (i.e., intentionally) incompetent, etc. —would not be the sort of individual with respect to whom someone like B could properly be said to have the sort of expectations I have been attributing to B in the examples given: in other words, there would be a failure of reciprocity, or higher order intentionality, of the sort required to make a moral relation go, because of either the outright lack of, or the undeveloped nature of, the requisite capacities. One might say that such an individual might simply not know the language of morality, whether capable of learning it or not. The issue of whether it is possible that an individual could have the capacity for verbal communication, as demonstrated by a command of many other particular languages, while lacking it for moral language, and could still be called a person, I shall leave moot for the present (see comments below in chap. 6, the section on moral persons and death).

The application of intentionality to moral actions follows along the lines laid out already. For the actions in question are, of course, the very actions I have been attributing to A (or whoever his/her counterpart might be). Thus the voluntary action x of A done in fulfillment of A's moral obligation to B, whatever this obligation might be in particular, would be said to be a moral action. This would entail that not only the particular voluntary action x would be moral, but that any action of that type would be moral, whenever performed, and with whatever morally responsible individuals taking the place of A. If A had chosen not to perform x (call this A's having done y where y is not morally equivalent to x), and B's expectation that A would perform x was not realized, then the nonperformance of x (or the performance of y), if not defeasible, would be described as a morally wrong action.

Moral reasoning, it may now be seen, would be parasitical upon the intentional conditions I have been describing with respect to individuals and actions. For example, A, in deliberating about his/her moral obligation with respect to B vis-à-vis performing x, and hence fulfilling B's expectation with regard to A's performing x, might indulge in reasoning which could lead him/her to the conclusion that there is an action z that is logically equivalent to x; and so A could decide, if z should also be morally equivalent to x, to perform z rather than x. Thus A would be said to have engaged in moral reasoning (and would have done so even in the event that A had discovered that z was not morally equivalent to x, but had then noticed that some other action was). If the moral reasoning in which A engages were to turn out to be unsound, what should be said about A from a moral point of view might be more troublesome: is one to be held *morally* responsible for having been misled by such reasoning into performing (or failing to perform) an action that is morally wrong in some objective sense? This is a fine point in moral theory to which we shall have occasion to return at a later stage in our deliberations; but that moral reasoning itself has an intentional connection should be clear enough.

To speak of an action as nonmoral would be to say of it that it in some way involves intentional entities and/or capacities but that none of them is moral.[2] For example, B could certainly have expectations with regard to A's actions, but they need not involve morality: if they are playing tennis, and B has just lofted a lob directly to A, who is located near the net, then B's expectation very likely would be that A would try to smash the ball as hard as possible at B's feet or at a corner of the court away from B; and B (or any knowledgeable tennis player) would believe that A believes that B's expectation would be as I have described it. And, of course A, believing B's expectation to be as described, might reason—in a nonmoral way—that a drop shot with enough backspin to cause the ball to hop back over the net would be the shot to attempt. B, naturally, could also, as an experienced player, believe that A would reason in the way described, and so might attempt to force A to bobble the shot by making a sudden anticipatory rush at the net while A is in the process of trying to execute it. Thus tennis, when played between those of equal intentional acuity and experience, might be said to reduce to skill in execution, or technique, unless luck intrudes itself in the form of a net-cord or bad bounce. There are numerous other examples of human performances involving (higher order) intentional matters but in no way connected with morality, although the just-mentioned matter of luck may also, as we shall see, play a variety of ubiquitous roles in morality.

It is perhaps unnecessary to point out that an individual may perform actions of a nonmoral sort in connection with his/her dealings with nonintentional material objects, and ordinarily does so many times each day. Some, at least, of one's expectations with regard to one's connections with nonintentional material objects, especially where they involve nonintentional causal or scientific relationships, may naturally require far less qualification than those that are connected with other human individuals (i.e., malleable higher order intentional systems). For example, my expectation that I would drown if suitably immersed in water for a period of time requires far fewer qualifications than my expectation that someone (even if there were several people around) would actually come to my aid if I were accidentally so immersed! One's expectations in game-playing contexts would appear to occupy a position intermediate between those one has in moral situations and those one has in the sort of relationships with nonintentional objects I have just described—as long as those involved do in fact play according to the rules of the particular game!

2. Intentionality and Moral Theory

Needless to say, I have not entirely avoided doing some theory in the preceding section, for the claim I have made that our ordinary use of moral language can be recast in intentional terms is, of course, in itself a theoretical point. But in so doing I have not engaged directly in what is sometimes called a certain kind of "moral theory," but instead in what has been termed by philosophers "meta-ethics": to say, for example, that a moral right is really nothing other than a certain kind of intentional object is to make a meta-ethical claim and not an ethical or moral claim as such.[3] An ethical or moral claim proper would be something on the order of "promise-keeping is (*prima facie*) morally right" or "the intentional killing of innocent persons is morally wrong." Moral theory of a certain sort thus makes its appearance when one proceeds to deliberate about, and to seek to find answers for, such questions as, Why is promise-breaking morally wrong? or What makes the intentional killing of innocent persons morally wrong? and Why is the intentional killing of innocent persons (usually) a greater moral wrong than the breaking of a promise? I shall, for my purposes in these investigations, include within the sphere of what I shall call "moral theory" not only questions such as these but also those such as, What is it about a certain sort of human action that leads us to describe it as a moral, as opposed to a nonmoral, action? What are the conditions under which a human individual is to be held morally responsible? or When does a human individual become—or cease to be—a moral person? or What is a moral person? In doing this I include within the same subject matter both ethical and meta-ethical concerns.

An important point worth calling attention to again is that in neither this nor the preceding section have I supplied any meaning (semantics) whatsoever for the term *moral*. All I have done so far is to give a sort of replay of some of our common usages of moral language and to propose that this language has certain intentional counterparts. Thus one of the tasks still outstanding is that of supplying in an explicit way a suitable meaning or semantics for 'moral', a meaning that will make it possible to sort moral from nonmoral intentional objects. This task falls, of course, to moral theory as I have just characterized it. But before proceeding with this task, I need to say something about certain problems to be dealt with by moral theory.

3. Moral Theory

Moral Theory, Problems: Moral Invisibility and Moral Semantics

There are a number of problems with which any general philosophic moral theory must be prepared to deal, but I shall here describe only a pair of these. The first, as it turns out, proves to be a problem particularly susceptible to the sort of intentional approach I have been developing, and the second also seems to be less recalcitrant when dealt with along these lines. The first problem has to do with the fact that the moral performances of human beings cannot be "read off" their performances in any simple way: in other words, whether a particular performance is a moral or a nonmoral one is not the sort

of thing that can be determined by a straightforward perceptual examination
of the performance. In a sense, the features of the performance making it
moral might be said to be "invisible." An example due to Gilbert Harman
1977 is instructive: he describes an individual who, upon rounding a corner,
comes upon some children setting fire to a live cat. While the individuals, the
cat, and the action of setting it on fire seem apparent enough, that what they
are doing is immoral is not apparent—at least in the same way. If it is true that
morality is a matter of higher order intentionality, as I have been urging, it is
clear why this is the case. For if morality involves, among other things, beliefs
and expectations about beliefs and expectations, and access to these must be
had only by way of verbal communication, then no matter what an individual
appears to be doing from a perceptual or behavioral point of view, one cannot
be sure what the individual intends to be doing without having him/her tell
us. Thus whether a performance is a moral one or not requires that the individual who is engaged in it inform us to that effect. For example, the video
tape of John Hinckley's attempted assassination of Ronald Reagan would presumably have *appeared* no different if Hinckley had been legally sane. This, in
spite of the special problems associated with confirming the veridicality of
expressions of belief, is the best that can be done.[4] The other problem is
connected with this one, and has to do more specifically with considerations
that might appear to be more difficult to deal with, because they turn upon
cultural and linguistic differences that cannot easily be dismissed.

This second and perhaps the more troublesome problem traditionally
facing moral theory has been found in the rather obvious fact that the employment of the word *moral* (or *ethical* and their putative equivalents in other
languages) is subject to extraordinarily wide variation, not only in a cross-
cultural way, but even within the same society or culture, whether over historical time or at a given time. It is a truism that what is *thought to be immoral* in
one culture or segment of a society may be *thought to be moral* (or nonmoral)
in another culture or segment of society. It is also a truism that such apparent
cultural and social relativism is widely viewed by philosophers, at least, to be
a rather hopeless position if it is taken in a serious philosophical sense as
constituting a moral theory, implying as it does a rather thoroughgoing moral
subjectivism or conventionalism easily leading to skepticism about the possibility of making any genuinely objective claims of a moral sort.

Anthropologists, sociologists, and social psychologists, it is sometimes
said, need not necessarily be concerned with such issues as whether a certain
social or cultural practice is "really" moral or immoral, and may be content
just to record what seems to be happening in a certain place at a certain
time. Two comments are in order here: *Firstly,* such researchers, interestingly
enough, may find in their own practice, especially if it involves any kind of

experimentation, that they may very well need to resolve issues of a moral sort, where the meaning of 'moral' cannot be left free to float in a completely unattached way. It would be a curious anthropological fact indeed if, say, British and Indian social psychologists could not reach *any* agreement as to whether a certain way of conducting an experiment on groups of people were moral or nonmoral. This is not to say that they need be in *total* agreement, for of course even the members of the British Psychological Association may fall out amongst themselves regarding the details of such matters, and must arrive at some sort of compromise between competing factions. Thus, while agreement upon the detailed application of the word *moral* might be difficult, it seems to be *thought appropriate* by those involved that an effort be made to limit in some manner at least the *range* of its applications in contexts involving social experimentation.[5] *Secondly*, anthropologists (and empirical linguists), especially, do run afoul of a problem we encountered earlier, the problem connected with the intentional circle and known as the indeterminacy of translation. How are they, as a matter of fact, to decide whether the terms in the language of a hitherto unknown people are to be translated into our language in a certain way? There are problems to be met with here even in what might appear to be easy cases, where, for example, the "natives" are found to use a certain expression in the presence of an easily seen animal: how can it be ascertained that the expression has an exact counterpart in our language? The answer, as might be expected in light of the troubles we noticed in connection with the intentional circle, is that we are expecting too much if we think we can always find an exact counterpart.[6] And, naturally, where the terms refer not to easily observable spatio-temporal objects but to abstract entities of any sort—such as intentional objects—the problems become more obviously difficult of solution, if not completely unsolvable.

Now even if we elect, as I have proposed in the first section of this chapter, to go with the claim that our ordinary moral language should be construed as referring to (unreduced) intentional capacities and objects, we have not solved the problems connected with moral semantics or the meaning of moral terms I have just been discussing: we have simply shifted the location of the problems. For we still need to know how to distinguish the nonmoral intentional capacities and objects from the moral ones—to start with in our own language—while recognizing that there will be, of necessity, problems of another sort when it is a matter of trying to find appropriate translations in our language for the (putatively) moral terms in other languages.

In the history of philosophical investigations of morality, Immanuel Kant also, in his own inimitable way, recognized that the meaning and application of moral terms required rather careful attention. He saw clearly enough that one could not simply read off, by a perceptual inspection of an individual's performance, whether it should be labeled a "moral," "immoral," or "non-moral" performance. He argued, in the complex fashion familiar to Categorical Imperative buffs, that the morality (or nonmorality) of a human performance could be discovered only indirectly, by first discovering the "maxim" or "rule" in accordance with which the performance was taken as an instance by the performer and then executed. Then, by a special process (the details of which have never been entirely clear even to many students of Kant), the maxim or rule was to be measured against an appropriate version of the Categorical Imperative.[7] At any rate he saw correctly enough that a behavioristic account of moral actions would not do (although he did not write in these precise terms). But in avoiding a behaviorist account he had recourse to what has become known as a rather "extravagant" ontology, an ontology which required the postulation of a "noumenal world" independent of space, time, and (nonintentional) causality, and housing a "Kingdom of Ends" in which Moral Agents were to find their proper home. This was in addition to the "phenomenal" world constituted by space, time, and (nonintentional) causality. He thus made it possible, he thought, to preserve moral autonomy in a world otherwise controlled by inexorable causality—or, in other words, he was able to argue that there is another, and a special, kind of "causality" relating to moral agents. But the price he had to pay for this was, in the opinion of many philosophers, rather too high, requiring as it did two apparently separate worlds as well as two kinds of causality, the meshings of which, the one with the other, have remained somewhat mysterious at best.

I rehearse this bit of history in order, I hope, to avoid repeating at least some of it. For the view I am formulating does, as did Kant's, make it possible to talk, as we have seen, about two kinds of causality, the intentional and the nonintentional, and is similarly nonreductive and nonbehavioristic, as I have argued. It does not, however, require that there be two ontologically different worlds: the domain of intentionality is, after all, just a part of the material domain. And there certainly is a kind of dislocation between the intentional and the nonintentional of the sort that shows up in Davidson's anomalous monism vis-à-vis the claim that intentional causality does not possess the law-like character of nonintentional causality; but this may be an epistemic rather than an ontological dislocation. It is simply the case that our knowledge of intentionality and of the workings of intentional systems is obtained in a different manner from the way in which we arrive at knowledge of the nonintentional and the workings of nonintentional objects.[8] As I have lately put it, it is a matter of employing differing belief-sorting or belief-regulating devices, devices which so far have been much better developed in science and mathematics than in the area of morality.

Before turning to the business of supplying a meaning or semantics for moral terms, which now has been shifted to the task of sorting moral from nonmoral intentional capacities and objects, I want to examine the very promising (meta-ethical) doctrine of moral realism, as it has been developed by Richard Boyd 1983. One of the virtues he claims for this doctrine is that it, as I have observed already, is modeled after scientific realism. Thus, if scientific realism has succeeded (in some version to some degree of approximation) in capturing at least some of the mechanisms responsible for the sorting and regulation of beliefs in its own area, and if the modeling is sound, then we might expect some version of moral realism to be able to capture some of the mechanisms which could make it possible for us in a similar manner to sort and to regulate beliefs in the domain of morality, i.e., the domain of moral intentional capacities and objects. With any luck, we might even be able to discern whether the prospect for a kind of "unified knowledge" encompassing both science and morality is a real one, a prospect that has been expressed in a variety of ways in the history of philosophy, from the dream of a "logically perfect language" to the more restricted notion embodied in the logical positivists' "unity of science." In the current idiom, this will very likely entail tracing the connections between knowledge of moral intentionality, folk psychology, and cognitive science. It is certainly clear enough that a knowledge of the appropriate means for performing a moral action frequently entails that information based upon scientific knowledge be at hand, so that in practice if not in theory, the two domains may be quite intimately joined.

*Moral Theory, Solutions: Richard Boyd's Moral Realism and
Homeostatic Consequentialism*

Moral Realism

Moral realism, according to Boyd, is a doctrine about moral judgments, moral statements and moral theories, and says that

> (1) Moral statements are the sorts of statements which are (or which express propositions which are) true or false (or approximately true, largely false, etc.); (2) The truth or falsity (approximate truth ...) of moral statements is largely independent of our moral opinions, theories, etc.; (3) Ordinary canons of moral reasoning—together with ordinary canons of scientific and everyday factual reasoning—constitute, under many circumstances at least, a reliable method for obtaining and improving (approximate) moral knowledge. (Boyd 1983, 1)

Boyd stresses the importance of the fact that moral realism, as he views it, owes its strength to recent developments in scientific realism. I shall not

here, to repeat my previous disclaimer, make any attempt to supply a definitive account of scientific realism or to examine the arguments brought for and
against it, but shall simply take Boyd's assessment of its contributions at face
value, since my primary interest is in the prospects for moral realism. Boyd's
capsule version of scientific realism is that it is

> the doctrine that scientific theories should be understood as putative descrip-
> tions of real phenomena, that ordinary scientific methods constitute a reliable
> procedure for obtaining and improving (approximate) knowledge of the real
> phenomena which scientific theories describe, and that the reality described by
> scientific theories is largely independent of our theorizing. Scientific theories
> describe reality and reality is "prior to thought." (Boyd 1983, 1)

According to Boyd, a sympathetic reading of scientific realism suggests a
number of constraints that need to be placed upon any account of moral
knowledge if it is, as moral realism, to inherit the advantages of scientific
realism. These constraints are roughly as follows (Boyd 1983, 34-35):

1. As in philosophy of science, where there must be an explanation of
   the fact that we started out with approximately true scientific beliefs,
   in order that we be able, by successively closer approximations to
   arrive at scientific knowledge, so in philosophy of morality, the account of moral knowledge must offer an explanation of the fact that
   we started out with a supply of "relevantly approximately true" moral
   beliefs. In neither area need it be the case that the initial beliefs are
   close approximations of the truth; but without the initial set of beliefs,
   it would not be possible for "reflective equilibrium" to occur. "Reflective equilibrium" refers to the complex reasoning process by means
   of which beliefs are constructed, modified, and brought into at least
   temporary equilibrium with one another, a process, according to scientific realism, requiring a (nonintentional) epistemic causal connection between the scientific theoretician and an independent reality
   (i.e., a reality not wholly of the theoretician's own making). Without
   this "realist" assumption, there would be no [nonmiraculous?] way
   of accounting for the possibility of successively closer approximations to the truth in scientific or moral knowledge.
2. There must be, in moral reasoning, something that is the counterpart to observation in scientific reasoning, a counterpart that supplies a basis for a realist as opposed to a constructivist approach to
   setting up the grounds for the sort of reflective equilibrium to be
   found in moral reasoning.

3. There must be a way to explain why it is that moral properties (for example, goodness) must have natural as opposed to conventional definitions. [Boyd, I take it, understands here a suitable adaptation of the sorts of definitions I earlier have characterized as requiring, for scientific purposes, the notion of natural kinds, properties, and relations, as opposed to conventional kinds, properties, and relations.]

4. There must be a way to show that real moral kinds, properties, and relations, by some sort of epistemic access via our ordinary use of moral language, control our use of moral terms in moral reasoning. The *initial* access by no means needs to be perfect, but it must be there to form a basis for the development of moral knowledge.

5. There must be a way to account for the sometimes indeterminate application of moral terms as a feature entailed by the character of moral reasoning. This would be in a manner similar to the way in which scientific realism accounts for the sometimes indeterminate application of scientific terms where these terms are of the "homeostatic cluster" variety.[9]

Now moral realism, as a doctrine subject to these constraints, could be implemented or instantiated in a variety of ways, depending upon the particular choice of substantive moral premises. Boyd has taken what he characterizes as "homeostatic consequentialism," a kind of nonutilitarian consequentialism, as an example of such an implementation or instantiation. I supply now a sketch of this view, which gives us a definite (if incomplete) semantics for our moral language.

Homeostatic Consequentialism

The way Boyd puts it, homeostatic consequentialism is the view according to which *moral goodness* is to be defined by a cluster of *human goods* and the *homeostatic mechanisms* which unify them (37). By "human goods" he understands things which satisfy important human needs such as, to start with, basic physical and medical needs, but also things which might be psychological or social, satisfying such needs as the "need for love and friendship, the need to engage in cooperative efforts, the need to exercise control over one's own life, the need for intellectual and artistic appreciation and expression, the need for physical recreation, etc." (37) And he adds: "just which important human needs there are is a potentially difficult and complex empirical question." (37) The "homeostatic mechanisms" he sees as unifying this cluster of human goods include such things as "cultivated attitudes of mutual respect, political democracy, egalitarian social relations, various rituals, customs and rules of courtesy, ready access to education and information, etc." (37) And again, he says, "it is a complex and difficult question in psychology and social theory just what these mechanisms are and how they work." (37)

The moral practice resulting from this view of morality, he observes, resembles good engineering practice in product design, where improvements in design result in large part because the homeostatic factors responsible for bringing the design to a certain stage of perfection themselves contribute to further changes, in spite of the sometimes conflicting demands placed upon the design. So also in moral practice, the conflicts which are frequently found in attempts to reconcile a variety of needs, each of which has corresponding to it something which is by definition a "good," tend by the process of homeostasis to resolve themselves, since moral goodness is itself constituted by a homeostatic unity.(38)

This feature makes homeostatic consequentialism an optimistic view, according to Boyd—or at least it might be said that those holding it might at times have to be doggedly optimistic in the face of so many disputes in the course of human history over the proper allocation of those things taken (at a given time) to satisfy human needs. (Boyd, in the remainder of his article, is concerned to show how to sketch a defense of homeostatic consequentialism against the objections of a variety of antirealist positions—e.g., J. Mackie 1977—in moral theory, and at the same time to show how this particular instantiation of moral realism might meet the constraints we have described above.)

What I shall do next is to give an indication of the manner in which considerations of an intentional nature seem to be required, in both moral realism and in any of its (correct) instantiations. I agree with Boyd's claim that an appropriately constructed version of moral realism could be given substantive form in a variety of ways, by the particular choice of substantive moral premises. And I think, although Boyd does not say this in so many words, that an optimum account of moral theory should be able to show that it is possible that there is, in the domain of moral knowledge, a form of *moral relativity* (modeled after Einsteinian relativity). I understand by this a way of expressing the conviction shared by many philosophers that, in spite of the quite apparent diversity in the deployment of moral language and the obvious explanatory problems to be faced in this connection, there must be such a thing as a "universal" morality, a morality whose fundamentals are *invariant* in some suitable sense with respect to individual, society, and culture. (Boyd's way of expressing this, it will be recalled, was supplied above as (2) [in the section, *Moral Realism*] in his list of three characteristics of moral realism.)

Capturing in the best way the precise form of this invariance is, of course, a very troublesome matter indeed, and not by any means so relatively simple a business as showing the respects in which all (normal) human individuals have physical structures and processes which are at least functionally invariant, such as their brains, metabolisms, and genetic components. The functional invariance of this set of structures, it is to be remembered, is one among the homeostatic cluster of features which taken together make it possible to assign human individuals to the natural kind we characterize by the label, *homo sapiens.* So I might suggest that what we require is a way of formulating some notion of an *intentional functional invariance* that would enable us to characterize as a *moral intentional kind* a certain class of human individuals. This would be a non-natural kind only in the sense that the features taken to define it would consist of unreduced intentional components: i.e., components some or none of which need be characterizable in terms of our currently most approximately true scientific theories. Whether these unreduced intentional components might one day, by suitable developments in scientific theories become reducible, which may or may not be required by the type of materialism I have in mind, is something upon which I shall not speculate. I shall postpone the business of dealing with the problem of intentional moral kinds until after I have indicated the manner in which intentional notions might, in a very natural way, be brought into Boyd's doctrine of moral realism and the homeostatic consequentialism he takes as a correct instantiation of it.[10]

Moral Theory, Solutions: Intentional Moral Realism and Intentional Homeostatic Consequentialism

Moral realism, as a meta-ethical doctrine about moral properties, kinds, and relations, says, in effect, that these moral entities are to be assumed to be real in some genuine sense independent of our beliefs and theories about them, but it leaves open the actual nature of the constituents or "stuff" of them. I have proposed the possibility of construing our ordinary moral language, whose syntax and usage can be charted without saying anything about its meaning or semantics, as an implicit way of referring to a variety of higher order intentions.[11] I think that this way of proceeding can be extended easily enough to the doctrine of moral realism, with the result that the moral kinds, properties, and relations under discussion may also be seen as intentional in nature. Moral kinds, properties, and relations thus become no more and no less real than the species of intentional capacities and objects with which they are associated. This species of intentional capacities and objects, of course, requires for its existence that there be a certain kind of higher order intentional system, so that moral realism on this reading turns out to be a doctrine about some features of such systems. One of the advantages of this way of operating is that it becomes quite clear that there need be no great chasm separating moral from other sorts of intentional activities: for example, the intentional capacity for having expectations may be viewed as a single capacity, at one time given employment in a moral, at another time, in a nonmoral rôle. In other words, one's moral expectations are just a special kind of one's expectations, subject, of course, to a set of conditions different from other sorts of expectations, such as one's scientifically based or one's game-playing expectations. (I shall continue to leave open the question, to which I have already called attention, as to whether an individual lacking, for whatever reason, this species of moral intentional capacities and objects, as demonstrated by an inability correctly to employ moral language, should be called a person.) I turn now to an examination, in intentional terms, of the constraints Boyd has proposed be placed upon any (correct) instantiation of moral realism.

The first constraint is itself already expressed in an overtly intentional form, viz., that there be an explanation of the fact that we started out with a supply of "relevantly approximately true" (putatively) moral *beliefs* (found in our so-called folk moral psychology), in order to make possible the particular sort of reflective equilibrium necessary for the development of moral knowledge. This constraint as it operates in the development of scientific knowledge (via another sort of reflective equilibrium involving another kind of beliefs) according to scientific realism, calls for what I am terming a nonintentional causal epistemic connection between the scientific theoretician and an independent reality. The epistemic connection for the case of moral beliefs must, of course, be described in a different manner, and be subject to different problems (e.g., the veridicality of belief), in line with the considerations I have already advanced about the nature of intentional causation and explanation.

The second constraint, that there be in moral reasoning something which is the counterpart to observation in scientific reasoning, could be construed as a call for the kinds of "observation" that are appropriate for intentional capacities and objects generally: direct observation of one's own intentional capacities and objects, or of others', by way of verbal communication. And again, there are, as we have noticed, difficulties here which must be coped with in whatever ways seem appropriate. *Moral* observation need, however, offer no peculiar or insurmountable difficulties.

The third constraint, requiring that there be a way to explain why moral properties must have natural—in the sense of nonconventional—definitions, also can be worked out in a fairly straightforward manner, again on the assumption that moral properties are a species of intentional entities, and that these intentional entities, as a part of suitable (material) intentional systems, have a kind of reality independent of the beliefs and theories of those who are said to have them. As I have noted, some care needs to be exercised in working out a suitable way of depicting what I have called "intentional kinds" as opposed to scientific natural kinds.

The fourth constraint calls for a way of showing that real moral kinds, properties, and relations control our use of moral terms in moral reasoning via some sort of epistemic access through our ordinary use of moral language. As I have already noted in connection with the second and third constraints, our access to the moral intentional capacities and objects which are constitutive of moral kinds, properties, and relations is, of necessity, by means of a particularized form of verbal communication, and thus nothing else would be capable of controlling our use of moral terms in moral reasoning. For even those actions of my own which I, presumably for sound reasons, have determined are moral actions, could not be *known* to be moral actions by anyone else unless I were to choose to communicate (verbally) this information. Because of the constraint imposed by the intentional circle, others could not, by (perceptual) observation alone (i.e., exclusive of verbal communication) determine that a performance of mine was really an *action* of mine, and if an action, a *moral* action.

The fifth (and last) constraint requires that there be an explanation for the sometimes indeterminate application of moral terms as a feature entailed by the character of moral reasoning due to the presence of concepts of the homeostatic cluster variety. Again, the nature of the type of higher order intentional systems capable of applying moral terms at all is such that one might expect, due to the network of higher order capacities required for the type, that the moral intentional entities would have to be of the cluster sort. That they are also of the homeostatic sort might be suggested by the fact that it is only by a suitable kind of mutual intentional interplay that such higher order intentional systems can continue to exist. That this must be the case is witnessed by the kind of breakdown in our ability to have such interplay when brain damage destroys a human individual's (intentional) capacity for verbal communication, or when an individual's capacities are diminished, say, by the effect of drugs.

An examination of Boyd's homeostatic consequentialism in light of the intentional considerations I have been amassing is even more revealing. For he proposes that this way of instantiating moral realism defines moral goodness as a combination of a cluster of human goods (where 'goods' are those things satisfying important human needs) and the homeostatic mechanisms which unify them. It is not altogether clear from Boyd's presentation what criteria might be called upon to classify human needs as 'important', and his mention of "basic physical and medical needs" by itself does not really tell us much. For, presumably, our interest in supplying such needs, whether for ourselves or for others, is not due simply to the fact that we are *human*—in a merely biological sense—individuals, but that we are, or may once again be, or may become, if we have not already been, human individuals who are also higher order intentional systems. That this must be what Boyd has in mind is suggested by his lists of both important human needs and homeostatic mechanisms. Recall his list of such needs: the "need for love and friendship, the need to engage in cooperative efforts, the need to exercise control over one's own life, the need for intellectual and artistic appreciation and expression, the need for physical recreation, etc." And the homeostatic mechanisms, which he says are to include such things as "cultivated attitudes of mutual respect, political democracy, egalitarian social relations, various rituals, customs and rules of courtesy, ready access to education and information, etc." It is clear that these needs and mechanisms are, one and all, not only characterizable only in terms of higher order intentions, but also possible only for a certain type of higher order intentional systems. Thus, with the qualification I have supplied to the physical and medical needs of human individuals, moral goodness, according to Boyd's version of homeostatic consequentialism, is a property definable only in terms of higher order intentional capacities and objects, since the "human" goods and homeostatic mechanisms unifying them, which are the constituents of moral goodness, must be characterized in intentional terms.

In order to have something like a complete semantics for moral terms, it would be necessary to add suitable ways of describing such notions as moral rights (and their correlated duties and/or obligations) and interests.[12] This would certainly be easy enough to do, since moral rights, and the duties and obligations connected with them, could be defined in terms of moral goodness. Thus we would have in hand at last a method for sorting moral from nonmoral intentional objects, and could differentiate the moral and nonmoral rôles to be played by the exercise of the intentional capacity for expectation. For example, when we speak of B's having a moral right as requiring that B have (or be capable of having) the expectation that A (or anyone in a suitable position) can be trusted possibly to perform an action x (or some morally equivalent action) in B's behalf, and that everyone (including A) believe that B has this right, this right is nothing else than a claim either to be given access to, or not to have withheld, some feature(s) of moral goodness, where moral goodness, of course, is defined in the intentionally modified terms I have just described.

One plausible account of the kind of interests relevant in this context has been supplied by Joel Feinberg 1974, where he argues that the attribution of rights to an individual presupposes that the individual have the capacity for interests, which are to be thought of as "compounded out of desires and aims, both of which presuppose something like belief, or cognitive awareness." (588) Here also it is the case that interests, if defined in this way, are quite explicitly intentional entities, and on the basis of some intentional version of homeostatic consequentialism, it could be maintained that the content of the interests in question—on the assumption that they are *moral* interests—would very likely be closely connected with nothing other than the features of moral goodness as depicted in that theory, at least as I have just characterized it.

I must in all honesty point out once again—and ask for the reader's forbearance in this respect—that I have not as yet dealt in an adequate manner with the still outstanding tasks of supplying a moral semantics, which would enable us to pick out the moral from the nonmoral of the intentional capacities and objects of persons, nor with the related matter of intentional kinds. In the next chapter I shall finally attempt to redeem these promissory notes, and in so doing make it possible to get on with the main purpose of these investigations: the business of characterizing the nature of moral personhood.

5

Moral Persons: I

We are now in a position, at long last, to try to show how to assemble into a unified sketch of persons and moral persons the bits and pieces of theory (and constraints upon theories) that we have accumulated over the course of our deliberations. To make it easier to do this, I shall, for the sake of exposition, divide the present task into two subtasks, starting with the schema for the making of a person, and then proceeding to the schema for the making of a moral person. It should be remembered that, while I am referring to this task as "theoretical," the ingredients I shall be using have not been concocted out of totally fictional materials: my use of the term *theoretical* here is simply to call attention to the need for further comparison of the present results with empirical investigations of the processes of intentional and moral development and decline as they are found to occur in human beings.[1] These schemata, in order really to be completed, would require a filling in of the gaps now present in our empirical knowledge of the actual mechanisms (both intentional and nonintentional) making possible the development of intentionality, and the failure of which produce the deterioration or demise of the intentional features of human beings. Investigations of moral development, as I have already noted, are to date neither as extensive as they might be, nor very conclusive, in part at least due to the fact that the nature of moral personhood (or the reality under investigation) itself has not been entirely clear. But the doctrine of moral realism, which I think is worth serious consideration, makes necessary, for the purposes of the sort of reflective equilibrium at work here, the constant confrontation of theory with the reality it presumably is charting. This reality, hopefully, will be in sharper focus after the following sections on person and moral person schemata. In the remaining sections of this chapter, I take up some features of what might be termed the "fine structure" of such persons, features having to do with the proper functioning of persons as persons or as moral persons: their identities and their malfunctioning as akratic or as servile individuals.

1. Moral Persons: Theory

How to Make a Person: a Person Schema

Before showing what is required to "make" a person, i.e., the template, schema, or conceptual functional framework needed, there is a piece of unfinished business that must be dealt with. This, it will be recalled, related to the questions raised by our reflections upon the nature of natural kinds. The suggestion, put forward as an hypothesis, that persons are material objects, certainly carries with it, by implication, the notion that it might be proper to think of them as occupying a natural kind (in the sense sketched above, chap. 2, sec. 2). There is no difficulty in saying that human beings, as the biological kind, *homo sapiens*, constitute a ɩatural kind, in spite of the fact that an account of the differentia of the kind must be given in terms of so-called cluster concepts, including those of the homeostatic variety. But in saying that persons are to be found among those material objects possessing the feature of (original) intentionality, we have introduced a characteristic whose features are not charted by biologists (at least in the way biology is currently done). This is in spite of the fact that there is (so far) no reason to suppose that intentionality is not in some manner a part of the genetic endowment of homo sapiens. Admittedly, some of us (following Noam Chomsky) may feel more comfortable in saying that the capacity for language acquisition is a part of this endowment, although we have at present very little idea as to how the actual mechanisms might work, or even what they might be. Since the capacity for verbal communication seems to be one of the essential intentional features of persons, it is tempting to smuggle it in along with the capacity for language acquisition, by taking out a kind of genetic loan. The hope is that one day it will be possible to pay off the loan in whatever genetic currency turns out to be acceptable (and as the history of the science of genetics shows, we must be prepared for surprises). So we might venture the claim that persons, as material objects possessing a certain type of intentionality, constitute a natural kind, subject to the eventual development of an approximately correct, genetically connected, scientific theory or theories.[2]

Or we might urge, pending the arrival of the right sort of genetic theory, that a different tack entirely be taken. For, while retaining the same materialist hypothesis as basis, we have seen that it is possible to treat the intentional features of human beings in an unreduced way, via an appropriate kind of psychological theory: witness the argument leading from folk psychology to cognitive psychology. Then the issue becomes one of determining whether cognitive psychology (or even something that might be called "moral psychology," as Morris 1976 has used the term, or what I have referred to as "moral science") is capable—as correct science—of supporting talk of cognitive persons as natural kinds.

Thus we can persist, however, even in the absence of the assumption of persons as a natural kind, in saying that they constitute an *intentional kind*.[3] All this does is to postpone the day of reckoning as to how best to sort the relevant beliefs, in view of our claim that persons are also malleable intentional beings. But the malleability of the beliefs and belief systems of persons is one of the features with which we are prepared to deal, via the notion of intentional selection. So, aside from calling attention to the possibility of the confirmation of the notion that human persons constitute a natural kind via some future, genetically based, moral psychology, I shall not further pursue the matter. There are similar issues that arise in connection with the question whether *moral* persons could conceivably constitute a natural kind, issues I shall postpone for a few paragraphs.

Now persons, we have argued, are to be looked upon as material, intentional, malleable things. Saying that they are material should, by this point in our discussion, raise no questions of any very troublesome type, provided that it is granted that their characteristic intentional features can be taken in an unreduced functionalist form: i.e., that it is not necessary to worry about the actual material "stuff" out of which they are constituted, but only about the functions performed by what are taken to be their essential features. Since the only persons with which we are familiar happen to be human beings, and since human beings have, in an evolutionary sense developed over a very long period of time, it seems one might not be entirely amiss in introducing hypotheses based on this background to support the particular way in which these capacities have in fact developed. This means that the capacities that human persons now have might be considered to be contingent, rather than necessary: this implies that had the evolutionary process gone in a different way, human persons might have had rather different capacities; but this possibility is something about which I shall not speculate. Saying that they possess intentionality and that they are malleable, as we have seen, raises other issues.

Saying that persons possess intentionality, à la Dennett, means (to review what we said above, chap. 2) that they are first of all to be viewed as *first order intentional systems*: i.e., the so-called intentional stance (as contrasted with the design and physical stances) can be taken toward them; they are rational, in the sense only that their actions appear to be in conformity with fundamental truths of logic (they need not know the rules of such logic); and it is possible to apply intentional predicates to them. But, and this is much more significant, they also possess the capacities making it possible for them to be viewed as *higher order intentional systems*, which means that they must possess, to start with, the capacity for reciprocity, or the ability which allows us to say of them that they not only have beliefs, desires, etc.(this is what we mean when we say of them that intentional predicates are applicable to them, or that they are first order intentional systems), but that they are capable of believing that other similar intentional systems also have beliefs, desires, etc. *about* their beliefs, desires, etc., and vice versa. With the capacity for verbal communication, it becomes possible for such higher order intentional creatures to say—in a Gricean way to other like creatures—one thing while meaning another thing, and to be understood when doing so. The capacity for verbal communication serves in turn as a necessary condition for the possibility of such creatures being both aware and self-aware: i.e., of being both conscious and self-conscious. It will be recalled that there was also introduced into this account of the intentional nature of persons the notion (due to Frankfurt 1971) of second order volitions, meaning that the individual possessing all the features we have just enumerated may also be in the position of being able to will or to desire to have a specific desire. This feature, as Frankfurt suggested, might well be seen as the feature essential to our being able to say of such individuals that they are, in an appropriate sense of that much-disputed term *free*, or that they have the capacity for free will. (There are, it might be noted, those who, like ad writers and drug pushers, desire to alter the desires of others!)

As an essential part of viewing persons as intentional beings, it is necessary to include as well the somewhat unnerving reminder that access to the actual beliefs of such creatures, other than that had by each creature with respect to his/her own beliefs, is available only by way of verbal communication. This, coupled with the possibility of there being a misreading of one's own beliefs to start with (accuracy of avowal is normative at best), introduces a factor of uncertainty into any transactions between such creatures.

The reasoning developed in connection with the circle of intentions supplies additional evidence that there can be no nonintentional (i.e., behavioristic) way of circumventing such uncertainty. These considerations led, as we noted, to Dennett's own rather pessimistic conclusion that knowing that someone—including oneself—is a person, is a necessarily problematic affair. Such pessimism might be viewed as unwarranted, as we observed, if one were to adopt a doctrine such as Davidson's anomalous monism. For doing so means that one will simply alter one's expectations with regard to how one charts the intentional behavior of persons, and will not seek law-like descriptions of their behavior (at least where such descriptions are modeled after the usual kinds of scientific accounts, where we have grown accustomed to expecting to be supplied with laws of a relatively reliable sort for charting the behavior of nonintentional objects). Personal behavior, on this reading of it, is said to be *underdetermined*. This means that there is no possibility of having knowledge of the scientific causal type, or of being in a position of knowing the sufficient conditions of personal action.

Saying that persons are malleable with respect to their beliefs and belief systems, it will be remembered, is simply a way of pointing to what seems to be a rather obvious feature of persons, a feature that also has rather disconcerting aspects. This is because there seem to be no initial limits at all on what a person can believe, or what a group of persons can believe. However, the capacity for malleability seems to be accompanied by—and this, we have conjectured, may have its basis in the evolutionary processes which produced both it and consciousness—the need to place limitations upon the nature and variety of beliefs and belief systems to insure the survival of the species. The hypothesis of intentional selection was proposed as a way of accounting for this need, by suggesting that the capacity for constructing belief systems seems to carry within itself the potential for adjustment and self-correction, a capacity seen at work in one of its most refined forms in the kind of reflective equilibrium found in the sciences and elsewhere. Indeed, the existence of such self-correcting belief systems as those found in mathematics and logic, but especially in the experimental sciences, can be taken as an indication of the success of intentional selection.

So malleability, via the evolution of intentionality, turns out not to be an unmixed evil. Malleability, where it is not circumscribed in suitable ways, can be blamed for some of the worst things that human beings have done to each other over historical time, and as such is, and continues to be, productive of evil consequences. But at the same time, since it (together with the capacity for consciousness) makes possible the ability for those having it to deliberate, or to consider (content-full) alternative sets of beliefs and possible courses of action, it seems as well to be a necessary condition for the sort of mind changing (or belief alteration) required in a variety of human contexts, but especially so in the domain of morality, where it may have good consequences.[4]

This appearance in human higher order intentional systems of the capacity for awareness and self-awareness meant that intentional selection did not have to be just the sort of unconscious, nonvoluntary affair found in natural selection, but could operate in a conscious (and self-conscious) voluntary homeostatic fashion, so that the modification of belief systems could come under a kind of self-control. The development of a field like genetic engineering, for example, is one of the more obvious and striking manifestations—due to its potential capacity for self-referentiality—of the way in which intentional selection has operated. It is early days indeed in this area, however, and we are a very long way from understanding the genetic mechanisms presumably underlying and making possible the features of intentional creatures I have termed "unreduced".

Thus in saying that persons, as material objects, are also malleable higher order intentional systems, we make possible a way of explaining both the difficulty we experience in understanding and explaining their behavior (because of the troubles with the veridicality of belief, the intentional circle, or the constraints imposed by anomalous monism) and their undeniable capacity for evil as well as good (because of the malleability of their beliefs and belief systems). Keep in mind that thus far I have still made no essential reference to what might be involved in making persons moral. Whether we like it or not, I think it is entirely appropriate to say that being moral is not a necessary condition of personhood. The figures we look upon as the most evil and morally depraved in human history were, no less than those of us who today consider ourselves to be persons, certainly persons. They possessed all of the features we have so far attributed to persons; it just happened that malleability, in their cases, led to results of a horrifying nature. Whether we would really want to say, as Dennett has suggested, that we all as persons and moral persons might properly be said to be located on the same continuum, is, because of this, a more troublesome claim, I think.

How to Make a Moral Person: a Moral Person Schema

To make a moral person, or to describe a moral person schema, we start with the person schema we have just completed, warts and all: that is, with the constraints imposed by the problem of belief veridicality, anomalous monism and/or the intentional circle, and the troubles with belief sorting generated by malleability.

Morality, we have proposed, is properly to be located in the domain of the intentional, and concerns itself with a particular subset of the beliefs, desires, expectations, etc. (and the capacities making them possible) of the type of higher order intentional systems we have described as persons. Our ordinary moral language, whose syntax charts the (internal) connections of our moral vocabulary (and against which we check the theorems we derive in formal deontic logic), and the putatively moral portion of our folk psychology, we have argued, can both in a felicitous manner be construed as referring implicitly to intentional objects or whatnots, i.e., the things and capacities pointed to or presupposed by the appropriate beliefs, desires, expectations, etc.

Moral theory, when construed as a theory about these objects and their associated capacities, is rich enough to generate a moral semantics. If one elects to espouse the doctrine of moral realism (in the form in which we have proposed it), then the correctness of moral theory will be judged by measuring it against the appropriate intentional objects and capacities, since they are taken as the reality here.

Now so far this remains rather abstract: how are we to go about the actual business of picking out the features which demarcate moral from nonmoral intentionality—and thus supply the meaning or semantics for 'moral' we have been postponing— and so finally arriving at the substantive moral premises that will drive moral theory? We have suggested that Boyd's proposal for doing this, in terms of what he has called "homeostatic consequentialism," which calls for defining moral goodness in terms of *human* needs, is really a disguised way of trying to pick out such intentional entities and their associated capacities. But, as we have noted, he leaves obscure some of the details: as I suggested, he apparently intends by talk of "human needs" to refer to what might better be called the needs of *persons*, since most of the needs he mentions are possible only for the sorts of higher order intentional beings we have characterized as persons. What I want to propose is that we describe two rather different kinds or classes of such "needs," which, when they are met, might be said to be productive of moral goodness, and when they are not met, might be said to be productive of moral evil.[5] Common to both classes of needs is the fact that the meeting of them requires voluntary action on the part of persons, and this makes these needs very different from such physical needs as those for food, air, and water, which may be met, certainly, by the relatively less sophisticated nonintentional devices developed over the course of evolutionary time in all living creatures.

The *first class* of these needs I shall call "basic enabling" needs (and this means, of course, that they can be seen as enabling only from the perspective of the second class): these are the needs of human individuals (those who have the appropriate genetic endowment, presumably) with respect to their being able actually to *develop* the very higher order intentional capacities essential to their becoming persons. Without these needs being met, there would be no persons, and hence no moral persons. On this basis I can suggest that there would be a kind of moral evil produced if certain things were voluntarily done (or voluntarily left undone) the result of which would be human individuals lacking the developed capacities required for their being persons. This might appear to be a curious sort of thing to say, since, of course, we run the risk, if we produce persons of the wrong sort, of having around individuals capable of generating moral evil. But this is a risk we apparently must run, since to try to insure, by some kind of intentionality "surgery" (i.e., brainwashing) that persons have only certain species of intentionality (even if it could reliably be done), collides with our intuition that this would not be the morally right thing to do. The possibility eventually of tracking intentional capacities to their genetic sources opens the Pandora's Box containing such gems as genetic surgery for altering these capacities, and cloning for producing to order individuals having such altered capacities. Sufficient unto the day are the moral problems thereof (cf. the alarms sounded by Jeremy Rifkin and others)!

The *second class* of needs, and the class upon which the morality of the first class is parasitical (those in respect to which the needs of the first class are relevant constitute one type of moral patient), has to do with the needs of those who already are persons, and this might be thought of as being much closer to the locus of morality proper. For these needs are those encountered in the lives of persons, needs the meeting of which are necessary for their *continued existence as persons*: these needs are met, indirectly, of course, by an array of nonintentional things (e.g., physical and medical), *but more significantly by a variety of intentional objects, ranging from everyday social rituals and customs to the most elaborate and refined legal structures.* Essential to a person's remaining a person is that he/she do nothing that would interfere with, or destroy, either the developed higher order intentional capacities upon which his/her own personhood depends or the conditions making possible their being exercised. A *moral person* might then be said to be the person who both recognizes that this is a fundamental fact of life about persons, and in addition, while recognizing that s/he has the power to interfere with, or even to destroy the like capacities of other persons as well as his/her own, yet (voluntarily) *chooses* to refuse to take actions having such consequences and chooses (whenever possible) to take actions contributing to the development and maintenance of these capacities—whether these actions involve nonintentional or only intentional devices—and *trusts* that others will choose in the same way.

Those who act in this way, or who instantiate the schema, might also be noted as exhibiting the characteristic of *caring*,[6] a characteristic which in our culture has apparently so far been allocated primarily to women.[7] It is due to the elective nature of these actions that those in a position to be recipients and beneficiaries of such actions must place their trust in the performer(s) of the actions. Even when the classes of such action are thought important enough by society that legal sanctions be imposed for failing to perform them (as in our expectations with regard to our treatment of children, accident victims, etc.), this cannot guarantee that those in a position to perform them (and able to perform them) *will* perform them. One aspect of the universality usually thought to be a necessary feature of morality is implicit in the observation that today's performer of a moral action is potentially tomorrow's recipient and beneficiary. In this way is revealed one of the intentional sources of the Golden Rule and other related principles, such as Richard Wasserstrom's second order right, or the so-called principle of respect for persons, all of which might be said, at least in part, to represent attempts to distill the essence of the sort of mutual expectation and trust depicted here.[8]

Thus, finally, is a substantive sense supplied for 'moral', a sense we previously connected (chap. 4, sec. 1) only with the theoretical proposal that, for example, having a moral right meant, in intentional terms, that an individual B might be said to have an expectation of a certain sort with regard to the beliefs, expectations, and actions of A vis-à-vis B, or anyone in the position of A (where some A, it will be recalled, *could* perform the action in question if he/she chose to do so). Being moral, in either an active or a passive sense, or *being a moral person*, is thus clearly a homeostatic affair, involving as it does the cooperation of like individuals. And since it is intentional in nature and voluntary as well, the metaphor depicting morality as a fragile fabric is quite apt. For even the developed capacities for moral intentionality, in a society where most individuals lacked them or few cooperated in supplying the conditions making possible their being maintained and exercised, would, in a sense, wither away or atrophy through lack of use, or simply be tossed to one side or even destroyed, as happens often enough in riots, violent political uprisings, and war. For it is again the capacity for malleability, manifesting itself in the kind of blind and self-destructive devotion to a cause that produces fanatics, that is easily capable of overriding the sort of moral intentionality we have just described. Malleability also shows itself in those described (in the manner of T. Hill 1973) as relinquishing certain of their moral rights in an unjustifiably servile manner by denying their own moral status (for a more detailed account of this, see below, sec. 2).

There is, in moral personhood thus depicted, a strong cognitive component, since it is implied, of course, that one *know* (in an appropriate sense) the consequences of one's actions. This is a component that has been recognized to be beset with problems since at least the time of Plato (or his teacher, Socrates), who wondered why it is, since no one would choose to do what he *knew to be evil*, anyone *ever does* anything evil. Part of the solution to this problem is to be found, surely, in the recognition that the concept of moral evil is quite evidently an open concept, which means that one's lack of knowledge in this area may not be simply a matter of not knowing something which one might have known, but of not knowing something of the sort of which it is true to say that there is no way one might have known it.[9] (This is connected as well with the concept of a crime, which is also an open concept if any concept is; clearly, the future contains crimes undreamed of by even the most imaginative writer of fiction.) In other words, it seems that our knowledge of the human endeavors that might interfere with or destroy our capacities to become or to remain persons is not limited just by our particular circumstances, but *essentially* limited. By the same token, moral goodness is also an open concept, and our knowledge of its forms as a consequence must also be essentially limited. Thus is set a fundamental problem for moral psychology: that of developing empirically sound ways of determining what types of voluntary actions on the part of persons will be productive of moral evil and moral goodness in the sense proposed.

Now knowledge of such knowledge may lead one to say rather extraordinary things, as it likely led Sartre to give it a kind of ontological status in human existence itself: the *pour-soi* is in the mode of being what it is not, and of not being what it is, and as such is (necessarily) in *mauvaise foi*, etc.. While there are certainly difficulties here, there are also important lessons to be learned from considering what ought to be said about the limit case, in practice, that confronts those unlucky persons who suddenly discover, because of accident or illness, that their lives as moral persons are very finite indeed, and who thus have the unexpected opportunity to choose to do what would otherwise be *prima facie* immoral: to bring about (or to arrange to have steps brought about by other persons, steps which will result in) their no longer being moral persons, or persons; that is, voluntarily to destroy their own capacity for moral intentionality. (I shall say more about this in the section below on moral persons and death, and in the concluding chapter.)

Matters are otherwise, although no less complicated to rationalize, with those who are not in such straits but who elect to terminate their own lives as intentional beings because of adherence to some cause, religious or political (or both), or because they care enough about another person to sacrifice themselves for that person. Writings on ethics are replete with such cases, with discussions of the sometimes irresolvable issues about conflicts of rights and duties entailed by these cases.

Before closing this section, I need to say something about the question whether moral persons, as I have just characterized them, should be said to occupy a natural kind, since I in the last section alluded to the need to deal with this issue. As with the similar question with regard to persons, I think the least that can be said is that moral persons also constitute an intentional kind, subject to the sorting of beliefs that this entails. *As a matter of fact, I view a part of what I am doing in these investigations as an effort along exactly these lines, or as I have urged, a study in moral science or moral psychology. The question whether this "science" will one day be taken as adequate to establish natural kinds I shall leave moot. By electing to adopt the version of the doctrine of moral realism we have proposed, one should at least be taken to espouse the view that there are moral kinds*, and since I am arguing that moral kinds are a species of intentional kinds, that is where the issue might best be left.

Finally, there are some rather interesting and useful consequences flowing from the way proposed here of describing the nature of moral personhood, or of providing a schema for moral persons, and in turn helping to flesh it out. For to characterize moral persons with anything approaching the "thickness" of the actual individuals we recognize others and ourselves to be, as opposed to the "thinness" of the abstract individuals found in a strictly theoretical account, requires attention as well to a variety of aspects of our lives together, in order to achieve the kind of reconciliation of theory with reality that is most desirable (at least if one speaks as a realist in such matters).[11]

For one thing, it can now be seen that at least part of our interest in human rights can be viewed as an interest in the first class of needs, the basic enabling ones, and as such, human rights would have a derivative moral status. In other words, what is really of interest to us about human beings in this sense is their potentiality for becoming persons, and, in particular, *moral* persons. The definitions of human rights, of course, have been so various that some of them have included the needs of our second class as well, so that, again, our interest in human beings may be related to the things required for them to continue to be persons, on the assumption that they have already become such.[12]

It is hardly necessary to remind ourselves that appeals to human rights, as a political or religious ploy, have tended in practice to be linked with one's favorite political and/or religious causes, and consequently may not have the sort of moral nonpartisan character that would appear to be desirable. Some Christian theologians have, I understand, discovered in recent years by "rereading" the *New Testament* that Jesus Christ was one of the earliest advocates of human rights. One is tempted to remark that surely these rights were for a time officially to be found attached only to Christians—at least the Church Fathers, if they had been apprised of the existence of such rights, probably would have promulgated some doctrine along these lines.

Moreover, our interest in the right to privacy, as well as our concern for those who are said to be unjustifiably servile (as I shall argue in more detail in sections which are to follow: for privacy, chap. 7; for servility, the next section of this chapter), may both be shown to be related to the classes of needs I have just described. Similarly, the nature of law, and the concept of punishment and the constraints appropriate to both, can best be viewed against the background of the schemata I have supplied here, as I will show below (chap. 7). This is even more true of the quality of life of moral persons; and, in extremis, of the deaths of such persons (sections 1 and 2 of the next chapter).

Before turning to a consideration of some of the fine structure of the concept of moral personhood, I might point out that the functionalist character of the moral person schema depicted here has been tailored to fit creatures like human beings as we know them. It is conceivable that there might be a class of beings of a functionally similar nature to human beings, but who might lack entirely the first class of needs: in other words, they might come to exist as full-fledged moral persons without their having gone through the process of development necessary for the appearance of human moral persons. I am not sure that it is conceivable that such creatures could be lacking the second class of needs and still fall under the concept of morality we have sketched, for this concept requires that the moral life be viewed as *essentially fragile* in nature, depending for its sustenance upon the good will and voluntary actions of the members of the moral community.

2. Moral Persons, Identity, and Moral Defects: Akrasia and Servility

It is time now to make good on another of the promissory notes issued quite early along the way. In the first chapter I alluded to certain problems connected with describing a variety of possible states of myself—for example, when I said that I hold certain opinions about how other persons might have treated me had I been born as, say, an anencephalic individual; or how they ought morally to treat me if in the future I, through accident or disease, should become the functional equivalent of such an individual. At issue in both of these possible cases (and in some of the others as well) is the question whether, and in what sense, my use of the pronoun, *I* in such contexts is justifiable as a way of conveying meaningful information about the person that I presumably am now, and have been for several years, or whether it is merely an honorific designation, or perhaps one among many possible ways of tracking a certain living human body. This use of the pronoun, it might be urged, seems to presuppose that it is both possible and meaningful initially to identify, and at a later date to reidentify, an individual as not only the same individual, but an individual of the same type. And these are only some among the aspects of the "problem" of personal identity, or as we shall address it, the problem of identifying and reidentifying through time certain individuals as individuals *and as the same (identical) persons or moral persons.*

Connected with—and perhaps even an essential part of— this problem are what might appear to be possible features of moral persons, features that, if they are understood in certain ways, might lead us to question whether what is ostensibly the same moral person actually is: the so-called moral defects, akrasia and servility. *Akrasia*, frequently translated as "weakness of will," has been recognized as a problematic condition since at least the time of Plato, and is connected with the fact that people apparently sometimes choose to do things they believe they ought not to do: they opt for courses of action that go against their better judgment.[13] Saint Paul is one of the more famous individuals who presumably fell victim to this condition—or at least his account in the New Testament (Romans 7) is usually understood to be one of the better depictions of the condition. *Servility* also is a rather curious business, since it has to do with the fact that some individuals apparently choose to deny their own status as moral persons (cf. Thomas E. Hill Jr, 1973). It has been urged that many individuals have exhibited and continue to exhibit this condition, including, for example, some members of racial minorities and some women. The very presumption that an individual *is* a moral person may be brought into question when either of these conditions manifests itself. For even if one were convinced that one were dealing with a moral person before these conditions made themselves evident, one might with good reason, as we shall see, have difficulty upon their appearance sustaining that conviction.

Deliberations by philosophers on the issues surrounding the nature of personal identity have sometimes proceeded in the absence of any explicitly formulated theory of personhood, and the same thing has been true of discussions of akrasia and servility. Again, as we shall argue below in connection with our discussion of the concept of privacy, one of the pieces of evidence lending support to the theory of moral personhood proposed here will be precisely that the adoption of this theory enables us to come out with some clearer ways of thinking about such matters as privacy, servility, and akrasia, too. As we shall see, the distinction that we have urged be made between the concept of a person and that of a moral person will come into play in a significant manner, as well. But we begin with the business of identity.

Moral Persons and Identity

Before assembling our views on the identification and re-identification of moral persons, I do need to say a few words about certain historical, logical, and what might best be called science-fictional, aspects of the so-called philosophical problem of personal identity.

John Locke may be held responsible for setting the direction of many subsequent discussions of personal identity (from Joseph Butler and Thomas Reid to the present) by his way of deploying his example of the prince and the cobbler.[14] He proposed that we consider what we would say if it were to happen that the "soul, carrying with it the consciousness of the prince's past life" were to take up residence in the body of a cobbler (with freshly departed soul): would we be willing to say that the prince continues to exist, in spite of the fact that his words and demeanor would present themselves with a cobbler-ish rather than a princely aspect?

More recently, and in a similar but somewhat more complex vein, Sydney Shoemaker (1963) proposed the curious case of Brown and Robinson:

these individuals, both suffering from some operable brain disorder, we are to suppose have had their brains removed for the difficult operations. Alas, the surgeon's apprentice mixes up the brains, so that Brown's brain goes into Robinson's body and vice versa. The individual with Robinson's brain unfortunately dies soon after the surgery, and the surviving individual Shoemaker proposed be referred to as "Brownson." Again, the identity question: Is Brownson the same as (identical with) Brown?

And further to complicate matters, we might add the much-discussed, science-fictional possibility that, because of what we know about the phenomena associated with split-brained (those who have undergone commissurotomy) human individuals, phenomena indicating that the cerebral hemispheres have a certain measure of autonomy, the bisected halves of one such individual's brain might be transplanted to the living bodies of two other (brainless or debrained) human individuals. The question now is not only whether the original individual whose brain was divided has survived, but whether the two remaining individuals are not only identical with her/him but identical as well with each other (this because of the property of identity known as its transitivity, reflected in the familiar saying, "Things equal to the same thing are equal to each other"). The case just described is one of "fission." Another permutation results in "fusion," on the assumption that the individuals with the separated brain halves might be operated on and the halves rejoined in the (brainless or de-brained) living body of still another human individual.

One of the factors that have figured in attempts to sort out these questions has had to do with the properties of what logicians refer to as the "identity-relation," or the logic of identity. Among the principles constituting this logic has been one known since Leibniz as the "Identity of Indiscernibles."[15] According to this principle, if a pair of things were to have every property in common (and to lack every property in common), then the "two" things would actually be indiscernible, and would have to be counted as one and the same (i.e., identical) thing. On the basis of this principle, the having (lacking) of every property in common, etc., counts as a *sufficient* condition of identity. There is another principle, however, sometimes known as the "Indiscernibility of Identicals," according to which the having (lacking) of every property in common is a *necessary* condition of identity: in other words, if a pair of things lacked this condition, they could not be said to be one and the same thing.[16]

Now, it can be argued, how one answers the questions raised with regard to the cases described in the previous paragraphs will turn upon whether one adopts one or the other of these two principles. Affirming the second of the principles would appear to commit one to urging that the individuals remaining after the changes have taken place are *not* identical with the original individuals. Espousal of the first principle, it might be claimed, would allow for the possibility that the remaining individuals might be said to be identical with the original individuals: falsity of the sufficient condition, i.e., that the individuals at the earlier and the later times have (lack) *every* property in common, etc., does not entail the falsity of the claim that the "two" individuals are the same. Thus it might appear that one could say that whether the individuals are the same at the earlier and at the later times depends upon one's choice of logical principles: application of the one principle seems to lead to the conclusion that they are; application of the other to the conclusion that they are not.

However, there are other alternatives, too: for example, one might argue that the identity relation needs to be read in a "tenseless" fashion. One could then propose that one and the same individual is, to take the case of Shoemaker's Brownson, at one time Brown and at a later time Brownson. Or, in still different terminology, that there could be an individual one of whose stages is at one time labeled "Brown" but at another (later) time has a stage labeled "Brownson." But then one might be tempted to respond that this seems to beg the very question at issue, which might be put in the form, What is *essential* to a thing's remaining the same thing over time? Or alternatively: Which stages are in some proper sense stages of the same, rather than of different individuals? It is clear enough that some kinds of changes would not lead us to say that there has been a change in identity, but that others could. We would have little or no inclination to say that anything affecting Brown's essential nature would occur if he were to receive as a transplant in his own body, say, the *heart* of some other indivdual. A brain transplant would surely be a different matter (unless the brain being used were in some way "reprogrammed" so that it actually was an exact duplicate of Brown's brain; but in this case there would no longer be a problem—except, of course, for the technological problem!).

Now how much headway can be made by sticking with the logic of identity alone is perhaps debatable, for the logical concept of identity resembles in some respects the logic of other higher order concepts, such as that of *number*. Number's being a higher order concept accounts for the fact that, for example, whether we refer to something as "one" or "two" depends upon how we have chosen to set up our (first-order) concepts. Thus (normal) human beings are said to have *two* hands, one left and one right, or *one* pair of hands: whether hands are one or two depends upon how they are counted, and either way will do, depending upon what our interests are. And so with identity: what counts as "one and the same" and as "two and different" similarly presupposes a choice in the way we have set up our (first-order) concepts. Whether the loafers I have on now are identical with the pair I had seven years ago depends upon my choice of identity concepts: one choice might be taken to suggest that there is an identity, the other that there isn't.

There seem to be needed, in addition to the notion of identity, certain other things as well, if we are to feel that we have properly got hold of all of the issues here. That this is the case is perhaps reflected in John Perry's observation (an observation with which Derek Parfit 1976, 101 concurs) that "the importance of identity is derivative. Apart from those other relationships it normally guarantees, it need be of no interest to us."[17] Our interest in knowing that we are dealing with the same person is, after all, because our dealings are always in a certain context: we will have, say, a legal or a moral interest in a person's being held responsible for things he/she has done in the past, for things now contracted for, or for those promised for the future. So the features of primary interest are those which will allow us to say of a certain person that he/she does (or does not) continue to be the same legal and/or moral person. This is not to deny, of course, that we might also have an interest in knowing whether a certain corpse before us is connected with a particular formerly living human being. Such identifications, while subject to difficulties of a multitude of sorts, need not present the difficulties—which we shall discuss shortly—that can afflict our reidentifications of legal or moral persons, for the reason that biological human bodies (whether living or dead), unlike persons, are nonintentional objects and have less troublesome identity conditions. Parfit (1976, 100-1) has put these points in the following way: "as a first approximation ... the truth of statements about personal identity just consists in the truth of certain statements about psychological and (perhaps) physical continuity. The fact of personal identity is not a further fact, apart from facts about these continuities." We shall modify Parfit's observation only by employing the notion of intentionality as a way of talking about the relevant type of continuity of interest.

However, before turning to an examination of some of the consequences resulting from bringing our theory of moral personhood to bear upon the matter of identity, I do want to comment upon one other aspect, so far not mentioned, of the literature on personal identity. Ever since Locke's introduction of the notion of *immaterial substance* to the discussion of personal identity issues, others again have followed suit, from Joseph Butler to Anthony Quinton (1962) and Shoemaker (1976). Locke supposed that there would likely be those who might want to argue that what remains the same over time is a specific kind of immaterial substance, sometimes called the "soul," and that it would be the continuation of this immaterial substance that would allow for an individual's in some sense surviving his/her death in a reidentifiable way. Locke, Quinton, and Shoemaker agree that such a position is not demonstrably, logically, self-contradictory (although putting the matter in this way of course falls far short of asserting the importance attached to the notion of immaterial substances claimed by Butler and many others).

Shoemaker (1976) has taken the greatest pains to try to show why it is that, even granted the logical possibility of the notion of an immaterial substance, there seems to be no way of finding out what different *kinds* of such substances there might be. For given the assumption—and this seems also clearly to be a logical possibility—that there could be more than one kind of immaterial substance, in the absence of any known way of acquiring conclusive knowledge about such substances there seems little to recommend an appeal to an unknown possibility as a way of profitably effecting the types of identifications and reidentifications that are of interest to us with regard to human persons. Shoemaker's suggestion that we must resort to a notion of "paradigmatic embodiment" as one of the only plausible courses of action open to us in solving personal identity problems may be connected with our own observation in chapter 2 about the possible role of the soul as homunculus. For to suppose that the soul/homunculus encapsulates already the very features of interest to us about persons is surely to involve us in either a *petitio principii* or an *argumentum ad ignorantiam*, and to plunge us as well into mind-body issues that we have purposely chosen to circumvent by adoption of our version of an intentionalistic (nonreductive) materialism.[18] Our theory of persons may thus be viewed as one way of providing some structural details for Shoemaker's concept of "paradigmatic embodiment."

Other than rehearsing some of the kinds of issues that have been under scrutiny by philosophers in recent years, and proposing a connection between Shoemaker's concept of paradigmatic embodiment and my own view, as I have just done, I shall make no further attempt to enter this particular area. My concern, of course, is that these discussions have for the most part proceeded under the apparent assumption that we already know as much as we need to know about the things—i.e., persons—under investigation. I shall now turn to the task of suggesting how it is that our recently developed characterization of moral personhood might be utilized in providing both a way of giving an initial identification for a moral person and enabling us as well to reidentify a given moral person as the same moral person over time.

It should be clear enough, given the view that a moral person is a higher order intentional system of the sort lately described (as a special type of malleable Dennett-person), that supplying an initial identification for such an individual will have as a necessary condition access to the individual's own beliefs, desires, expectations, understandings, etc. This access, by the conditions stated, must be via some type of verbal communication, whether orally or by some form of written means. Coming to know *that* a particular human individual is a person or moral person thus presupposes a developed capacity for verbal communication; to be able to identify a particular individual, and to distinguish that individual from others requires coming to know the particular beliefs, intentions, etc., and belief systems held by that individual: those beliefs, intentions, etc. which presumably, as a matter of fact, would not be held by every other individual.

What, after all, allows us to say of several individuals that they are all moral persons requires that they all have certain higher order beliefs, etc. in common; what distinguishes them from one another will be not only the additional beliefs, intentions, etc. that they hold, but also the particular *manner* in which they might be said to hold the characteristically moral beliefs, intentions, etc. (and belief systems) that make it possible *ab initio* for us to place them in the class of moral persons. We discover, according to our proposal, that a particular person is a moral person (moral *agent*) when we discover—by access to his/her beliefs, intentions, etc.—that s/he both recognizes that by a voluntary action (or inaction) s/he could influence in a causal way (where the causes may be either nonintentional or intentional, or both) either the development of an individual into a person or the continuation of an individual as a developed person or moral person, and attempts to act in accordance with this recognition.[19]

Such moral persons, while typically differing from one another precisely because of the other (i.e., nonmoral) beliefs, intentions, etc. that they hold, will also differ in the manner in which they hold the higher order beliefs which themselves constitute the criterion for their being moral. For example, one moral person might choose to act to preserve the rights of another person even if this should mean some diminution in the free exercise of the rights of still other persons, not excluding her/himself; another might opt for a course of action the result of which could be expected to be a state of affairs in which the exercise by some person of his/her rights might be curtailed in the interest of a group of persons. In other words, it must be the case that individuals can be moral persons and at the same time adopt or reject utilitarian ways of reading beliefs, intentions, expectations, etc. And the same thing would be true for other ways of choosing to perform moral actions, although the parting of the ways reflected in the distinction between a rights-based and a utilitarian ethic is probably among the most deep-seated ones in our moral thinking. Indeed, it seems not unreasonable to allow for the possibility that one and the same individual might, on different occasions and without any inconsistency, choose courses of action in conformity with one or the other of these two approaches. And in a related way, as Bernard Williams has tried for many years to coax us into thinking, our choices of actions might also reflect a departure from some abstract principle of fairness when the persons involved in an actual situation are some of them more intimately connected to us in a variety of ways than the others, and be no less moral for all that.[20]

The reidentification over time of a certain moral person as the *same* moral person thus presupposes the possibility on separate occasions of correctly accessing the individual's (moral) beliefs, expectations, etc, and determining that they have not changed in any crucial way.[21] Since this access is necessarily by way of verbal communication, the (normative) assumption is that the individual in question will not encounter insurmountable problems re the veridicality of his/her own beliefs, nor (normally) will there be any reason to suppose that he/she will deliberately misrepresent these beliefs to someone else.

We should notice in this connection the difference between the inaccessibility of belief and the *absence* of belief, since this suggests something about the *retrospective nature* of personhood: "I was once not a person" is not (logically) meaningful as an utterance for one who has not yet become a person; nor, of course, is its meaningful utterance possible for one who is no longer a person. Ignoring this feature of personhood can produce extraordinary confusion (as a case in point, cf. Hare 1975).

The discovery that an individual is an instance of the type we have referred to as exemplifying akrasia or servility could certainly have a bearing upon answering the question whether we ought to reidentify such an individual as the same individual over time for moral purposes. This is a question we must now consider, and we begin with the case of servility.

Moral Persons and Servility

The servile individual, as portrayed by Thomas E. Hill, Jr., as we have noted, is one who is in the position of (voluntarily) denying her/his own moral status. This condition may manifest itself in various ways, some of which Hill supplies in his depictions of "the Uncle Tom," "the Deferential Wife," and "the Self-Deprecator" (the names of which are rather self-explanatory). The feature common to all individuals of these types is that they consider themselves not to be the moral equals of other persons with whom they are directly related. In other words, they voluntarily forgo exercising rights to which they are entitled as moral agents (or patients), in each case deferring to other persons, not because they think this is something they should do as an instrument or temporary policy for accomplishing some particular goal, but as a continuing stance. There need be nothing abnormal about someone who, on occasion, would adopt as an expendable strategy the willingness to have certain of her/his rights overridden; what would be abnormal would be the doing of this routinely.

In terms of the vocabulary we have developed, we would describe the servile individual as one who elects to decide, with respect to a whole class of higher order beliefs and expectations—namely, the *moral* ones, that they are no longer to be held in a universal way. In particular, the servile individual would be in effect saying that certain other persons need not take a moral stance toward her/him in the sense of recognizing and choosing to act in such a way as not to interfere with, and to do things that are positively causally related to, her/his continuing to be a person or a moral person. The servile individual might be said to be in the awkward position of both recognizing and trying to act in such a way as to preserve the (moral) personhood of everyone except her/himself.

To maintain such a position, however, would be not only awkward but even paradoxical, for it would not be entirely clear that such an individual really understood what is required of a moral person. Thus one might well wonder whether one ought initially to identify as moral such an individual. If an initially moral person (one who by definition clearly was not servile) were discovered to have become servile during some intervening time span, then one would have good reason to wonder whether s/he ought to be reidentified as the same moral person. For one who has come to think it appropriate as a matter of fixed policy to remove her/himself from the status of having moral expectations about the way in which others ought to treat her/him seems not to be thinking in a manner consistent with the sorts of expectations quite widely assumed to be appropriate on the basis of the usual sort of moral theory, which stipulates as a general rule that there can be no such exceptions granted.

In another way of putting it, we might say that an essential part of the logic of morality seems to dictate that one has an obligation not to be servile, that this is a duty laid upon every putatively moral individual. Otherwise, we would be in the position of at least implicitly condoning the existence of a class of individuals all of whom might be servile, and who by being so might serve to help to perpetuate forms of injustice we have come to recognize in the historical treatment of a variety of minorities. Clearly, the existence of servile individuals does entail the existence of individuals other than the servile individual—for it is these others who make it possible, by their forbearing from helping the servile individual to repair her/his defect, for her/his servility to continue. It could even be proposed that in a sense a moral society has not only the right not to have servile individuals present in it, but moreover a responsibility and a duty to see to it that conditions contributing to the development of such individuals be prevented from arising.[22]

Most such conditions are likely to be intentional in nature, and servility may have, as a disorder of certain higher order beliefs and expectations, a higher order intentional etiology as well. Certainly the correction or "cure" of servility entails the acquisition of insight of a higher order sort: one afflicted with the condition must be brought to see *what* the condition is, in order to understand why it is not desirable to be in the condition. This in turn presupposes that a suitable higher order capacity has been or can be developed.

The recognition by a previously servile individual of his/her own defect would entail the developed capacity to detect the particular sort of inconsistency at work (the actual inconsistency might be put in the form of saying that while everyone ought to be treated morally, there is nevertheless at least one individual who need not be so treated. And the "at least one" could easily turn out to be a whole group of individuals). This would presuppose, of course, a developed capacity to detect inconsistency as such: in the absence of this developed capacity one would have good reason to wonder about the status of the individual as a person. Happening not to be aware of an inconsistency at a particular time would not be a source of concern, for we know all too well that there have been (and presumably always will be) unrecognized inconsistencies; inability to see *any* inconsistency as an inconsistency would be another matter entirely. Thus one might say that servility would have to be a repairable or curable defect, or a kind of fixable blindness, as blindness to a particular inconsistency would be a kind of temporary blindness. Once cured or fixed, however, it seems unlikely that one who had been so afflicted would suffer a relapse.

Now the possibility of there being servile individuals is a real one only on the assumption that there is a difference of an essential sort between being a person and being a moral person: for the servile individual, while clearly not countable as a full-fledged member of the moral community, is nevertheless a person in the sense we have proposed. In other words, being servile is a possibility only for those with sufficiently developed capacities as persons (i.e., malleable Dennett-persons), for the conditions that are necessary for our being able to say of someone that he/she is servile would be ones that would at the same time be necessary for our being able to describe her/him as a person. Among these conditions, it will be recalled, is the higher order condition making possible voluntary action itself: the capacity for having second order desires or willings. Servile individuals, in voluntarily denying their own moral status, will (or desire) to have the desire that others so treat them. There can be no servile dogs, horses, or small children, for the reason that none of them can be persons in the proposed sense: while small children might be said to be potentially capable of developing higher order intentions (including higher order desires), dogs, horses (and most other creatures) apparently lack this potentiality. Thus servility is a defect only for higher order intentional systems with developed capacities, and might most accurately be described as a higher order intentional defect, but a defect of a curable type.

Moral Persons and Akrasia

The morally akratic individual, as opposed to the servile individual, seems to be one more likely to be met with—in others and in ourselves—at least if we are to take as accurately representing this type of individual the views developed in Davidson 1970b. For the akratic person, or the akrates, is the individual who on occasion—and not all the time, since if s/he did this all the time it would be a habit or a character defect—voluntarily selects, by employing what philosophers have often called "practical" reason, a course of action s/he believes not to be in accord with what s/he believes to be the best action, or to be in his/her best interest.

It is clear enough that the akrates is necessarily a higher order intentional creature, as well as a malleable one. And as Davidson has pointed out, it is clear enough as well that such an individual may manifest the syndrome in nonmoral as well as in moral contexts. In terms of our way of characterizing morality, this means that the courses of action elected need not involve interfering with the meeting of either of the two classes of needs involved in anyone's becoming or remaining a person or moral person. Common enough is the picture of the athlete on the playing field (presumptively nonmoral) who has gone with a course of action obviously contrary to his/her better judgment, resulting in the loss of a point, a match, or a meet. When asked afterwards why s/he chose to do what s/he did, no rational explanation is forthcoming: whence the titles for David Pears' and Alfred Mele's books on akrasia: respectively, *Motivated Irrationality* and *Irrationality*.

It is not at all clear what should be offered as the best theory of moral akrasia: this is apparent from the struggles engaged in by philosophers from Aristotle to the present time. What is clear enough is that if its onset is not (as it seems necessarily not to be) predictable, then we have yet another parameter to be reckoned with in our moral deliberations. Akrasia seems to be a part of the collection of features that contribute to what we earlier on alluded to as the "underdetermined" character of personal behavior. And if akrasia is a part of what it is to be a moral person, there is a kind of indeterminacy built into the identity over time of moral persons. Such indeterminacy is perhaps more a ground for pessimism than Dennett's remarks about the difficulties to be met with in determining whether anyone—including oneself— really is a person. There is some ground for optimism in our being able to know that there is such a thing as akratic action, and so being able in advance to prepare ourselves for its possible appearance in ourselves and in others.

Discovering that someone else is an akrates, like discovering that someone else is servile, presupposes the possibility of the type of verbal communication that is found only in higher order intentional creatures of the sort we have characterized as persons. Thus akrasia, like servility, seems to be a condition not likely to be present in nonhuman animals. But akrasia, unlike servility, at least on our reading of these two conditions, seems not to be a "curable" feature of persons. Like a New Year's resolution, resolving that in the future one will not be an akrates, viz., that one will always choose to do what one thinks best, seems to commit oneself to the doing of something that cannot be guaranteed to be carried out.

6

Moral Persons: II

In this chapter, I continue to develop considerations of a mainly theoretical sort, beginning with a brief account of the manner in which talk of possible worlds seems to be pertinent to the nature of moral personhood as we have begun to describe it. I then proceed to discuss some matters related to the deaths of, and the quality of life of, moral persons.

1. Moral Persons and Possible Worlds

With a sketch for a theory of moral personhood in hand, it becomes possible to shed some light on the notion of certain relevant possible worlds. I begin with a characterization of our actual world—which, in the manner of speaking customary among possible-worlds semanticists, has to be a possible world—and then turn to a description of some of the features which would be found in a perfect moral world. Then I consider features which, if they were present, would insure that at least one kind of possible world could not be a moral world.

Our actual world seems to be such that it is one in which it is possible that there are some persons who can conceive of performing moral actions but who cannot bring themselves to carry them out. There is, of course, a question as to whether such persons should be described as moral persons, since they would seem to suffer from permanent paralysis of their capacity for actually exercising their (moral) practical reason. This world also contains, presumably, immoral persons, nonmoral persons (some of them suffering from akrasia), and akratic moral persons. It also would seem necessary to include in this world servile persons (since, as we have argued, a servile person *is* a person, and might possibly be cured of her/his servility); and of course, akratic servile persons, about both of which types there seems to be some doubt as to their status as moral persons (cf. the section above, Moral persons, Identity, and Moral Defects: Akrasia and Servility).

Such a world presupposes causal efficacy, of both the intentional and the nonintentional sorts. A world where there are effective intentional causes itself presupposes a world where there are effective nonintentional causes and nonintentional states of affairs. [By 'effective' I understand a cause that is *known* to be a cause, as contrasted with causes of the unknown (but knowable) variety. Without such knowledge, one person could not go to the aid of another (or, for that matter, him or herself): for what one thought to be aid could turn out to be harm.] This world is, however, one to which Davidson's anomalous monism is applicable: this may be read as a reminder that we must have a different level of expectation with regard to our ability to forecast the behavior of natural kinds from that we seem to be entitled to have with respect to the behavior of intentional kinds. For example, if my going to the aid of someone required first securing the help of another person as my assistant, my expectations vis-à-vis my assistant would have to take into account the anomalous character of the behavior of persons, and so prepare me for the possibility of being let down.

In the actual world, it is not clear whether it could ever be the case that there would be either the resources (intentional or nonintentional) or the intentional mechanisms that could insure that *all* potential persons could become persons, or that even all moral persons could be maintained as moral persons. This world remains a moral world, however, in spite of the fact that it contains instances of unsuccessful moral practical reasoning and of immoral actions. A world might be said to be a minimally moral world provided it contained persons of the sort for which we have provided a schema, persons capable on occasion of performing morally, where this capability is both (higher order) intentional and effectively causal. There would be, in such a world, intentional states of affairs. It would likely be the case that not all minimally moral worlds would survive, since it would probably be true that some lower bound would have to be placed on the number of persons required to sustain such a world.

An ideal or perfect moral world is conceivable, certainly. It is not clear, as Kant seemed to think, that such a world would require immortality, for there seems to be nothing inconsistent in the notion of an immortal complete akratic individual, or a world made up of such individuals.[1] What such a perfect world could not have, of course, would be moral akratic individuals, or servile individuals, or individuals both akratic and servile. Nor could it have immoral individuals. The perfect moral world would be one, presumably, where one's moral intentions and the consequences of one's actions never came apart (perhaps this is a way of depicting the world longed for by deontologists!). This is quite unlike the actual world, where, because of the limitations placed upon our ability to predict intentional behavior, we can never be absolutely sure that even our most carefully selected actions will have the consequences we hope them to have, especially if, as we have noted, they require other persons for their implementation or if these other persons, or we ourselves, might be subject to (partial, or standard) akrasia. In such a world, bad—but not necessarily morally bad—things could still happen to persons and to potential persons.

A description of a possible world which could *not* be a moral world might include at least this feature: no person in this world who could conceive of performing moral actions ever could carry them out. One version of this world might be characterized by universal complete akrasia. By "universal" complete akrasia is to be understood a world in which *every* individual is a complete akratic. In such a world there would be no causal efficacy of the requisite intentional type. (It is not entirely clear whether an individual suffering from complete akrasia could even be said to be a person in the intended sense: Compare the idea of an individual who is physically totally paralyzed, and so incapable of any causal action or of any (physical) action. The complete akratic might thus be described as an intentional paralytic, in much the same way as the servile individual might be described as being afflicted with a peculiar form of intentional blindness, or agnosia.) Consistent with the hypothesis that persons are material (physical) things, of course, *total* physical paralysis would entail complete akrasia, and would be equivalent to death.

A world in which a certain individual has ceased to be a moral person— one who has died (in any of the senses outlined below, sec. 2) would, of course, not be a moral world *for that individual*. This is consistent, as we have noted, (also see sec. 3 below), with there being other persons who might elect to try to treat some kinds of potential, partial, or former persons *as if* they still were moral persons, whether justifiably or not.

2. Moral Persons and Death

One quite appropriate way of initiating a discussion of a topic is to start where someone else has left off. In the present case, I have chosen to take up where Jay Rosenberg 1983 finishes, with probably one of the most definitive characterizations of human death in the recent philosophic literature.[2] He proposes that the type of death of interest here be described in the following way:

> The permanent and irreversible loss of syntropic capabilities which is the death
> of a living member of the species *homo sapiens* . . . is a functional change which
> constitutes a change of natural kind—from a human being to the remains of a
> human being—and which, in consequence of our moral practices, also results in
> a simultaneous change of ethical kind—from a person to a person's corpse."(122)[3]

Perhaps as important as what appears in this account is what is not
explicitly said: by this I mean the carefully executed argumentative steps taken
by Rosenberg in the preceding three chapters of his book, steps which lead
him to reject any characterization of death that would take the form of proposing that the death of a person be thought of as a "change of condition,"
and as a consequence, allowing for the possibility of some form of "life after
death." For example, one of the most ancient (dualistic) ways of depicting
death was to suggest that when a person dies what happens is that "the soul
departs the body": the change of condition is that from an embodied to a
disembodied soul, which appears to imply that there would be something
which might be said to survive death.

I shall not rehearse here the additional argument by which Rosenberg
seeks to demonstrate the impossibility of there being any coherent dualistic
theory of the sort that seems to be presupposed by such talk of death as
change of condition (and as a consequence, that no sense can be given to the
notion of life after death), since I think it is clear enough where my own
sympathies lie. For, as I have already indicated (for a variety of reasons in
other contexts), in connection with espousing a theory of personhood requiring a suitable form of materialism, I have, of course, rejected the sort of talk
that would purportedly support bodies and souls as ontologically differentiable entities (chap. 2 "Material Persons," above).

Before raising some issues about what I consider to be deficiencies in
Rosenberg's characterization of death, however, I do first need to spell out
what I take to be the meaning of his proposal—which is coupled with a reasonably coherent view of the nature of persons and their moral or ethical
dealings—and to point to areas of agreement between his account and our
moral person schema.

In the discussion surrounding the quoted passage, Rosenberg has tried
to make clear several points: (1) that our "moral practice" calls for making *all*
human beings persons (at least all those from birth on)(119); (2) that there is
justification—in "our implicit moral theory"—for this, since there is a continuum of both structural features and developmental capability among members of the species, and as a consequence it would be "morally abitrary" to
make cuts between persons and nonpersons (although, he says, it is morally
permissible to place constraints upon the full exercise of some moral rights

on the ground that an individual—a child, for example—has not reached a certain developmental stage)(119); (3) that to call an individual a 'person' is to "bestow a status" (as to call an individual a 'citizen' is to bestow a status upon someone—although this "someone" could be Caligula's horse, who was made a Roman citizen by imperial decree)(114); (4) that the particular *kind* of things to which persons are assigned by this bestowal is an ethical kind; and that the criteria for assignment to this kind are that the thing in question be the subject of certain rights (in particular, the so-called human rights) and be the beneficiary of the correlated obligations on the part of others to respect those rights. "To count some being as a person, in short, is to grant to that being the sort of respect and treatment due persons, to acknowledge it as having a certain ethical or moral standing." (115) "We do not . . . discover that some entity is or is not a person. We acknowledge that some entity is a person, or we do not acknowledge it. Personhood is a bestowed status." (140) (Presumably, although Rosenberg does not say this, Caligula could have elected to count his horse as a person, too.) The ethical kind, person, is "transmitted" from parents to offspring (as is the legal kind, citizen) by our moral practice (119). (5) These considerations taken together thus entail, in our most generally accepted moral practice— which is that which is justified by our implicit moral theory— a connection between the natural kind, *homo sapiens*, and the ethical kind, person: whence the connection between the change of natural kind (from living to dead) and the change of ethical kind (from person to person's corpse).

I take it that Rosenberg's reference to "our moral practice" is in part a way of registering the fact that in the ordinary use of our moral language, the words *person* and *human being* are used pretty much interchangeably in a wide variety of contexts. I think not too much rides upon this, but I think it does make more difficult what might be termed the public relations task of the moral philosopher, especially if s/he tries to apply some of the desirable features of the analytic method Rosenberg himself extols. As a case in point, I think some of the parties who have been engaged in debates about abortion have not had much of a chance of arriving at a real meeting of minds precisely because of the conflation of the meanings of these two locutions.

A great deal more rides upon talk of "our implicit moral theory." At least I assume that what we are talking about here, while it might *begin* with some of the views lying behind our moral practice, and so capture a kind of "folk" moral philosophy or ethics, must at least aim at a much more refined outcome. This outcome, of course, whatever shape it may finally take, must certainly intersect with something like the moral person schema we are proposing. It is not entirely clear where Rosenberg himself really stands on this matter, at least given his authorial stance as the analytic philosopher who never advances any substantive views of his own, but whose primary function is to clarify existing views. But no matter. I shall direct my remarks at the hypothetical holders of "our implicit moral theory," whoever they might be. But to simplify my discussion, I shall in what follows adopt the authorial stance of referring to them collectively by the name 'Rosenberg', in honor of the anonymous philosophical anthropologist who might be credited with having unearthed the particular version of the theory discussed in Rosenberg 1983.

Rosenberg's suggestion that membership in the ethical kind of interest to us relies upon the criterial features of a being who is the subject for (human) rights and their correlated obligations is one that is itself made possible, I think, by our moral person schema. For what is required in the first place for there to be such things as rights and obligations, which on our recently developed view are aptly characterizable as higher order intentional objects, are the sorts of higher order intentional systems we have characterized as persons and as moral persons. On our view, the concept of a moral or ethical person requires the concept of a person, which means, to join the vocabulary in Rosenberg's view with that in ours, that his concept of an ethical kind is parasitical upon that of a particular sort of higher order intentional kind.[4] We, unlike Rosenberg, wish to drive a wedge between the concept of a person and the concept of a moral person; the justification for doing this was referred to much earlier, and was employed to good effect more recently in the discussion of certain moral defects (see above, chap. 5, the discussion of akrasia and servility).

By taking the notion of intentional kinds seriously enough to be able to employ intentional causes and explanations, we further diverge from Rosenberg's characterization of an ethical kind as something having (merely) a "bestowed status." Explanations and predictions of the behavior of higher order intentional kinds (e.g., persons), we have urged, can be no less effective— although subject to certain limitations—than explanations and predictions of the behavior of natural kinds (e.g., chemical compounds). However, no matter how diligently we might try to bestow the higher order intentional features we have linked with personhood upon Caligula's horse, we would be unable to explain and predict its behavior in anything at all like the manner in which we can do so for authentic persons. We might, of course, propose that the horse be called an "honorary" person; but honorary persons are by no means equivalent to actual persons (in our sense), any more than (to use one of Rosenberg's favorite examples) a counterfeit driver's license is equivalent to the genuine article. Trying to bestow personhood upon a horse would be, of course, somewhat less nonsensical than trying to bestow it upon, say, the statue of a man, since the horse, unlike the statue, at least is an intentional system rather than an artifact produced by an intentional system. We have left open the possibility that there could be higher order intentional systems other than human ones; they also could be said to be genuine persons, without any need for bestowing the status upon them, simply by discovering, through the successful taking of a higher order intentional stance toward them, that they have the required features.

Furthermore, Rosenberg's claim that because there is a continuum of structural and developmental capacity features of human beings it would be "morally arbitrary" to make cuts between persons and nonpersons, is one, given our theory, that need not be sustained. He, in fact, does himself make just such a cut (an intentionalistic one) in describing the constraints ordinarily placed upon the autonomy of children. Such cuts are not only possible, but are justifiable on the basis of our theory of moral personhood. As an example (as we have recently seen), it is quite important that we make the kind of cut entailed by our being able to sort servile from nonservile persons, in order that we might both eliminate the conditions (especially the intentional ones) leading to the appearance of such persons, and when we find such persons on our hands, hope (with their cooperation) to effect a change in them. Similarly, our (and Rosenberg's) way of dealing with children (and other functionally equivalent humans) by placing constraints upon their autonomy reflects our belief that they are not fully moral persons (in our sense), however much we might wish to bestow such a status upon them.

We certainly can subscribe to Rosenberg's suggestion that it would be morally arbitrary to effect cuts merely on the basis of the kinds of structural dissimilarities reflected in skin color, nose or eye shape, etc. But surely it must be because we would encounter great difficulty in explaining and predicting the behavior of children (or other humans with equivalent forms of behavior) by bestowing upon them higher order intentional features they do not have, that we feel it inappropriate to place them fully in an ethical or moral intentional kind. This is in spite of the fact that many children (unlike Caligula's horse) will some day become persons (and, it is to be devoutly hoped, moral persons!). Thus it is no accident that our first class of (enabling) needs (as described above, chap. 5, sec. 1) is keyed to individuals characterizable as potential—in the sense of potentially having certain higher order capacities that might be developed—persons. The pony who eventually became Caligula's horse at no point could have been described as having had such needs, and someone's having bestowed upon the pony the title of 'potential person' could not, in fact, have magically created these needs, nor the rights or entitlements we feel it appropriate to connect with them.

Rosenberg's suggestion that membership in the ethical kind is automatically "transmitted" from the parents of human beings to their offspring in our moral practice is one I think it difficult to find very plausible on the basis

of our schemata. Surely it would be more accurate to say that such membership would be of a conditional type (conditional, that is, upon development of
the appropriate capacities), although it can easily be granted that sorting out
the conditions in a precise manner and determining when they are applicable
can be a sticky business. Because of the malleability of persons, it need come
as no surprise that there are persons who are willing to bestow the status of
membership in an ethical kind upon even anencephalic human infants or their
functional equivalents. The issue *whether* such bestowal is morally justifiable
is one the resolution of which seems not to be aided by an implicit moral
theory that simply justifies such a practice in an unqualified way. I comment
in passing that the notion of bestowal carries with it the notion of withdrawal
of status, too: just as citizenship is a status that may be revoked, so it might be
claimed, is personhood (in Rosenberg's sense, membership in an ethical kind).[5]
The demonstrated failure of resolution of the issues here by our existing implicit moral theory is one that has been carried over into our legal practices
as well.

I want now to comment upon features of Rosenberg's characterization
of the death of persons that I think can be viewed as deficient in light of our
moral person schema. There is a deficiency of sorts in Rosenberg's approach
to death in that his argument to the effect that there can be no coherent
dualistic theory of death—and that this entails that there can be no coherent
notion of an afterlife—does not touch what seems to be a fairly obvious fact: it
is not too likely that those who are predisposed (for whatever reason) to
believe in the existence of some form of afterlife are going to have their belief
shaken by Rosenberg's or any other similar argument. Our moral person
schema, with its account of the malleability of belief of persons, provides an
explanation for this and for similar sorts of beliefs and belief systems.

I think, to begin with Rosenberg's explicit characterization of death,
that there is no problem if the individual we are describing is one who has
suffered "permanent and irreversible loss of syntropic capabilities." Since on
our view, too, such an individual would have ceased to manifest the malleable
higher order intentional features necessary for the characterization of either
personhood or of moral personhood.

Problems do make their appearance, however, when we fail to realize
that it is quite possible to say that not all deaths (in Rosenberg's sense) of
human beings are deaths of persons (in our sense). Given our person schema,
it makes good sense to say that an individual's remaining a person is not
something that tracks invariably with a certain living human body (or even
with a certain living human brain, assuming the sort of science-fictional stance
referred to earlier in our discussion of personal identity). The death of a person (in our sense) may be said to be the sort of thing that can precede in time

the death (in Rosenberg's sense) of a certain human being. Such a death of a person can be brought about by a variety of irreversible neurological disorders, the net result of which is to render an individual permanently incapable of functioning as a malleable higher order intentional system, although there may continue to be a certain living human body.

Similarly, the change of ethical kind in our moral practice signaled in Rosenberg's account by the change from person to person's corpse does not convey the fine structure made visible by our person-moral person schemata. It is true enough, certainly, that on our schemata, too, the appearance of a corpse does indicate the impossibility of there continuing to be a certain specific malleable higher order intentional system. But we do need as well to be able to mark the change in ethical kind that may make its appearance *prior to* the appearance of a human corpse, when we have on our hands a living human body but not a malleable higher order intentional system. As a matter of fact, I think it has become clear that even a segment of our legal practice has left behind the implicit moral theory adumbrated by Rosenberg. For since January, 1985, by a decision of the New Jersey Supreme Court it has become possible legally (in the state of New Jersey), to withdraw not only the usual life-support apparatus, but feeding and hydration tubes as well, from certain types of comatose human individuals, where the prognosis is that such withdrawal will result in death (in Rosenberg's sense).[6] This, of course represents a change from the earlier decision by the same court in the case of Karen Ann Quinlan, which was itself precedent-setting in allowing the removal of certain life-support equipment and making those responsible for this action immune from prosecution for homicide if she had died as a result of taking this action.[7] How quickly and how widespread these legal practices may become remains to be seen, of course. Nor is it clear how quickly and how widespread might be the changes in medical practice the 1985 New Jersey Supreme Court decision alone appears to make possible.[8]

Now while it seems conceivable on the basis of our moral person schema that there could be such a thing as the death of a moral person at a time prior to the death of a person, this does not appear to be too likely in practice. Such a possibility would require that we be able to describe an individual such that up to a certain time s/he has functioned as a moral person, i.e., one manifesting the features associated with a malleable higher order intentional sytem of the moral sort, but after that time never again is capable of functioning as a moral person, although continuing to function as a person for some indefinite period. There would be, in other words, an onset of a type of permanent moral blindness or moral "agnosia." Such an individual, even if s/he were capable in some sense of remembering what it had been like to function as a moral person, would be incapable ever again of engaging in successful practical reasoning of the moral sort. That there are such individuals, and that some of the individuals we label as psycho- or sociopaths might be said to be like this in some respects, seems clear enough; what is not clear at all is how they get to be the way they are, or what their prospects are for again becoming moral persons, if ever they were to start with.

While it seems we need to leave open the conceptual possibility that a moral person could die but that there still could remain a person, it would appear to be more plausible to say that the deaths of moral person and person would coincide. It is likely that our unwillingness to allow individuals—those who have undergone the sorts of changes we have been describing—to function as moral persons would also extend to our consideration of their functioning as persons. In other words, the degradation in capacity both to hold and to act upon the beliefs, expectations, etc. that we couple with moral capacity is one we might expect to find as well in the capacity to hold and to act upon nonmoral beliefs, expectations, etc. And as seems to happen, for example, in those afflicted with something like the more advanced stages of Alzheimer's disease, we would feel no more confidence in trusting such individuals to abide by the rules of a nonmoral activity like playing a game of checkers than we would in trusting them to abide by moral rules or under-standings.

Talk of the kind of deterioration of higher order intentional functioning found in Alzheimer's patients and others who have suffered similar irreversi-ble brain damage is (as we have noted earlier in our discussion of personal identity) intimately related to the problems encountered in reidentifying a person as the same person over time. To call an individual the same person before and after the onset of such conditions would be at best an honorific description, on the assumption that genuine reidentification of persons re-quires access to an individual's beliefs via verbal communication. One might better say, at the very least, that the person who was formerly there has died, and this in not only a metaphorical sense. Whether one might want to say that a "new" person could make an appearance, i.e., a new malleable higher order intentional system with identifiable and reidentifiable beliefs and belief systems and with the capacity for second-order desires, would not be so sim-ple a matter as it could be in the case of an otherwise normal individual who has suffered some form of near-total and irreversible amnesia. For one might, in the case of such an amnesiac, want also to say that there has been both the death of a person and the appearance of a "new" person, provided there has been no degradation in function of higher order intentional capacities.

On a related topic, talk of the death of the "old" person and the appear-ance of the "new" person of the type associated with religious accounts of conversion experiences is certainly possible on our account of the nature of personhood: one of the necessary provisoes would be that the individual in question remain a person after the experience. The point of this is to rule out the legitimacy of counting as conversion experiences changes of the sort associated ordinarily with the onset of some form of serious and debilitating psychological dysfunction. The presence of permanent or full-time glossolalia (speaking in tongues), for example, would not be compatible with one's remaining a person.

Adoption of an account of the death of persons that would make it appropriate to talk of it in the terms we have just been proposing would carry with it as well a revision in our conceptions of the *process* of dying and of the nature of our moral deliberations in that connection. For we would have to be able to describe some dyings of persons in relation to an account of the processes correlated with the gradual loss of the features making an individual a malleable higher order intentional system, and not just with the gradual loss of the sorts of syntropic physical functions characteristic of the natural kind, *homo sapiens*, à la Rosenberg.

In all fairness to Rosenberg, it should be noted that he does describe what he refers to as the possibility of loss of rationality. By 'rationality' he understands more than behavior consistent with logical rules, in the sense of first order intentional systems, but actually features made possible in our schemata by the capacities for reciprocity, verbal communication, and awareness or self-awareness. In terms of our schemata, of course, these capacities are necessary conditions, each one in turn for the next, and all together in turn for a thing's being describable as a person, which is itself a necessary condition for a thing's being describable as a moral person. Such loss of rationality he thinks is connected with our moral deliberations, but not in a way such as to affect our categorization of an individual as a person, since this categorization, he says, is not one that is discovered but is one that is bestowed, as we have noted. Where Rosenberg would say that an individual with permanent rational incapacitation remains an ethical person, we would say that there would be a change of kind from person to partial or former person. In terms of our schemata there would appear the possibility of a kind of differential ethical treatment of partial or former (who could be living as well as dead) persons. On Rosenberg's account, such differential treatment is called for only upon the change from person to person's corpse.

Because Rosenberg does take this position, he is unable, I think, to come up with an entirely persuasive story on such death-related matters of moral concern as euthanasia, "letting die," and rational suicide (Cf. his chapters 6, 7, and 8, respectively). Our implicit moral theory, he suggests, would have us try to sort out such issues by appeal to a pair of principles: would we, in opting for a certain course of action do something that would result in (1) an increase or decrease in intrinsic disvalue, or (2) an increase or a decrease in intrinsic worth? If one assumes, as he does, that suffering or pain of a physical sort might be taken as a paradigm of something having intrinsic disvalue, and that the exercise of moral autonomy might be taken as paradigmatic of something having intrinsic worth, then a resolution of what morally ought to be done would turn in large part upon how we choose to operate in terms of these considerations. We might be inclined to decide, in a particular case, such as his hypothetical candidate for euthanasia, the rationally impaired and suffering Alric, that Alric's constant and apparently unrelievable suffering would call for our putting him out of his suffering by killing him, and thus weighting the first principle over the second. But, of course, one could just as well take the other side in the dispute, and argue that the possibility (remote as it is) of Alric's being able to exercise moral autonomy would outweigh the disvalue of his continuing to live in pain. Thus the proponent and the opponent of euthanasia could be said to agree on the principles involved, but to disagree on which of them might be said to take precedence, and there would seem to be no clear way to resolve their dispute. The parties to the dispute, by adopting our implicit moral theory, which calls for treating all human beings as (moral) persons, have set themselves up for problems. Of course, once Alric dies (in Rosenberg's sense), with the connected change of ethical kind called for by our practice and our implicit moral theory, the dispute would likely come to an end (save for some minor disagreements over the proper treatment of human corpses).

The adoption of a view such as ours that allows for speaking of a change of ethical kind upon the permanent disabling of the higher order intentional capacities of a human being at a time prior to the individual's death (in Rosenbergian terms) would make it easier to resolve the case of Alric (and all the cases his typifies). By Rosenberg's description of Alric, it is clear enough that what is suffering in this case is not (and will not in the future be), by our proposal, a malleable higher order intentional system at all, but only something that once had such features. So the ground might be cut from under the anti-euthanasia argument that calls for forgoing killing in this case, since the exercise of moral autonomy is something that is possible only for a functioning (or functional) malleable higher order intentional system.

I think, incidentally, that destruction of the higher order intentional capacities calls as well for a rethinking of what constitutes suffering. On our view, the moral justification for thinking that something ought to be done about the suffering of a malleable higher order intentional system is that suffering—and this can be not only physical but intentional in nature—is one of the things that could either interfere with the development of the capacities of such an individual, or if the individual had already developed these capacities, could interfere with their continuing exercise (see above, chap. 5, sec. 1). So whether the suffering that Alric is said to have is a morally relevant sort of suffering is a question that needs to be considered, as is the question as to whether maintaining him in a suitably deep stage of anesthesia in order to "stop" his apparent suffering would be essentially different from killing him.[9]

Attempts to resolve the moral issues surrounding the "letting die" of certain individuals being sustained by life-support mechanisms I think would also fare better if one were free to operate with the possibility of treating these individuals as something other than full persons (in the sense of our proposal). Rosenberg is correct enough in suggesting that the morality of the decision whether to withdraw life-support mechanisms is parasitic upon the initial decision that such equipment be deployed. This initial decision would certainly, in some cases, be vastly easier if one had the option of saying that there had already been a change of ethical kind from a person to something other than a person.

Connected with these observations is, of course, the manner in which it would be necessary to modify the assignment of *rights* to such candidates for either euthanasia or "letting die." Our moral practice seems usually to call for withholding from adults in general positive passive absolute rights (rights to have someone act in their behalf), just as this same practice approves of assigning such rights to human infants and making their parents the bearers of the correlated obligations. Thus it seems generally to be the case that no particular persons are assigned the obligations one would ordinarily expect to be correlated with positive passive absolute rights for adults; in the absence of such correlated obligations it falls upon no one in particular to have a duty to render the sort of assistance assumed to be appropriate vis-à-vis parents and their children. Saying this is not to deny that there may be particular sorts of adults—for example, automobile accident victims—who are assigned positive passive rights because of their special condition, by correlating with these rights obligations placed upon a certain class of people who may be required by law to be "Good Samaritans" (e.g., professional medical personnel).

There are obscurities here aplenty, so far as standard human malleable higher order intentional sytems are concerned, which our moral practice and our implicit moral theory are slow in clarifying (cf. the case of pregnant women, who, given certain assumptions, might be said to be compelled to be Good Samaritans [Thomson 1971]). This process of clarification might be accelerated in the case of the sorts of candidates for euthanasia and "letting die" we have considered, by recognizing that such individuals are no longer persons, and thus need not have to have assigned to them the positive passive rights deemed appropriate for infants (or with suitable constraints, certain special kinds of adults). For that matter, one might also wonder about the appropriateness of assigning even negative passive rights to such individuals, since it is not clear in what moral sense one might be capable of *harming* them.[10] In allowing for the possibility of with-holding from such individuals either positive or negative passive rights, we make allowance for the moral permissibility of certain kinds of actions with regard to them, such as killing them or "unplugging" them. We do not need to say that someone is morally required to perform such actions under any normal circumstances, although we can allow for the possibility that there might be circumstances where doing so would be morally obligatory.

In the matter of (rational) suicide, the individual who might with good reason determine that this is the way to go might well decide that sufficient conditions would be supplied by the prospect not just of a protracted (and possibly painful) dying, but by an indefinitely long period of (pain-free) existence as something less than a fully functioning malleable higher order system. In other words, knowledge that the future will with very high probability bring conditions that one could not control, and conditions that, if they were present, would be incompatible with one's remaining a malleable higher order system (although one might remain alive indefinitely), would supply a good reason for electing for suicide.[11] More difficult to sort out would be the possible role of other persons in the case where the person wishing to commit a rational suicide is for some reason incapable of doing so. What is troublesome is that even if a certain person is morally justified in committing suicide, but is unable to do so, it is not clear upon what other particular persons could fall an obligation to assist her/him in the enterprise. In the absence of positive passive absolute rights, there could be at most only conditional such rights, rights correlated with obligations falling upon only special groups of persons, such as relatives or friends (or court-appointed friends?).

We shall now draw together our deliberations on the death of moral persons and some of the related moral issues. To begin with the concept of death, it would seem to be appropriate to propose the following account: A fully developed human moral malleable higher order intentional system might be said to have died under a variety of circumstances:[12]

1.(a) When the entire physical system has died, à la Rosenberg, with permanent destruction of syntropic capacity, or (b) when the brain of the system is almost entirely and irreversibly damaged.

2. When the physical system has not died [in the sense of either 1.(a) or (b)], but (a) the system is not functioning in its full sense as a moral malleable higher order intentional system due to the fact that it is no longer capable of exercising its specifically moral capacities, but is capable of exercising its nonmoral capacities (we have suggested this as a conceptual possibility only, since in practice it seems unlikely that there would be loss of capacity to have moral

expectations but not a loss of capacity to have [nonmoral] expectations);[13] or (b) the system is not functional: there is an irreversible loss of higher order intentional capacity (in practice, there probably would be a coincident [irreversible] damage to some critical part[s] of the higher brain); or (c) there is a moral malleable higher order intentional system that is functional, but it can no longer be reidentified as the one it once was: i.e., it is no longer possible to reidentify it as having the same beliefs, expectations, etc. (this condition is compatible with saying that a "new" person has appeared, so long as there is no irreversible loss of higher order capacities, as in the case of near-total [irreversible] amnesia).

Our moral deliberations with regard to individuals who have died, or who will shortly die, in any of these senses, must be shaped appropriately, and will allow us to arrive at resolutions of the issues typically putting in their appearance in connection with such matters as euthanasia, "letting die," and rational suicide. These resolutions could range from making it morally permissible to making it morally obligatory to practice certain forms of euthanasia, to allow certain individuals to die, and to allow (and perhaps to assist) certain individuals to commit suicide, and would turn heavily upon making a judgment call as regards the possibility of satisfying our second class of (maintenance) needs (see above, chap. 5, sec. 1).

Now the loss of the features making an individual a malleable higher order intentional system in turn will connect with the way in which we would have to describe the changing quality of life—by which we understand the quality of malleable higher order intentional life—of individuals in the process of undergoing loss or diminution of higher order intentional capacity. We turn now to a consideration of the quality of life of persons, and in particular, of moral persons.

3. Moral Persons and Quality of Life

The proper application of the expression, 'the quality of life', like that of 'the right to _____', is something upon which almost everyone feels qualified to express opinions. After all, who but oneself could be better qualified to have an opinion about his/her own quality of life? And so far as creatures of other species are concerned—or for that matter, members of one's own species who are not fully developed, or who, because of genetic defects, will never develop beyond a certain point—who is a better measure of the quality of life of the creature than the creature itself? Who are *we* to say that a bat doesn't have a perfectly good quality of life, in spite of being genetically blind?[14] Who is better placed than the satisfied pig to measure its quality of life? Or even the apparently happy, well-fed, dry-diapered human infant its quality of life? Is it not hopelessly and indefensibly presumptuous even to think about making quality-of-life comparisons between members of the same species, much less across species?

One way of responding to such questions might result in a relativism of a rather invidious type that would have us forgo any attempt at all to make such comparisons. One might even elect to adopt and to follow a Butlerian aphorism to the effect that "each individual's quality of life is what it is and is not another thing." As a matter of fact, however, there are probably few who use the locution 'the quality of life' who do not think that such a straight individual relativism is simply false, and that one is perfectly well entitled to make comparisons, and to devise rankings, certainly within species, and to some extent across species. But how is one to do this? Probably among the first serious candidates might be a proposal that an appropriate standard for the quality of life of an individual should be determined by what is "normal" for the species.

To show what might be meant by this proposal, consider the following example. The quality of life of an individual bat with malfunctioning sonar would be said to be inferior to that of the "standard" bat with normally functioning sonar: the poor creature might be constantly banging into things, and might certainly starve to death if it didn't fracture its skull first, or suffer some other terminal or permanently disabling injury. And even if there were some incredibly improbable genetic anomaly that simultaneously disabled its sonar and resulted in an individual bat's being equipped with operating eyes and optical nerves, unless there were an even more incredible and coincidental genetic fluke that modified the other necessary (visual) information-processing parts of the bat's brain, the quality of life of such a bat would likely still be deemed inferior to that of the "standard" bat, since the outcome would be rather much the same as that for the case of the bat with malfunctioning sonar. A pig that remained unsatisfied after a bountiful repast would be a sad spectacle, indeed—or even one that was satisfied after receiving some paltry, abnormally small feed dispensation. The presence of a raucously distraught infant, in spite of being dry-diapered and well-fed, might presage either a serious or a trivial quality-of-life problem in the sense proposed, ranging as it could from an open diaper pin to a terminal disease.

An apparent virtue of this approach to answering comparative questions about quality of life within a species is that it does, of course, rest entirely upon *non*intentional explanation and causation: one simply reduces the concept of quality of life to matters connected with defining natural kinds. The highest possible quality of life for an individual then becomes identified with normal functioning for the species. Deviations from such normal functioning result in a lower quality of life. Employing this criterion for judging quality of life would make it possible to move away from the mammals that have comprised our examples so far to other types of animals—and, of course, even to plants.[15] And, since normal functioning always depends upon the individual's being located in an appropriate environment for making its functioning possible, one might readily assume that a full account of a natural kind would include an account of the surroundings without which the kind itself would be incapable of existing. Thus on this view the quality of life of a fish placed into a world devoid of water in its liquid state (or a world where the available water no longer could dissolve the oxygen required for piscine respiration) would be harsh indeed (its life would be mercifully short, one might be tempted to say, on the (probably mistaken) assumption that fish are capable of feeling or experiencing the quality of acute respiratory distress[16]). Similar comments would apply to the quality of life of a plant placed into a world devoid of available carbon dioxide, or light—or to an individual plant with a genetic defect leaving its cells incapable of fabricating chlorophyll.

Talk of the quality of life of plants, or even invertebrates, for that matter, likely would provoke the response, "Well, that's not quite what I had in mind." It is clear, I think, that we need to look further than to a description of such normal functioning of a species or natural kind for the meaning of, or for a criterion for applying the expression, 'the quality of life'. This is not necessarily to say that an account based upon natural kinds must be abandoned: only that it needs at least to be supplemented by some other account(s), especially if one wishes to be able to speak, say, of an individual's being *entitled* to a certain quality of life in a sense other than that the individual be able to function as a standard member of its species or natural kind (in an environment conducive to its so functioning). Our primary interest in this essay, certainly, is in the quality of life of human persons and human moral persons, and this means that we cannot ignore the fact that humans constitute a natural (biological) kind, and that we should expect to be able to develop a pretty good description of what constitutes normal functioning for members of this kind. What is of particular significance from the perspective we have been exploring is that those human beings who become persons (/moral persons) constitute an intentional kind as well. I shall urge that it is functioning as a "standard" member of this latter kind that allows us to employ 'quality of life' in the primary sense intended by those who use the expression. It is then by analogy with this primary sense that 'quality of life' is to be made to apply to other sorts of things, beginning with intentional beings of other than the higher order sort, and possibly moving on to others.

To be a member of an intentional kind, as opposed to a natural kind is, as we have indicated, to be a member of a kind of things whose very existence depends upon there being intentional systems of the right sort. The reader might recall the discussion (chap. 3. section 3) in which we employed the example of Ronald Reagan: Reagan as former professional movie actor is a member of an intentional kind, or as President of the United States is a member of a different intentional kind; he is the sole member (so far) of the class of Presidents of the United States who are former professional movie actors.[17] But his being a member of any of these kinds is entirely dependent upon there being suitable sorts of higher order intentional systems of the type we have characterized as persons. Members of any of these three kinds, since the kinds themselves require higher order intentions for their characterizations, are themselves of a higher order intentional nature. One's explanations of how these kinds come into being and how they operate must be given entirely in intentional terms: 'professional movie actor' and 'President of the United States' are expressions referring to intentional objects of an ineliminably intentional sort, the explanations of which are subject to the intentional circle, since they involve necessary reference to higher order intentions such as beliefs about the beliefs of those who do things with certain kinds of cameras and projectors, etc., or expectations about the beliefs of those who are frequently found at a certain address in Washington, D.C., etc.. However, 'Ronald Reagan' understood as referring to a particular member of the biological species, *homo sapiens* (Kripke: 'Ronald Reagan' understood as a stand-in for a rigid designator) is an intentional object of the eliminably intentional sort, since we are dealing with a natural kind. To say of *this* individual that at a certain time in his life he has nonmalignant colon polyps or that he has a nasal basal cell carcinoma is to remain within the boundaries of the sorts of non-intentional explanation and causation appropriate for accounts of natural kinds of this particular type. And by our first proposal for characterizing quality of life, we could say that an individual who comes to have either of these conditions would have an alteration in the quality of his life, but not so much so if the polyps were malignant or the skin cancer a sarcoma. To say of a professional movie actor (or a President) that he is a good or a bad sample of the type, or that certain actions of his in this capacity were praiseworthy or blameworthy, or that he might (in this capacity) be expected in the future to take (or not to take) certain kinds of actions, is to refer to matters requiring higher order intentional explanation and causation. And in a manner that we have not yet spelled out, such actions (/inactions) could presumably have an effect upon his quality of life as a higher order intentional being.

So let us see if we cannot develop a better proposal. To start with, let us suggest that we keep the first proposal but make it subject to the following modification: the features that make an individual human being a normal member of its species or natural kind will *some* of them, when taken together, constitute a necessary condition for defining the quality of life for that individual, but do not also give us a sufficient condition for doing so. What we have in mind by such features are those in particular connected with both the genetic endowment (and the proper development of this endowment) of the human brain and the neurophysiological appurtenances necessary for cognition (including awareness and self-awareness) in the individual, along with, of course the equipment and motor skills needed for demonstrating the presence of a developed capacity for verbal communication (in the sense defined above in chap. 2, sec. 2). What we have tried to do in stating this condition is, as much as possible, to describe only features of the nonintentional sort to be found in giving an account of a natural kind. For these purposes we also are assuming that in some suitable way the so-called representation problem has been solved: the type of developed neurophysiological system we are referring to successfully encodes, and successfully retrieves, representations of things in the nonintentional world, although the full details of this solution so far seem to elude us.[18]

But being a human person, and so having the quality of life of a person, requires also the successful operation of a variety of developed intentional capabilities of the sort we have been at some pains to describe. How these capabilities actually develop, and how they might be lost, either permanently or temporarily, as we have previously noted, are also among the matters of which all of the details presently escape us. Presumably, the representation problem for intentional (including higher order intentional) objects is also solved in normal human persons, although whether the encoding and retrieval mechanisms for beliefs about beliefs, etc. are the same as those for beliefs about nonintentional things is not known either. Human persons do, in fact, succeed much of the time in being able to differentiate among their own beliefs, expectations, and their orders, etc.: for, as we have suggested, without differentiable intentional *content*, or malleability, awareness or consciousness presumably would not have been a permanent result of natural selection, and would not have made possible the sort of intentional selection we have earlier described.

To sum up our results: Let us add to our new proposal the requirement that a complete account of the quality of life of human persons and human moral persons must include not only the necessary features found in the description of the natural kind *homo sapiens*, as we suggested above, but also the features needed to describe a human person as a malleable higher order intentional system, or as a member of the relevant intentional kind with a developed capacity for intentional selection.

A feature that seems significantly to capture the particular sense of 'quality of life' we are seeking and one that clearly requires higher order intentionality, can be expressed in the following way: *a quality of life is something* that can appropriately be the object of a desire. A higher order intentional sytem is capable of consciously desiring one quality of life rather than another (unlike other [first order] intentional systems, such as fish, which appear to lack the capacity for doing this). Such a quality of life will have as one of its components not only the having of desires but the desire to have certain desires: hence the higher order nature of a desire for a certain quality of life. We might even urge that the capacity for such higher order desires is an *essential* feature of the type of quality of life that we are seeking.[19] In this sense, quality of life considerations have been around at least since Socrates raised his celebrated question re the kind of life one ought to live (cf. Williams 1985 for an argument to the effect that there can be no answer to this question that could be acceptable for all human beings). And these features, we have argued, are not reducible [at least by any plausible current theory] to any account of natural kinds.

We realize that describing matters in this way will infect our account of the quality of life of human persons with the difficulties we found to be inescapable in our account of persons: in particular, the problems of the veridicality of belief and of anomalous monism, and in general the difficulties having to do with intentional causation, explanation, and prediction, that are to be met with by remaining within the intentional circle. But so be it!

7

Moral Persons, Rights, and Law

In civilized societies, relationships between moral persons and some of the numerous actual varieties of legal institutions are no less inescapable than are the moral relationships in which they find themselves entwined. Some features of these legal institutions have developed over a period of many thousands of years, and have had to deal with most of the matters that have led to the full range of differences, sometimes acrimonious ones, that have come to exist between persons. In the resolution of these differences a number of concepts have surfaced and have proved to be quite useful, perhaps none more so than the concept of legal right. In chapter 4 we sketched in a general way how the concept of right fares in the context of talk of higher order intentionality, and suggested that rights actually should best be thought of as a certain kind of higher order expectations or beliefs, presupposing for both their existence and their apprehension suitable types of higher order intentional systems of the sorts we have identified in chapter 5 as persons and moral persons. What we shall do initially in this chapter and its appendix is to look more carefully at the concept of right, and especially at the way in which legal rights and moral rights might best be connected with one another. This we begin to do in the section entitled Legal and Moral Rights: Wellman's Theory of Rights. And then, in order to try to come to understand a right that has come lately in United States Constitutional Law to loom as perhaps one of the most fundamental and important ones, we examine the right to privacy in the section, Moral Persons and Privacy. Finally, in the appendix, Some Possible Connections between Law and Morality, we resume our full stance as theoreticians of higher order intentionality, and offer some considerations to support the claim that law and morals, when each is viewed in an idealized,

noninstitutional and objective sense, should be seen as more closely connected with one another than has sometimes been thought by some writers in
the separate domains.

1. Legal Rights and Moral Rights: Carl Wellman's Theory of Rights

Rights-talk, like talk about religion and politics, is something that is and
has been indulged in by almost everyone in the United States and in other
countries with democratic forms of government (or with aspirations to such
forms of government). In the course of this talk, especially in recent years,
rights of some description have been ascribed by someone to almost anything, whether animal, vegetable, or mineral (and to things that are none (or
all?) of the above, such as branches of government, institutions, organizations,
corporations, and the terrestrial ecology (or parts of it). In many instances,
little apparent thought has been given either to the propriety of the ascrip-
tions or to the nature of rights themselves.[1]

A refreshing exception to such flaccid discourse is Carl Wellman's *A
Theory of Rights: Persons Under Laws, Institutions, and Morals*.[2] In this book
Wellman develops out of the often-cited but seldom fully exegeted analytical
work of W.N. Hohfeld, in an original, meticulous, and persuasive way, a model
for rights, beginning with legal rights, moving to institutional rights, and
thence to moral rights.[3] In briefest terms, his proposal (following in part, he
says, one due to H.L.A. Hart 1973) is that rights be viewed as relatively complex *constructions* out of (modified) Hohfeldian elements. My own interest,
of course, is in trying to locate Wellman's proposal in an appropriate place on
the map of higher order intentional concerns I have been fabricating in connection with my own investigation of moral personhood. But before doing
this, a more detailed account of Wellman's approach to characterizing rights
is needed.

Wellman reads Hohfeld as having taken the position that an examination of legal practice (at least in Britain and the United States) reveals that
there exist only a small number (*eight*, actually) of basic legal notions or conceptions, out of which the whole fabric of the law—or as Hohfeld preferred to
put it, the full assortment of "legal positions" possible in our society—may
be constructed: the so-called Hohfeldian elements. These elements may be
described as assigning to individuals legal "advantages" or "disadvantages."

Under the law, according to Hohfeld's analysis, it turns out that one
may have any of the following advantages: a claim, a privilege, a power, or an
immunity. But as soon as any one individual is in the position of having any
such advantage, another (or others) is (are) relatively (and correlatively) at a
legal disadvantage. Hohfeld's idea was that these elements could not themselves be broken down into any more fundamental conceptions, but that they

do sustain certain relations with one another. These relations he summed up in a pair of tables, a table of "jural correlatives" and a table of "jural opposites". Wellman (13)[4] represents the table of correlatives (having replaced Hohfeld's use of the term *right*, with the term *claim*[5] as follows:

claim	privilege	power	immunity
duty	no-claim	liability	disability.

Correlated, for example, with a legal *claim*, which some individual may have as an advantage, someone else must have a *duty* to satisfy that claim (which places her/him at a disadvantage), and so on for the other correlatives. Furthermore, the *existence* of a claim entails the existence of the correlated duty, as happens in the case, for example, where someone extends a line of credit to someone else: the coming into existence of the creditor's claim for repayment against the debtor brings with it the existence of the debtor's duty to repay the loan. The creditor could also have other advantages, in the form of certain privileges, powers, and immunities vis-à-vis the debtor, who would have the correlated disadvantages in the form of no-claims, liabilities (perhaps to repay on demand), and disabilities (say, having no immunity from being prosecuted in a court of law).

Hohfeld's table of jural opposites is as follows (Wellman, 14):

claim	privilege	power	immunity
no-claim	duty	disability	liability.

In these pairings, the significant thing is that the existence of a jural opposite implies the *non*existence of its opposite: e.g., an individual subject to law cannot have both a *power* and a *disability* with respect to the same thing, or while occupying the same legal position.

Wellman argues (chap. 2), for what appear to be good reasons, that Hohfeld's claim that the eight notions he describes as irreducible is false, and that, as a matter of fact, they may be reduced to just two: a legal duty and a legal power. Such economy, however, would make our talk unnecessarily prolix, so for practical purposes the tables of correlatives and opposites survive, but in a slightly changed shape. Wellman's own version of the table of opposites receives the following form:

[Advantages]	[Disadvantages]
a claim of X against Y	a no-claim of X against Y
a liberty of X in the face of Y	a duty of X to Y
an ability of X over Y	a disability of X over Y
an immunity of X from Y	a liability of X to Y

[To which Wellman adds the following pair (54):

a duty of X   a contrary liberty of X
a power of X   an impotence of X]

Wellman's re-worked table of correlatives (53) appears as:

a claim of X against Y   a duty of Y to X
a liberty of X in face of Y   a contrary no-claim of Y against X
an ability of X over Y   a liability of Y to X
an immunity of X against Y   a disability of Y over X

But what sort of a thing, precisely, is a *right*, in Wellmanian terms? Wellman proposes taking *legal* rights as the paradigm for explaining the general nature of rights, since legal rights have been both defined and have had their detailed structures rather carefully worked out in practical terms over a lengthy period of time. A legal right can best be characterized as being constituted of legal positions, such positions in turn being themselves constructed out of the (modified) Hohfeldian elements we have just been describing. Each such right can be shown, Wellman thinks, to possess a certain Hohfeldian element or position as its "core," or central element, with other elements clustering around it.

He thinks also that such rights are essentially *adversarial* in nature: a right is asserted by a first party (or parties) against a second party (or parties), and there must be present as well a third party (or parties) who will take an interest in the confrontation and defend the position of one or the other of the first two parties. But in addition to being adversarial, rights give to the right-holder a kind of *dominion* (in a nongovernmental sense), provided they are respected.

Wellman points out that his characterization of rights is similar to one developed in Hart 1973, although, he says, Hart did not bring out either the adversarial feature or the dominion-if-respected feature urged by Wellman; Hart, instead, elected to emphasize the freedom of choice placed upon the right-holder, generally in the form of a bilateral liberty: the liberty to choose to perform, or not to perform, a certain action. Wellman sums up his account of our talk of rights in the following passage:

> On my interpretation of the language of rights, every assertion or denial of a right presupposes some possible confrontation to which the right is relevant. At the center of any right stands a defining core, a legal position that defines the essential content of the right, that to which the possessor has a right. Around

this core cluster a variety of associated elements, other Hohfeldian elements that, if respected, confer upon the right-holder freedom and control concerning the exercise or enjoyment of the core. There are three parties or classes of parties to any right. A first party is anyone who possesses the right. A second party is anyone against whom the right holds. A third party is anyone in a position to intervene in the presupposed confrontation between a right-holder and a second party and side with one principal adversary against the other. The essential purpose or function of any legal right is to confer upon its possessor a specific sort of dominion over one or more potential adversaries. The right achieves its purpose only if the legal norms that define and confer it are respected by those subject to the law—hence, my dominion-if-respected model, constructed out of Hohfeld's fundamental legal conceptions, somewhat reinterpreted. (102)

As examples of classes of legal rights, Wellman (again following Hohfeld and Hart), discusses liberty-rights, power-rights, claim-rights, and immunity-rights. In each case, the Hohfeldian element conferring an advantage upon the right-holder, and forming the core of the right, is identified in the designating expression. To get some idea of the complexity of a legal right, one might consider again the example of the creditor-debtor relationship. One could in this case suggest that the creditor has against the debtor (and this is an adversarial feature) a claim-right. But, as we have noticed, the existence of a claim is connected with the existence of a correlative duty, bringing in another Holfeldian element, and is connected as well with the nonexistence of a claim or the existence of a no-claim on the part of the debtor. Nor is that the end of the matter: the creditor is also said to have a liberty, for at his/her choice, the debt could be cancelled, or repaid in some other manner than originally specified, or by someone else. The creditor, too, has a power against the debtor, and, in addition, an immunity against anyone's interfering with the debtor's fulfilling his/her duty to the creditor, thus bringing into the picture the third party. It is possible, of course, to describe elements other than those picked out here, a selection intended only to suggest the complexity of the features of a right.

Wellman calls attention to the fact that legal rights so characterized are not neatly pinned down in a simple and rigid definition, for in the law it may happen that in the course of actual judicial proceedings some Hohfeldian elements may receive more emphasis, or may be thought to be more important, than others. He suggests that this way of describing rights be understood as supplying a model—rather than a strict definition—for rights generally, whether within or without the law. He urges that a model allows, as a definition could not, for the inevitable changes that make their appearance over the course of time in the development and application of actual laws.

Before moving to an account of moral rights, Wellman sketches some of the considerations suggesting that any kind of institution or organization that has rules or norms governing its operation and the behavior of its members might in a similar way characterize its own particular kinds of rights by supplying its own readings of the Hohfeldian-elements as adapted to its own positions. Thus individuals who are members of such institutions might find themselves possessing locally defined rights, exercising these rights against various (locally defined) second parties, and in the presence of (locally defined) third parties who would be capable of taking an interest in the confrontation between the first two parties. Members of clubs, churches, and academic institutions would thus have suitably definable positions vis-à-vis their roles in these organizations, positions which, in analogy with Hohfeldian legal positions, would place them at certain advantages and disadvantages, and assign rights to them. These rights, like the legal rights we have just described, would be constructions out of a number of elements, with the particular content of the elements depending upon the rules and regulations currently in effect in the organization; and as with legal rights, the particular way in which some element or position might occupy the core of the right would be subject to change over time. For example, in most American colleges and universities, elevation of a faculty member to (permanent) tenure has been understood to define a position whose central core might best be described in terms of an (institutional) immunity-right. Such a tenured faculty member has been understood to have immunity against a variety of institutional reasons (ostensibly having to do with an interference with academic freedom) for ending his/her employment (although not against every possible reason: financial exigency on the part of the institution, or gross neglect of duties, and/or moral turpitude on the part of the professor in his/her relationships, especially with his/her colleagues or students are typically not excludable), but also to have certain privileges, powers, liberties, and claims—Hohfeldian-type elements clustered around the core element.

In Wellman's account, the move from legal rights to institutional rights is relatively straightforward, since institutions, including the actual institutions in which the law is of necessity located, are also products of particular times and places. The move to an account of moral rights is more complicated, due in part, he suggests, to the fact that in ordinary usage 'morals' and 'morality' refer ambiguously: (1) to time and space-bound moral codes and understandings, and (2) to concepts and principles which it might be suggested have some claim to objectivity, or might be said to be in some sense invariant with respect to time and place. Wellman's assumption in this book[6] is that it is possible to assign a consistent and coherent sense to 'moral objectivity,'[7] and having done so, to be able to expect to give a description of moral rights that would not be restricted to any particular times or places. Thus one might aspire to develop a characterization of moral rights in terms of a construction of them out of moral positions or elements that are definable in some objective sense, in a manner somewhat comparable to that involved in the construction of legal rights out of Hohfeldian elements or legal positions.

To distinguish between the two senses of 'morals' and 'morality' alluded to in the previous paragraph, Wellman (chap. 5) elects to employ the expression 'a morality' to refer to the conventional or received moral norms of a given society, and the expression 'morals' to refer to "a body of norms of conduct and character that are noninstitutional, objectively valid, and specifically moral" (121). The "norms" he has in mind in the latter sense he suggests actually are nothing other than *moral reasons*, the "practical reasons to which one appeals to justify a moral judgment" (122). Again, he thinks a comparison with the law is illuminating: ordinary folk (and lawyers) may express judgments of a variety of sorts about the law, but what makes such judgments (legally) authoritative are actual judicial decisions. Ordinary folk (and moralists), too, may make judgments about morality, but in this case what makes them (morally) authoritative is the appeal to moral reasons that are not confined to any particular society, to the *norms of morals* rather than to *morality norms* (unlike the legal case, where one is necessarily confined to some actually existing legal system).

The two types of norms share two features, he argues, the first of which is that both are what he calls "dual-aspect" norms. A dual-aspect norm is one that provides reasons not only for action but also for reaction. One individual's (or a group of individuals') *actions* as directed by moral norms or reasons will ordinarily produce *reactions* in other individuals, and these reactions also will be directed by moral norms or reasons (123). The one set of norms function as guides to action, the other set as guides to the appropriateness of reaction, and may involve positive or negative sanctions (Wellman goes on to say, actually, that the presence of such sanctions is *essential* to defining morals (125)). The presence of such dual-aspect norms, governing both conduct and reaction to conduct, also reflects the *essentially social* nature of both morality (time and place-bound) and of morals (not time- and place-bound) (124).

The other feature both types of norms share is that they are "nonelective." What Wellman understands by this is that it is impossible for an individual to "opt out" of either a particular society, or morality, or out of morals (124). Whatever action an individual chooses to perform, it can and likely will be judged by the prevailing norms (whether those of morality or those of morals) even though the individual may view his/her own action as falling outside the norms. Wellman does not say this, but I assume that he would allow for the possibility of genuinely new types of action making their appearance, and so bringing about a change in the existing (morality) norms or in their application (see the appendix to this chapter, *Some Possible Connections between Law and Morality*).[8]

Wellman proposes that it is on the basis of the sharing of these two features by morals (noninstitutional) norms and by morality (institutional) norms that he can do what few other moral philosophers have been able to do, and that is to explain what it is that makes a moral duty or virtue *moral* (126). He discusses and rejects the familiar view that distinguishes between "positive" and "critical" morality, defining critical morality as an idealized set of rules that it would be reasonable for any society to accept as modifications of its existing rules (its positive morality).[9] (Actually, he voices strong objections to any approach to delineating the nature of morality by formulating a set of rules.) I have no argument with his views on this count, but I shall raise and shall shortly discuss an objection to his claim to have shown what it is that makes moral duties and virtues moral by pointing to the feature as essential to defining 'moral' that the norms of morals and the morality norms share the same two properties: i.e., they are both dual-aspect and nonelective. My objection, simply put, is that in so doing he begs one of the fundamental questions at issue: namely, that of singling out the meaning or semantics of 'moral'. The discussion will follow shortly.

In order, then, to be able to define moral rights, Wellman proceeds to characterize the moral counterparts of the Hohfeldian elements: moral claims, moral liberties, moral powers, and moral immunities. Central to this enterprise is the notion of a *moral duty*, which is, as he puts it, "the constraint imposed upon a moral agent by some applicable moral reason that is both a reason for the agent to act and for other members of the moral community to impose negative sanctions in the event that the agent fails to act in accordance with this moral reason" (136). The "reasons" he refers to here are, as we have noted, nothing other than the norms of morals.[10]

A *moral claim* can easily enough be defined as the correlative of a moral duty: one individual has a moral claim against another just in case that other individual has a moral duty to the first (143).

A *moral liberty* is nothing other than the absence of any contrary moral duty (and this he notes, has a parallel in the law, where a legal liberty is also nothing other than the absence of any contrary legal duty) (146).

Defining a *moral power* turns out to be more complicated, and Wellman suggests the following characterization:

> X has a moral power to effect some moral consequence C if and only if some specific act of X implies C, given the background facts about X and the circumstances of the act, *and* this implication is contingent upon either, whatever inten-

tion of X is required for the efficacy of the exercise of some host power or the reasonably imputed intention of X to effect some such moral consequence. (157)[11]

Finally, a *moral immunity* may be described as an immunity against one or more second parties (158).

Taken together, the notions of a moral claim, a moral liberty, a moral power, and a moral immunity, thus defined, give us, in a Hohfeldian way, *moral positions* analogous to the legal positions already described. And, as the corresponding legal positions allow us to model legal rights, so one can proceed to model moral rights in an analogous manner. As with legal rights, so with moral rights, we have different moral rights characterized in terms of the positions constituting their central cores, with the other positions or elements clustering around them: viz., moral claim rights, moral liberty rights, moral power rights, and moral immunity rights. What makes moral rights unusual, as compared to legal rights, is of course the fact that we are to understand the 'moral' in 'moral rights' to refer to something that is non-institutional (having the feature of objectivity) in a way that actually existing legal rights cannot. Moral rights do share with legal rights, however, their essentially social nature and their adversarial nature, and their conferring of dominion if they are respected. Moral rights, too, are to be understood as being held by a first party against a second party, with a third party in a position to take sides with either the first or the second party to a confrontation.

Wellman's "dominion if respected" modifier does not, when applied to moral rights, undermine either the existence or the importance of moral rights. Moral rights that are not in fact respected do not because of that cease to exist, he argues. For moral rights exist so long as moral reasons (the norms of morals) exist. For example, in the case of a simple moral right such as that of the promisee to have a claim against the promise-maker, the fact that a particular promise-maker fails to keep his/her promise in no way brings about the nonexistence of the norm of morals in accordance with which promises ought (generally) to be kept. Nor would the fact that a particular promisee might not exercise his/her moral liberty right to relieve the promise-maker of his/her duty to keep the promise bring about the nonexistence of such a right. Nor, again, would it be true that failure on the part of the promisee to exercise the moral liberty right to relieve the promise-maker of his/her obligation would empower some third party to do so in the promisee's behalf without his/her permission. For the promisee is also understood to have a moral immunity right against precisely such actions on the part of *anyone* in the moral community.

While the account of Wellman's proposal I have supplied here is necessarily too brief, and certainly does not fully convey the detailed richness of his vision, I believe my account should make it clear enough that he has succeeded in a most admirable way in dealing with many of the theoretical complexities of the nature of rights. In fact, if I might be forgiven for putting it in such a banal way, I stand in awe at what he has been able to do, and must admit that my own thinking has been profoundly altered by following the course of his analysis. My primary concern in what is to follow is not with the fine structure of his proposal, nor with the arguments that might be mounted for and against it, so much as it is with certain matters that, in a manner of speaking, have been staring us in the face the whole while. These are matters I am sure Wellman would agree, if he were to stand back a bit, merit the sort of careful attention he is so patently capable of giving them. These matters are as follows:

(1) Wellman does not offer us any insight on the proper way of dealing with what might be called an "ontological" question about the instances of Hohfeldian notions, whether one is thinking of those found in the law, in institutions, or in morals: What sorts of things (in reality) *are* these Hohfeldian elements?

(2) He mentions only in passing the notion of a "moral right to privacy" (163) in connection with his brief discussion, as an example of such a right, of a woman's right to have an abortion (and in another context, of "a kind of sphere of privacy" created by each right) (196), but does not tell us nearly enough for us to be sure how such a "right" should be fitted in with the moral rights he does define, and in turn with the law. Since the ontological position of rights is, on his theory, presumably parasitical upon the Hohfeldian notions, a clarification of this matter turns, at least in part I think, upon a satisfactory response to (1).

(3) I alluded a few paragraphs back to the fact that in my opinion Wellman has begged an important question with regard to the matter of explaining what it is that makes moral duties and moral virtues moral: he has not, I think, really supplied us with what I have earlier referred to as a semantics (or meaning) for 'moral'.

(4) He acknowledges, on the last page (220) of his book, that he has not adequately dealt with the great variety of questions that make their appearance in relation to the problem of determining what sorts of beings are capable of possessing rights, moral or otherwise. Thus the "persons" in his title are left without anything like a formal definition, and are defined only implicitly in the context of talk of Hohfeldian notions.

I shall propose that the solution to this last problem, the answer to the ontological question raised in (1), the clarification called for in (2), and the remedy for the begged question alluded to in (3) are all connected, and that illumination can be shed upon all of these matters by our approach to moral personhood. I shall conclude my examination of Wellman's theory of rights by briefly discussing each of them, beginning with (1).

The question as to what sorts of things, ontologically speaking, the instances of Hohfeldian notions are, is one I think can best be answered in terms of our account of higher order intentionality. For to speak of claims, liberties, powers, and immunities, whether in law, in institutions, or in morals, is to refer, surely, to things of the sort we have shown how to describe as requiring higher order intentional capacities and talk of higher order intentional objects. By 'intentional objects' we have understood the objects of belief, understanding, desire, hope, expectation, etc., objects the apprehension of which requires an intentional system having the right kind of developed capacity. And, it will be recalled, the object of a belief, desire, etc., could be related either to an intentional or to a nonintentional thing. For example, I might desire that it not rain on the picnic I have planned for next week, where the absence of rain would constitute a particular sort of nonintentional thing. However, I could also have the hope that the friends I have invited to the affair are looking forward with pleasure to being there (since they should have the expectation of a pleasurable experience), and so in this case the object of my hope would be not only an intentional thing, but a higher order intentional thing: my hope has as its object not a nonintentional thing, i.e., its not raining, but another intentional thing, namely, my friends' expectations re their anticipated feelings at my picnic. I can refer to the intentional object of my desire, that it not rain on my picnic, as *eliminably* intentional; the intentional object of my hope that my friends have pleasurable expectations as *ineliminably* intentional. The rationale for this distinction has its source in the fact that whether (or why) it rains (or not) has nothing to do with intentionality, since this is a matter for the usual sort of nonintentional causal explanation—although whether it rains on *my picnic* is certainly an intentional affair (and an ineliminably intentional one).[12] Because of the intentional circle, there is no way of eliminating talk of intentions (and of intentional causation) from my hope about my friends' pleasurable expectations, and talking instead of nonintentionally causal matters.

When one speaks of a Hohfeldian notion, a *claim*, for example, one is also referring to a certain type of intentional object, which in this case is to be related to a possible (higher order) belief on the part of the person said to have the claim that another person has a duty (itself a higher order intentional thing) correlated with this claim. Or, when speaking of a Hohfeldian *liberty*, one is making reference to a belief on the part of the person having the liberty that he/she will not, in choosing to act in certain ways, be restrained by the contrary expectations of other persons.

Similar observations may be made about the other Hohfeldian elements, and what is clear is that they all make essential reference to intentional rather than to nonintentional things. The Hohfeldian notions take as instances, in other words, intentional objects only of the sort that are ineliminably intentional in nature. For the claims, liberties, powers, and immunities all must have reference not to any nonintentional things (such as the presence or absence of rainfall), but to the beliefs, desires, hopes, etc. of a certain class of higher order intentional systems (a class that includes my picnicing friends). This is not to say that nonintentional things cannot enter into the Hohfeldian picture, for they certainly may figure prominently, sometimes as vehicles of intentionality: for example, the physical object that may have been borrowed with the promise of its return (as when my neighbor borrows a tool of mine); it is, of course, not the borrowed object itself but the fact that the promisee has a claim upon the promise-maker that is of significance.

Thus the instances of Hohfeldian notions constitute a particular variety of higher order intentional objects, requiring for their existence and for their apprehension the right sort of intentional sytems with suitably developed capacities. These Hohfeldian constituents thus construed might be thought of as possessing a kind of neutrality, but they will in turn be differentiated in accordance with the (intentional) context in which they are to be found, and so might be variously legal, institutional, or moral.

Now if we adopt Wellman's proposal with regard to characterizing the nature of rights, and the account just given of Hohfeldian elements and notions is assumed to be plausible, it will follow, since Wellman-rights are themselves constituted of Hohfeldian elements or positions, that they also will be describable as another variety of higher order intentional objects. Rights, as constructions out of constituents that are themselves already higher order intentional objects, will be locatable in the class of higher order intentional objects the next level up. And as usual, the apprehension of such objects will require the existence of higher order intentional sytems with the right kind of developed capacities. To say, for example, that a creditor has a legal claim right against a debtor is to say that a Hofhfeldian element, i.e., a claim, constitutes the core of the creditor's position (as first party) against the debtor (who as second party has a duty to repay), a position that can legitimately be defended by a third party. The claim, and the duty that is correlated with it, are both higher order intentional objects, referring as they do to ineliminably intentional things, and so the assertion that in this case the claim constitutes the core of a right is itself a higher order intentional thing. Needless to say, the "parties" all must be suitably developed higher order intentional systems. Or, to use another of the examples we have already encountered, the institutional immunity right held by a tenured faculty member is also a higher order intentional thing of a similar type, where the right, as do all Wellman-rights, gives, if respected, a certain kind of dominion to the right-holder. In this case, the only individuals in a position to respect (or *not* to respect) the right would be those having the requisite kind of developed capacity for apprehending such a higher order intentional object and standing in an appropriate position in the institution. Similarly, 'dominion' itself designates a higher order intentional thing, and requires the correct kind of higher intentional system for its apprehension. To speak of a moral right, then, in the Wellmanian sense, is to designate a certain kind of higher order intentional object, a kind of object found at the same level, presumably, as the legal and institutional rights referred to in the last paragraph.

Now in Wellman's view, as we have seen, what makes moral duties and virtues distinctively *moral* is that the norms of morals share with the norms of morality two features: they are both dual-aspect and nonelective.[13] These features would presumably be found in the Hohfeldian-type elements that go into making a position a moral position, and from thence into the making, via a core element or position, of a moral right. Thus a great deal rides upon pinning down exactly what is to be understood as the meaning (semantics) of 'moral'.

In charging Wellman with begging the question in the way in which he has claimed to point to what makes moral duties, moral virtues, and now moral positions, moral, what I find troubling is not the fact that there is a sharing of features of the sort claimed between the norms of morality and the norms of morals: I earlier at least implicitly endorsed a view similar to this one in remarking upon the development of a more refined moral psychology (via a type of reflective equilibrium) out of our folk moral psychology. The difficulty that Wellman has not dealt with—except, in my opinion, by begging the question—is that it may well have turned out to have been the case that not all the supposedly moral features of our received morality norms may have been correctly described as being *moral* in the first place. While the sort of non-institutional objectivity and universality that he takes to be essential to morals —as opposed to moralities—is a legitimate requirement, I think, the fact that we find these features desirable does not by itself insure that we have thereby isolated what it is that may be taken to constitute what are sometimes called "moral-making" features, features that might be not only individually necessary but in some sense conjointly sufficient for pinning down the meaning of 'moral'. We need some way of deciding which candidates for moral positions in our morality norms are genuinely moral in order that we might jettison the pretenders, and might thus insure that the norms of morals might be as free as possible of imposters. And there certainly has been no shortage of such imposters.

To show the sort of thing I have in mind, let me flesh out a bit the example of the "aqueous believers," used in connection with our account of intentional explanation and causation given above (chap. 2, section 2) in order not to give offense to any actually existing group. Let us call our mythical group of aqueous believers the "Society of Aqueous Practitoners" (SOAP, for short): As before, the members of this society share the belief that their God/Goddess requires of them, as a test of their faith in Her/Him, that they completely immerse themselves in water for extended periods of time. In this Society, this requirement readily becomes an "ethical" imperative, something that they ought (morally!) to do, and to encourage others to do by positive and negative sanctions (children may become full members of SOAP at the age of twelve, and then are not only entitled, but are expected to practice the immersion rite). Presto, we have a dual-aspect, nonelective "morality" norm. (A feature of this group that some nonmembers find off-putting is that there never have been any survivors of the immersion rite! And as we remarked before, this fact seems not to have deterred the living members of the society from practicing the rite.)

The proposal we have offered for pinning down the meaning of 'moral' is the one that appeared in our "moral person schema." It will be recalled that what this schema calls for as a way of "making" a moral person is that one begin with a modified Dennett-person, or a malleable Dennett-person, (or a material, malleable, higher order intentional system of the Dennett type), with all of the difficulties built into that notion vis-à-vis the veridicality of belief, anomalous monism, and the intentional circle. Such a person becomes a moral person through the realization that s/he possesses the capability of performing actions that may interfere with, destroy, or assist in the production or maintenance of persons (/moral persons), by way of meeting (/failing to meet) the needs the voluntary meeting of which is necessary for the existence of such persons, and elects to try to perform in this context only those actions that contribute to the production or to the maintenance of persons (or moral persons). These needs, it will be recalled, include ones that are nonintentional, but more significantly, ones that are intentional—and especially higher order intentional—in nature.

We pointed out, too, that determining how these needs manifest themselves, and how their being met contributes to the production and maintenance of persons and moral persons, is by no means a simple matter. We must not only await the results of further empirical investigations in moral science or moral psychology, but we must cope, of course, with the fact that in dealing with the higher order intentional features of human beings we must expect to discover that the beliefs, hopes, expectations, etc. of an individual may have unexpected (and sometimes unpredictable) effects upon the behavior of that individual. This is a failing, one might say, that is built into taking the (higher order or personal) intentional stance. But whatever the drawbacks, we do at least have a way of supplying a semantics for 'moral person', and consequently for 'moral'.

With such an understanding in hand, we can then evaluate our received morality norms and abandon the imposters, or at least modify norms that do not capture what is involved in the voluntary meeting of the needs that are essential to an individual's becoming or remaining a person or moral person, and so feel more confident that we are arriving at norms of *morals*, norms also having the requisite sort of noninstitutional objectivity and universality. Moreover, we might also venture to form new norms, as conditions of the lives of human persons change over time. Our rejection of the SOAP immersion norm as a genuine moral norm would be based upon the observation that the norm in fact encourages beliefs and voluntary practices that insure that some children do not become (full) persons, and that some among those who are full persons are not maintained as persons. We can notice, too, that the immersion norm would be not a harmless nonmoral norm, but a palpably immoral one, unlike other possible norms, such as dietary restrictions of a sort having no significant effect upon the physical well-being of the members (cf. the SOAP view that the ingestion of ice on any day but Tuesday is a fundamental no-no).[14] And, as we suggested, we would also be in a position to evaluate the formation of new norms: for example, with regard to the rational decision of an individual person (/moral person) to bring his/her own existence to an end, a norm that might approve such a decision whenever one is faced with the prospect of a fast-approaching existence devoid of a desirable quality of life (as we have proposed this be characterized, chap. 6, sec. 3 above).

I have spoken explicitly so far to the matters under the headings (1) and (3) in my list of things needing attention in Wellman's theory of rights, but certainly implicitly to the others, especially to (4), since an essential part of my argument is that the moral person schema does provide an account of a paradigm for the sort of being to which it *literally* makes sense to attribute moral rights.[15] I would urge that the ascription of rights of any type to other sorts of beings (including nonliving ones) would be metaphorical at best, and in any case that the existence of any such "rights" would depend entirely upon the existence of individuals of the paradigm sort, since the recognition that an individual has a right involves an intentional object of the ineliminably intentional sort, and is necessarily a higher order intentional affair.

I shall make only a few comments about (2), since I say much more about both the nature of the moral right to privacy and the conditions making it possible in the section to follow, *Moral Personhood and Privacy*. There I argue that the type of privacy that is relevant here is of the higher order intentional sort, of course, but that it is also associated with the process of intentional selection. It is this process which, when it is successful, enables individuals possessing the (developed) capacity for "previewing" and pre-selecting their beliefs and their actions via awareness and self-awareness to avoid interfering with the meeting of the needs of themselves and other individuals, needs the voluntary meeting of which is necessary for their becoming or remaining persons and moral persons.

An important problem of an unavoidable sort is certainly present, but it is one with which we have good reason to be familiar: what is to be counted as properly "private" in the higher order intentional sense depends at least in part upon the beliefs of the particular person. Consequently, what actually counts as a violation of privacy probably could not be pinned down in any kind of general formula. But it seems, if one were to be able to rank moral rights, and thought it plausible to link moral rights with the types of needs referred to in our moral person schema, that a moral right to privacy would be one of the more fundamental—and one of the more important—such rights. I am not entirely clear how such a right should best be described in Wellman's Hohfeldian language. For I think it could be argued that the moral right to privacy might be said to require for its realization *all* of the advantage-marking Hohfeldian elements: it might be said to represent a claim, a liberty, a power, and an immunity. Or, better, perhaps, that *its* being respected represents one of the necessary conditions for any person's or moral person's *other* rights being respected. I believe that it is clear enough, however, whatever its locus in relation to the Hohfeldian-type moral elements and moral rights, that the moral right to privacy is a higher level intentional thing, requiring for its existence, recognition, and support, obviously, suitably developed higher order intentional systems.

2. Moral Persons and Privacy

Some Existing Views on Privacy

There is a formidable body of literature[16] that has arisen with respect to the notion of privacy, both as a legal and as a moral concept.[17] While all of those who have written on the subject agree upon its fundamental importance to matters of human concern, that is about as far as the agreement has gone; it would be unquestionably difficult to formulate any more detailed thesis about the concept of privacy that would receive general approval. For, as Ruth Gavison 1980 (Schoeman 1984, 348) suggests, discussions of privacy have dealt with it sometimes as "a situation, a right, a claim, a form of control, [or] a value," and have related it "to information, to autonomy, to personal identity, to physical access," with a notable lack of coherence. Some of the reasons for this state of affairs will surface as I proceed. All of the discussions implicitly—some of them explicitly—make use of the concept of a person (or of "human" in the sense of "person"); none does much in the way of explicating the details of what a person is, aside from observing that persons are connected in a significant way with privacy in some of its forms. Some writers suggest that without an appropriate form of privacy, persons as such (at least as we now know them) could not exist;[18] others seem to imply that our world would be a better place in the absence of certain familiar forms of privacy (see n. 23).

However, a survey of the literature, of the sort supplied by Ferdinand Schoeman 1984a, suggests that our attention to the concept of privacy has been brought primarily by a variety of legal considerations, beginning with the oft-cited article by Samuel Warren and Louis Brandeis 1890 who were concerned to show that the "yellow" journalism of the day was making unwarranted intrusions into the privacy of certain members of Boston "society" (Warren's family in particular). Written in reaction to the piece by Warren and Brandeis, and in addition to it perhaps one of the articles having had the most influence upon the actual development of the law is that of William Prosser 1960, in which he argues that the proper legal place for privacy is in tort law.[19] Edward Bloustein 1964, in direct response to Prosser, claimed that Prosser had unduly narrowed the legal concept of privacy and in so doing not only failed to capture the connection between privacy and human dignity but made it impossible to employ it, as one might reasonably expect, in nontort as well as in tort law: e.g., in U.S. constitutional law: the Fifth Amendment privilege against self-incrimination, and in common law: where "a man's house is his castle."

One of the more recent, and possibly the most definitive, treatments of these matters is the comprehensive discussion by Ruth Gavison (in the paper mentioned above), in which she judiciously covers most of the points at issue in the existing literature and adds some eloquent observations of her own with regard to the importance of having an understanding of a concept of privacy rich enough to capture not only the fullest range of its legal instances but also its source in the nature of human beings (i.e., persons). She proposes (Gavison 1980 at Schoeman 1984, 347) the need for a coherent view of privacy that would meet three requirements: it would provide (a) a neutral or descriptive characterization of what privacy is, prior to supplying (b) a value description of it, in terms of the kinds of interferences with privacy that are undesirable, and in turn (c) a useful legal account of it: that is, one picking out those undesirable occasions appropriately calling for legal action. I propose a way of satisfying these requirements at the end of the section, *Moral Person-*

hood and Privacy. I shall first make some remarks about the notion of reductionism in the context of the notion of privacy, and then discuss some views of Reiman and Wasserstrom which relate privacy to persons.

One of the main bones of contention in the legal discussion has centered upon the question whether privacy is to be viewed as a basic entity of some sort or whether it is itself derivative from some more basic entity or entities. For example, if privacy is viewed as a right, the question is whether or not there are other rights from which the right of privacy might be obtained; or if privacy is associated with torts, whether it is to be connected with a tort of its own (as Bloustein 1964 argued) or is to be found in other more basic torts (as in Prosser 1960).[20]

The view that privacy is to be constructed out of more basic ingredients has been labeled "reductionism," and has figured in this form in discussions of a more explicitly philosophical sort, such as that of Judith Thomson 1975[21] in support of a form of reductionism, as well as that of Gavison[22] in favor of an unreducible notion of privacy. For present purposes, I think little is to be gained by examining the details of arguments of this type in regard to the reducibility of some types of privacy. This is a perplexing matter of possible importance, certainly, in the attempts of those working in the area of legal theory to arrive at a more unified and coherent way of employing the notion of privacy in legal contexts, although it is not likely that the actual development of the law would come to a halt without its being resolved. I have already, in discussing the concept of a moral right, been concerned to sort out certain aspects of the sort of reductionistic claims that might show up in connection with the irreducible nature of intentionality.[23] I shall make some comments about reductionism, intentionality, and law at the end of the section, *Moral Personhood and Privacy.* Next, however, I shall describe two of the proposals about privacy supplied in the literature insofar as they relate explicitly to the notion of personhood.[24] These proposals are due to Jeffrey Reiman and Richard Wasserstrom.

Jeffrey Reiman 1976 proposes that there is an intimate connection between the notions of privacy and personhood, a connection he puts forward in the following form:

> *Privacy is a social ritual by means of which an individual's moral title to his existence is conferred.* Privacy is an essential part of the complex social practice by means of which the social group recognizes—and communicates to the individual—that his existence is his own. And this is a precondition of personhood. To be a person, an individual must recognize not just his actual capacity to shape his destiny by his choices. He must also recognize that he has an exclusive moral right to shape his destiny. And this in turn presupposes that he believes that the concrete reality which he is, and through which his destiny is realized, belongs to him in a moral sense.[25]

That Reiman intends his thesis in an empirical sense is perhaps indicated by his subsequent remarks:

> the relationship between privacy and personhood is a twofold one. First, the social ritual of privacy seems to be an essential ingredient in the process by which "persons" are created out of prepersonal infants. It conveys to the developing child the recognition that this body to which he is uniquely "connected" is a body over which he has some exclusive moral rights. Secondly, the social ritual of privacy confirms, and demonstrates respect for, the personhood of already developed persons. I take the notion of "conferring title to one's existence" to cover both dimensions of the relationship of privacy to personhood: the original bestowal of title and the ongoing confirmation. And of course, to the extent that we believe that the creation of "selves" or "persons" is an ongoing social process—not just something which occurs once and for all during childhood—the two dimensions become one: privacy is a condition of the original and continuing creation of "selves" or "persons."[26]

Reiman supports his claim by an appeal to the work of Erving Goffman 1961 upon the effects of certain types of institutions upon individuals.[27] How "scientific" was Goffman's study (of what he referred to as "total institutions") is perhaps a debatable matter, in view of generally accepted ethical prohibitions against placing human beings in experimental conditions of total deprivation of privacy for extended periods of time, but it is clear that Reiman himself holds the view that there is evidence (albeit somewhat speculative) for the thesis that privacy, as a "social ritual," is a necessary condition for the possibility of personhood. This leads him to say, finally, that on this assumption the "right to privacy is a right to the existence of a social practice. . . . It is the right to conditions necessary for me to think of myself as the kind of entity for whom it would be meaningful and important to claim personal and property rights."[28] I shall not at this point comment upon the strength of Reiman's thesis, or his employment of the expression "moral right"; I shall shortly (in the following section) be very much concerned to examine the notion of moral rights in terms of the moral person schema I have recently sketched. I turn first to Wasserstrom's views about persons and privacy.

In Wasserstrom 1979a, the proposal is made that

> one rather plausible conception of what it is to be a person carries with it the idea of the existence of a core of thoughts and feelings that are the person's alone. If anyone else could know all that one was thinking or perceive all that one was feeling except in the form one chose to filter and reveal what one was and how one saw oneself—if anyone could, so to speak, be aware of all this at will, individuals might cease to have as complete a sense of themselves as distinct and separate persons as they have now. For a significant, if not

fundamental, part of what it is to be an individual person is to be an entity that is capable of being exclusively aware of at least some of its own thoughts and feelings.[29]

Wasserstrom's comments here are suggestive, but it is not clear how they might connect with the thesis advanced by Reiman according to which privacy is the source of an individual's *moral* existence. However, Wasserstrom suggests that this way of thinking about persons does, as he puts it, illuminate some of the puzzling features of the Fifth Amendment privilege. For, he says, the sort of testimony one should be allowed to escape giving by appeal to the Fifth Amendment is precisely that concerned with one's private thoughts and feelings, the revelation of which would diminish "the significance or role of the concept of individual personhood within the society."[30] Wasserstrom is silent, however, on the sorts of connections one would expect to find between guilt and personhood, and between what he calls "individual" personhood and moral personhood. The implication is, presumably, that both individual personhood, with its sort of privacy, and the legal roles of such persons are in some way connected with society, and in turn with morality.

In the course of his discussion Wasserstrom does point to the fact, however, that we lack a *theory* of privacy. An indication of this, he says, is shown in the reflection that we do not really know how to respond, for example, to a hypothetical proposal to the effect that we would be better off if we were socialized in a manner different from the way we in fact are. He supplies a brief sketch of some possible changes in socialization and their effects upon such everyday matters as our sexual relationships (and our thinking about erotic matters generally) together with the claim that such changes would be desirable. An appropriate theory would enable us to appraise such a normatively framed proposal, and to make recommendations with respect to possible changes in the way in which socialization takes place. I put forward the reminder at this point that we have also been lacking a theory of moral personhood, and that however such a theory is constructed, it could well join in a variety of ways with a suitably defined notion of privacy. It will not be altogether surprising if theories of moral personhood and of privacy should turn out to be parts of the same theory, as I shall now proceed to suggest in the following section.[31]

Moral Personhood and Privacy

The theoretical considerations that have been amassed in producing the sketch of the moral person schema (supplied in chap. 5, sec. 1) I think can be shown to provide a basis for evaluating the views of both Reiman and Wasserstrom, and will make it possible as well to speak to areas either omitted or left vague in their discussions of persons and privacy. The legal discussions of privacy, too, I believe can profit from such observations (see my comments at the end of this section, and also the other sections in this chapter).

According to the person schema, it is among the essential features of persons that they, as higher order intentional creatures, be depicted as having private access to their own intentionality: to their own beliefs, desires, expectations, etc., via their capacity for self-awareness; public access (such as it is) to these things is to be had only by verbal communication, subject to the constraints imposed by the veridicality of belief, the intentional circle and anomalous monism. These constraints need not, as we have observed, necessarily be a source of pessimism with regard to understanding and explaining the performances of persons, but they certainly make more difficult such understanding and explanation. In addition, an essential feature of persons is their malleability with respect to the beliefs and systems of beliefs they may hold, and this also is a source of difficulty. But offsetting this difficulty, I have argued, via the hypothesis of intentional selection, is the capacity formed over evolutionary time on the part of persons thus characterized to develop various belief-sorting devices, devices which, I have been urging, need not be limited to the kind of reflective equilibrium that has made its appearance in the experimental sciences and mathematics, but which may extend as well to what I have called moral psychology, or better, the theory of moral intentionality. And this, as we have seen, may be profitably connected with the version of the doctrine of moral realism we have described.

Thus the form of self-conscious privacy that Wasserstrom takes to be an essential feature of what he calls "individual" persons is built into their nature, if one adopts as an approximately correct description of this nature the schema I have proposed. And if one takes seriously the suggestion that this schema, although in a sense theoretical, must be measured against the reality of material higher order intentionality as it is embodied in normal adult human beings, it appears that this privacy of intentionality is confirmed by one of the only sorts of observation available: the palpable failure of the only kinds of behaviorism so far proposed in being able to reduce intentionality to perceptually observed behavior, which is in effect equivalent to saying that the intentional circle is found here, too. So privacy of this sort seems to be an irreducible part of human persons, at least if they are taken as instantiations of the proposed schema.

However, if this schema is accepted, it is not clear why an instantiation of such privacy in an actual person should, as Wasserstrom suggests, be connected with the kind of privacy safeguarded by the Fifth Amendment privilege allowing one to refuse to give testimony one believes to be self-incriminating—at least for the reason he gives that such testimony might diminish "the significance or role of the concept of individual personhood within the society." For one need not, under any nonintrusively coercive circumstances, communicate what one's beliefs are, if one chooses not to do so.[32]

However, if the moral element enters the picture, i.e., the moral element as I have proposed it be defined in terms of the moral person schema, then one might, if one *believes* that a certain kind of testimony might impair the exercise of one's higher order intentional capacities and/or capacity to function as a member of a group of persons capable of intentional reciprocity, deem it quite appropriate to forgo giving such testimony. For, of course, if one's higher order intentional capacities were in some way diminished, then one's ability to function as a credible member of a set of persons having undiminished forms of such capacities would indeed be curtailed. If something along these lines is what Wasserstrom has in mind by "the significance of the role of the concept of individual personhood in society," then things become clearer. However, I may be reading things into Wasserstrom's account, because, as I have already noted, he is silent on the subject of moral personhood.[33]

Now so far as Wasserstrom's speculations on socialization and the lack of a *theory* of privacy are concerned, I think the following comments are in order. The moral person schema (and the person schema it presupposes) are sufficiently flexible to allow for quite wide variations in the ways in which actual human persons might be socialized; this is implied by the property of malleability. But if this schematism is correct, privacy of belief remains an unalterable feature of persons, *whatever the particular form their socialization assumes.* What actual persons take to be damaging to the exercising of their intentional capacities in terms of their roles in their groups of fellow persons can of course be expected to vary with the particular nature of their socialization, and so they might indeed, because of their actual socialization, *believe* that certain ways of dealing with their essentially private intentional features would be damaging, and hence, on our theory, consider them to be morally evil. Whether or not there really would be moral evil is something that can be determined, so long as one is operating with an appropriate version of moral realism; but this is quite consistent with discovering that one's intentional capacities are diminished for the reason that one believes that they are diminished. In other words, an intentional cause, in this context, is no less real than the standard sort of (nonintentional) cause in a nonintentional context. For example, my *belief* that my capacity to make judgments, or to understand certain things, has suffered an impairment may affect the exercising of the capacity just as much as my actually having an impairment due to the use of a drug. The hypothesis (under which we are operating) that there is a material basis for intentionality is, of course, quite consistent with just this sort of thing, since at an appropriate level there presumably are neurochemical (or whatever the appropriate adjective) changes taking place, whether due to the having of a belief or to the presence of a drug.

Now privacy (of the type being referred to by Wasserstrom) on the theory I have been advocating, as an intentional object, might best be described as connected with an open concept, and as such possessing features not all of which are capable of being scheduled in advance. A theory of privacy would have to take this into account, and as this can be done by our proposed schema, I would suggest that the schema itself constitutes a foundation for such a theory of privacy. Thus whether or not something like a so-called invasion of privacy will be thought to be (i.e., believed to be) productive of moral evil will vary with one's socialization; but whether one's capacity to function as a higher order intentional being has been impaired or destroyed by the voluntary action (or consequence of such action) of some person or persons is a matter that would be invariant with respect to socialization. Such invariance would indicate as well an invariance in terms of the immorality of the causative voluntary action. It is possible that there could be, as the result of involuntary actions on the part of persons, impairment or destruction of higher order intentional capacity; this would be nonmoral in nature. Among the most fundamental problems for moral psychology probably are those of trying to discover sound empirical ways of establishing, firstly, whether such impairment or destruction of intentional capacities has actually occurred in a person, and, secondly, whether there are morally permissible steps which might appropriately be taken to repair such damage (some form of empirically sound intentional therapy, a therapy which could employ nonintentional elements as well as intentional ones).

Reiman's views on the nature of privacy are, unlike Wasserstrom's, explicitly connected with the concept of personhood, at least as Reiman sees the matter. For, as he suggests, privacy as a "social ritual" seems to function as a necessary condition for personhood: truly a condition without which human individuals could neither become (it is the way in which "an individual's moral title to his existence is conferred") nor continue to be persons. I have troubles here with two things: (1) the use of the term *moral* and (2) the rôle of the social ritual. I begin by discussing (2).

The legal metaphor of title conferral is picturesque enough, certainly, but suggests a kind of arbitrariness that I think is inappropriate in this, a presumptively moral context, as does the ascription *social ritual*. What is lacking is a way of showing how to justify, in a nonarbitrary way, the existence of *this* social practice. And also I have misgivings about describing this social practice as a necessary condition of personhood, for the reason that it seems that human individuals might be quite capable of acquiring personhood without it, if personhood is understood in the way I having been urging. There is no doubt, of course, that there are and have been social (and/or religious) ways of producing "nonpersons", but the primary reason for our being able to see the hypocrisy of this practice is precisely because we realize the injustice of making personhood so capricious a thing. Reiman's intent, perhaps, is not to speak of the social practice in this way at all, but in normative terms: there *ought* to be a social recognition of the fact that an individual has fully become a person (and even more significantly, a moral person). If this were the case, such a practice would amount to an endorsement of an intentional state of affairs that had already come into existence: namely, the development of the higher order intentional capacities I have depicted in my account of the person schema. There is no doubt that social practices, because they are essentially intentional, and as they can be observed to operate in the actual world, may either contribute to this development or impede it. And there certainly are practices with the capability of destroying personhood once it has come into existence. Determining in a sound empirical way what these practices are and how they operate would be another of the matters to be dealt with by moral psychology. We already have, in fact, some very good ideas here to build upon. What is more elusive, of course, is discovering the practices that might contribute to the development of personhood, and whose absence are productive, say, of the criminal individual (cf. Herrnstein and Wilson 1985).

Reiman does not define 'moral', but I think it is significant that the term shows up in his discussion in connection with the acquisition and maintenance of personhood. For, of course, on my view, moral personhood presupposes personhood, but is not equivalent to it. As I have proposed in the description of the moral person schema, the moral person is the individual who is capable of recognizing (both in his/her own case and in others of the same type) that s/he has acquired certain higher order intentional capacities, and that it is within his/her power to maintain, or to diminish or to destroy, these capacities (or the conditions making them and their exercise possible), but who chooses not to do so (and trusts that others will do likewise). This sort of personhood is not, I think, a kind that can be conferred solely by social practice, although it is clear enough that there are not only social practices involved in its development but also those that can impair or destroy it, whether these practices are purely intentional (for example, the practice of "shunning" or psychological abuse) or whether they employ nonintentional means (for example, the use of drugs, physical abuse, or torture).

In closing this section, I want (1) to suggest how the person-moral person schemata might be employed in connection with the three-part coherency thesis proposed by Gavison with regard to the nature of privacy, and (2) to make some comments about the reduction of rights, intentionality, and the nature of law.

(1) The person schema, I think, *first of all* provides a *neutral* way of describing a quite fundamental form of privacy. For it is the privacy that, on the assumption of the hypothesis of intentional selection and the higher order capacity for awareness and self-awareness, has been an essential part of the developed capacity of individual persons for "seeing" into the future, or for deliberating about possible courses of action and attempting to avoid those potentially harmful to themselves. Even cooperative endeavors on the part of groups of persons entail this sort of private deliberation in advance of, and during the course of, the formulating of plans. In some ways, of course, things would be far less complicated if groups of persons did not operate in this way, but could operate as non-Skinnerian hardwired creatures, as do bee hives or ant colonies. Interestingly enough, it is when human individuals are caught up in the sort of hysteria that occurs in mob behavior that they manifest features of a type totally in opposition to the form of private deliberation just described, for they are in such circumstances incapable of exercising the kind of fore-sight characteristic of the best individual instances of the process of inten-tional selection. If the hypothesis of intentional selection is sound, it would appear to be the case that there is an evolutionary interest built into pre-serving the sort of privacy which is an irreducible part of persons, although it is clearly possible for various forms of privacy to be overridden (even voluntarily, as in the case of those who affiliate themselves with certain types of cults).

Secondly, explaining the *value* of such privacy (apart from the evolu-tionary perspective) is, because of the malleability of belief of persons, a more troublesome matter. For it is the same privacy that makes possible the enter-prises both of persons we have come to prize most highly and of those we look upon with utmost horror and shame. But, as we have suggested, this is one of the facts of life built into the nature of persons, at least as we have described them: in order to have moral persons, we must first of all have persons. The moral "production" of persons, as we have noted, requires run-ning the risk that there will always be some persons produced who are capa-ble of bringing into the world more moral evil than moral goodness. The value then, of this sort of privacy, is of a piece with the value we place upon the production of persons, and once they have appeared, their maintenance.

Privacy assumes a *moral* value when it is a part of the deliberations of those persons who are moral in the sense we have proposed in the moral person schema. And privacy, in the sense associated with persons and moral persons, is an intentional object as well: in other words, what a person *believes* to be private *is* for him/her private, and because of this fact he/she will sort harmful from helpful influences on the part of other persons upon the main-tenance and the exercising of his/her own intentional capacities, and will thus judge them in terms of moral good or evil. Establishing proper ways of justify-ing such beliefs is, of course, another matter.

Thirdly, the associated *legal concept* of privacy would be connected with the supplying of the needs necessary for the development and maintenance of persons and moral persons. And again, because of the fact that there are open concepts associated both with the things that persons employ to meet these needs and as well with those which frustrate them (things generative of moral goodness and moral evil), the legal concept also will be an open one. There is no possible way of formulating laws today that could cover all possible future ways of interfering with, or destroying, the capacities necessary to the existence of the higher order intentional human individuals we characterize as persons and as moral persons. Our laws should be formulated, however, on the basis (in so far as possible) of the invariant features of intentional capacity development and destruction we have referred to as being recognized by empirical investigations in moral psychology. The Fifth Amendment privilege, for instance, may be viewed as a particular way of acknowledging the acceptance of the *risk* to be encountered in connection with the development and maintenance of persons. The main price to be paid, after all, is simply more diligence in prosecutorial efforts to establish by other evidence the guilt of the individuals who abuse the privilege.

(2) I would propose, as a way of adjudicating disputes about which (legal) rights are the most "basic," that the following considerations be taken into account: Rights are, one and all, intentional in nature; they are, it will be recalled, on our reading of them, certain kinds of (higher order) expectations. Law may be viewed (and I shall argue for this in more detail in the appendix to this chapter) as itself an intentional realm, and related in a variety of important ways to morality. On the assumption that one of the functions of the law is that precisely of ensuring that moral rights be taken seriously, it would seem plausible to carry over into legal deliberations considerations connected with the setting of moral priorities. In particular, these considerations would include those we have outlined with respect to the production and maintenance of persons, and especially of moral persons. One of the difficulties here, as we have observed, is that there will inevitably be a certain degree of variability with regard to what might be considered by a particular person to constitute an injury to his/her intentionality. Thus while the law itself must also await the appearance of more detailed knowledge from the science of moral psychology, it would not appear unreasonable to suggest that the legal rights taken to be basic be those connected with assuring the production and maintenance of persons, whatever the details turn out to be.[34]

Appendix to Chapter 7: Some Possible Connections between Law and Morality

I begin this section by examining three sets of propositions which I shall suggest might together go some way toward capturing the general nature of a few of the many types of relations that may be said to hold between morality and the law. My understanding, for this purpose, is that 'morality' and 'law' refer to normative or idealized, relatively unstructured concepts; precisely what I mean by saying this will become clearer as the examination proceeds.[1] It has happened that in some actual court decisions reference has been made to the bearing of morality upon the law, but such references have not been ordinarily thought by all legal practitioners to be crucial to the legal points at issue. My interest here in connection with my deliberations upon moral personhood might best be viewed as falling under the heading of the philosophy of law, or jurisprudence, since what may actually be legal in a technical sense in common or statute law, which is always (and necessarily) a function of particular times and places, need not correspond to what one might with good reason want to argue *ought* to be legal. I shall return, at the end of this section, to a few considerations of a more practical sort.

The three sets of propositions are as follows:

I. Crime/Injury—Law
   A. If x is (or would be) a crime or an injury, then there is (or ought to be) a just law prohibiting x.
   B. There is (or ought to be be) a just law prohibiting x only if x is (or would be) a crime or an injury.
   C. X is (or would be) a crime or an injury if, and only if, there is (or ought to be) a just law prohibiting x.

II. Moral Rights—Law
   A. There is (or ought to be) a just law prohibiting x only if x is (or would be) a violation of a moral right (or a right derived from a moral right).
   B. If x is (or would be) a violation of a moral right (or a right derived from a moral right), then there is (or ought to be) a just law prohibiting x.
   C. X is (or would be) a violation of a moral right (or a right derived from a moral right) if, and only if, there is (or ought to be) a just law prohibiting x.

III. Moral Rights—Crime/Injury
   A. x is (or would be) a crime or an injury only if x is (or would be) a violation of a moral right (or a right derived from a moral right).
   B. If x is (or would be) a violation of a moral right (or a right derived from a moral right) then x is (or would be) a crime or an injury.
   C. x is (or would be) a crime or an injury if, and only if, x is (or would be) a violation of a moral right (or a right derived from a moral right).

Before considering the import, and possible truth, of these propositions, a few preliminary observations are in order. In all the propositions, the "x" is understood to be, as logicians say, a "placeholder" for voluntary human (person) actions (or inactions) or types of such actions (or inactions), or for pronouns referring to them.[2] For example, in IA., one might find an instance of what is claimed by the proposition by putting in place of the x, say, the type of voluntary action commonly referred to as murder. Thus, 'If murder is (or would be) a crime or an injury, then there is (or there ought to be) a just law prohibiting it.' Or again, an individual might, by way of electing for a certain kind of inaction, provide an instance of criminal negligence. Thus the propositions may be viewed as purporting to capture certain general connections between pairs of concepts, known instances of which might be found fairly ready to hand.[3] One reason for wording them in this particular way— and this is indicated also by the qualifiers "would be" and "ought to be"—is to capture the fact that *new* crimes or injuries, and hence new forms of illegality and of immorality, may come into existence at any time (e.g., computer crime). It perhaps needs to be pointed out, too, that part of the intent in employing the expressions 'is a just law' and 'is a violation of a moral right' is to distinguish them from the possible locutions, 'is *thought* (in society or culture z) to be a just law' and 'is *thought* (in society or culture z) to be a violation of a moral right', which are expressions one might employ to avoid objectionable forms of social or cultural relativism (Cf. chap. 4, sec. 3. *Moral Theory, Problems. Moral Invisibility and Moral Semantics*).

The notion of *injury* employed in these propositions is intended to operate in a wide-enough sense to capture injuries in addition to the usually designated criminal ones, injuries to be found typically in the civil jurisdiction covered by tort law, but not excluding those suffered because of breach of contract. What actually counts as an injury is a troublesome matter to determine, as the concept seems to be one of the defeasible or open variety (as one might expect via the connected open concept of moral evil). The sort of battery to which professional boxers and football players are subjected in carrying out their professional activities is a case in point. Such injuries inflicted in the ordinary course of events off the playing field involving nonathletes, or athletes and nonathletes, would likely be actionable at law (in California law, I am told, the fists of professional boxers are considered lethal weapons). Injuries of the type suffered due to nonhuman forces or agencies, such as storms and volcanic eruptions, are also excluded, the vagaries of the insurance industry and its regulatory laws notwithstanding.[4] I think there is good reason to say, as we shall see shortly, that the propositions in III. go a good way toward capturing at least some of the features that might be thought to be *essential* to an action's (/inaction's) constituting an injury.

The expression 'derived from a moral right' is intended to capture the following consideration: if one were to show, say (as I have already suggested and shall shortly argue in more detail), that what has sometimes been termed a "human" right, the right to some basic level of physical and psychological *well-being*,[5] is more properly thought of as a *moral* right, then one might from it derive a variety of rights, e.g., water rights; the right to have access to pertinent information in one's file in a credit bureau (or a college registrar's office, etc.). Both of these rights, depending upon the particular circumstances of the individuals concerned, may have a great deal to do with their well-being, where this well-being can be characterized in terms of the voluntary meeting by persons of certain needs, both intentional and nonintentional.

Now for the promised examination of the sets of propositions: the choice of the 'if . . . then' logical structure here is premeditated, and designed to suggest that there are logical relations between, to start with, an action's (/inaction's) being a crime or an injury and its being prohibited by a just law. According to IA., an action's (/inaction's) being a crime or an injury would have as a necessary condition that it be prohibited (or that it ought to be prohibited) by a just law. Consideration of the possible truth of this claim focuses attention upon the meaning of 'crime or injury'. One could, of course, argue that one of the very points being made by advancing the proposition is precisely that it is part of an attempt to formulate what we are to understand by calling an action a crime or an injury *in a legal sense*. Thus understood, it could serve as well to remind us of the familiar convention in law that one who is subject to a law is entitled to know in advance of performing a certain action whether or not it would count as a (legal) crime or injury (although with ignorance of the law not generally counting as a defeating plea).

IB. differs from IA. in suggesting that an action's (/inaction's) counting as a crime or injury function as a necessary condition for counting it as an action (/inaction) prohibited by (or that ought to be prohibited by) a just law.

IC. represents the very strong claim resulting from the logical compounding of IA. and IB., a claim making each condition both necessary and sufficient for the other. The truth of IC. thus depends upon the truth of the propositions out of which it is compounded, and thus focuses joint attention upon each of them.

We might now observe that IA., if true, could represent what some might view as an excessively legalistic approach to matters, and might interfere with the stipulation mentioned above, that our conception of law must be rich enough to allow for new forms of crime and injury making their appearance. The "or ought to be" qualifier presumably would accommodate this possibility, but there might remain the feeling that there could be some forms of crime or injury that might be lacking the serious features calling for the enacting and the enforcing of law. In order to deal with such a consideration as this, one might best look at the third set of propositions, which does do something in the way of connecting crime or injury to violations of moral rights (or rights derived from moral rights). But it will be noticed that the propositions in the third set bear logical relations to those in the second set, relations which (if they hold) set up some of the possible connections between morality and law. The reader might observe, for example, that IIA. and IA. together, by a simple type of chain reasoning, imply IIIA. Thus the truth of IIIA. is logically connected with the truth of IA. and IIA. So, before reaching a final opinion about the propositions in I., it would be wise to look carefully at those in II.

IIA., on my reading of it, has certain attractions. For in proposing that an action's (/inaction's) being a violation of a moral right (or a right derived from a moral right) be a necessary condition for the action's (/inaction's) being prohibited by a just law, one might make it easier to examine existing and proposed laws with a view to eliminating those that do not meet this requirement. Thus one could show, by demonstrating that a certain action (/inaction) or type of action (/inaction) does not really amount to a violation of a moral right (or a right ... etc.), that a law prohibiting it would not be desirable. Additionally, it could also be argued that such a requirement does indeed capture *part* of what ought to be meant by calling a law a *just* law.[6]

Now, as we have already noticed, IIA. together with IA. yield IIIA., which connects crime or injury with violation of moral rights (or rights ... etc.). And here, as with IIA., our saying that a certain action counts as a crime or injury has as a necessary condition that it be counted as a violation of moral rights (etc.). As with IIA., I think there are considerations of a sort similar to those that supported it that are to be found here, too. According to IIIA., an action (/inaction) could not be claimed to be a crime or injury unless it could be shown to be a violation of moral rights. A difficulty is, naturally, that one needs to be very clear about what constitutes a moral rights violation (and this entails being very clear about the meaning of both 'moral' and 'rights').

As with IA. and IIA. together yielding IIIA., so it is the case that IB. and IIB. logically imply IIIB. And again, our willingness to accept IIIB. would be contingent upon our willingness to accept both IB. and IIB. In this case, I think there could be difficulties to be met with in accepting IIB. For while one might say that IIA. is somewhat moralistic in tenor, IIB. might be said to be a rather legalistic proposition. For IIB., if injudiciously(!) implemented, could produce an excessive number of laws, in the manner, perhaps, of the Jewish Talmud. Whether a proliferation of laws and rules is thought to be a defect might be a matter of disputation, of course—especially in the computer age, where those subject to such a system of laws might be supplied with portable computers, so that knowing whether one's actions should be described as law violations might possibly be quickly determined by a few key strokes. Already itinerant, devout, and sophisticated Moslems may today avail themselves of such electronic devices to inform them of the location of Mecca relative to whatever geo-coordinates at which they may find themselves located, in order that their prayers be offered while facing in the mandated orientation! The law-applicability case is of course more troublesome: whether among the proposals in Artificial Intelligence research for designing "expert systems" there should (or could) be included such a project is not entirely clear. Perhaps, as with medical diagnostic systems, such a system could provide an initial—if not the final—word. Impaneling a jury together with an expert system would surely require some getting used to, to say the least.

If we assume, as we have done for present purposes, that the concepts of law and morality under examination are both, after all, idealized ones, ones having some claim to being, in Wellman's terms both noninstitutional and objective, then perhaps we do not really have to worry about the business of implementation. It is instructive nonetheless, I think, to deliberate about possible connections between an admittedly idealized morality, which seems the more plausible notion, and an idealized notion of law, no matter how difficult its realization in some actual society might be.

To facilitate further an understanding of the relations set out in the three sets of propositions, I think it is useful to call attention to some of the implications for them of our moral personhood schema. Moral and legal concepts, whether idealized or actual, have as instances certain kinds of higher order intentional things. The notion of a moral right, as we have already suggested, concerns a specific type of expectation (which we described as itself a species of belief) that one person might be said to have with respect to the beliefs, understandings, expectations, etc. of all other (moral) persons.[7] This, as are all expectations, is a higher order intentional thing, since it can be thought of as a belief about a belief (or an expectation about a belief or an expectation). As such, references to such rights can be said to require intentional objects of the ineliminably intentional type, as we have seen.

The fundamental moral-making feature as we have depicted it is defined by reference to the type of malleable Dennett-person who realizes that by his/her voluntary actions he/she can control the meeting of the types of needs (especially higher order intentional needs) that are essential to the production or maintenance of persons (/moral persons). In this context, a violation of a moral right would occur whenever such a person voluntarily performs (/fails to perform) an action whose consequence, directly or indirectly, is a failure to meet these types of needs. By way of the proposition sets (depending upon which ones are accepted, of course) one establishes connections between such (voluntary) failures to meet these needs and the concepts of crime or an injury and of a just law. The possibility of such connections, we can now observe, presupposes that the concepts of crime/injury and of law are also higher order intentional ones. This seems plausible enough, since crimes/ injuries and laws require for their description and their apprehension higher order intentional systems with suitably developed capacities. Thus just laws would be precisely those designed to prohibit—or at least to discourage—the voluntary failure to meet these types of needs, where such voluntary failures would count as crimes or injuries.

As we have already noted, there is no simple way of determining what count as voluntary failures to meet such needs, since we do not—and perhaps cannot—know in advance either the nature or the full extent of these needs, or all of the ways in which failure to meet them might affect those who are, or who are to become, persons or moral persons. Thus the concept of a rights violation cannot be defined in advance except in a schematic way. Nor can that of what counts as a crime or an injury. This deficiency is inherited by the connected concept of law—but this should not be surprising, since crime/ injury and law, as higher order intentional things, are also subject to the irreducibility restrictions imposed by the intentional circle.

The observations we have just made, while admittedly concerned with idealized notions of moral rights, crime/injury, and law, can certainly be useful in the assessment of actual laws and of actual actions claimed to be criminal or injurious. For example, the New Jersey State Supreme Court has since 1976 pushed ahead in the absence of any explicit and coherently formulated theory of personhood or moral personhood to make it possible to enact into law the notion that there do exist human individuals—*former* persons, we might suggest in most cases—who in a perfectly appropriate sense cannot be legally injured, and who thus cannot be the victims of criminal activity (cf. n. 3 and 4). The theoretical deliberations we are amassing here, I believe, do provide one form of justification for such legal outcomes. The individuals in question seem no longer to have, or to be capable of having, either of the types of needs we have proposed as crucial to the producing or to the maintaining of persons or moral persons. However, the gap between a state supreme court decision (or even a series of them) and appropriate legislation at any level is a wide one, and often enough results in laws that are defective, at least in part—but this should be no cause for alarm, since the higher courts themselves exist in large measure precisely for the purpose of pruning away or correcting such defects, either in the law or in its applications, as these defects make their appearance over time.

I conclude this section by making a pair of remarks and issuing a confession of puzzlement. As I have indicated in examining the sets of propositions appearing at the beginning of this section, there might be good reason for saying that the relationships delineated in these propositions would appear to entail a closer connection between morality and the law than some may be comfortable with. I have in mind a well-known piece dealing with the "enforcement of morals" (Devlin 1965[8]) that has acquired a certain degree of notoriety for suggesting that the law, which is frequently depicted as concerning itself only with "public" matters, should concern itelf with certain "private" matters as well. I think it imperative to insist again on the assumption under which I have been operating: the "law" and the "morality" which are the subjects of my sets of propositions are both idealized. Since this is the case, I would find nothing terribly objectionable to thinking in an idealized manner of law as a way of "enforcing" morals, whether "public" or "private": the necessary qualifier, of course, is that the enforcing also be of the idealized sort, perhaps by way of the higher order intentional causation produced by the *threat* of enforcement.[9] I certainly believe that there may well be certain kinds of human actions that may always escape the sanctions of any actual law, and by calling for laws that are actually unenforceable, show that no just law is possible in such cases. But then I wonder whether such actions could properly be said to fall into the realm of morality, either.

The second remark is connected with the first, and it is that I think it helpful at the least to view law instrumentally, as a way of taking morality (and moral rights) seriously—provided, again, that one is thinking of the idealized notions. In turn—and this brings us back to the actual world again—the taking of laws seriously by the people who live in our actual world seems to require that the laws have actual sanctions attached to them. Indeed, the enforceability of an actual law seems to *require* the appending of sanctions to it, and there is some truth to the familiar observation that a law that is unenforceable is in some sense an unjust law. This is perhaps a sad, but nevertheless an accurate, commentary upon the nature of persons and the possibility of at least one type of utopia.[10] Thus, taking morality seriously in our actual world entails the need for the sanctions that insure that our actual laws are taken seriously.

The confession of puzzlement has to do with the view, which I suppose is a possible one (although this is part of what I find puzzling), that at least a portion of the law, other than that dealing with second order legal affairs, is concerned with first order matters of a totally nonmoral nature. I readily admit that there have been and that there remain laws like this, if one is speaking of actual laws (think of laws with regard to so-called victimless crimes, laws that prohibit actions that apparently harm or injure no person).[11] What puzzles me is whether it ought to be the case that law (in an idealized sense) should be like this. My current inclination is to say that law (in an idealized sense) should not be like this, but I am prepared to be persuaded otherwise.

8

Not Quite Back to Square One: Reconsiderations

I at this point resume the stance I took in section 1 of chapter 1. The difference now is that I shall show how the talk I indulged in there (as I said there, "for the sake of argument") about certain actual and possible states of myself, and about the beliefs and moral opinions that might be held (by myself and by others) about those states, might some of it be given both explanation and justification, and some of it be modified or rejected, in terms of some of the theoretical points developed in the intervening chapters.

When I said that I believed that I am presently a moral person, and that I have been one for some time and shall remain one for some indeterminate but finite time in the future, the possibility of my being able to speak in this way may now be seen to entail the following things: By assuming the characterization of 'moral person' supplied in the schemata in chapter 5, I can describe myself as a certain kind of malleable material higher order intentional system, or *malleable Dennett-person*. It is only on some such basis as this that I can say that I have a developed (higher order) capacity for the necessary self-awareness, that is, for the having of beliefs about my own beliefs and also for the having of beliefs about the beliefs of other persons (and about their beliefs about my beliefs, etc.). But as a *moral* person, some of my higher order beliefs take on a particular *content* as I realize that I, by voluntarily choosing to do so, can do or arrange things (intentional or nonintentional) that can *interfere* with my remaining in this condition, and that other persons, too, have the same capacity with regard both to themselves and to me. I, and these other persons, also have the capacity to choose to do or to arrange things, some of

151

them of a nonintentional and some of them of an intentional nature, that will contribute to the *meeting* of the needs that must be met if I am to remain a moral person.

But our actual world being what it is, I realize also that there can be occurrences (of both intentional and nonintentional origins) which are capable of completely destroying me as a moral person—these occurrences might range from a tree falling on me (through no human agency) with fatal results, to nuclear holocaust. The variety of the possible worlds in which I could not continue to exist as a moral person is, it hardly needs saying, extraordinarily large.[1]

The plausibility of my stated belief that I may not have been a moral person (or a person) for the whole of the time since my birth is demonstrated also by the adoption of the schemata in chapter 5. Only now I would be more accurate in saying, not just that I *may* have been in such a condition, but that there was a time when I was definitely *not* either a person or a moral person. For on the assumption that higher order intentional capacities must be *developed* (via the meeting of the first class of needs mentioned in chap. 5.), there must have been a time when I had at most only the *potential* for developing these capacities. And as we have noticed, one of the dismaying things about human existence is the fact that our recognition of the development of these capacities is something that is itself spread over time. For example, ordinarily something more than a period of eighteen months has to elapse before the judgment can be safely made that a John Storar (cf. Preface), who lives for fifty-two years, is never going to develop mentally beyond the level of an eighteen-month-old child. But such judgments can, and at times must, for various reasons, be made. You, my dear reader, simply by your being able to read (and presumably to understand) what I write here, have sufficiently demonstrated your developed personhood—if not necessarily your moral personhood!

It is, alas, *only in retrospect* that we can say with confidence that you or I were at one time potential persons or moral persons. The John Storars of the world, because of the nature of identity as it applies to moral persons or persons, could never be in the position of meaningfully employing the expression, "There was a time when I was not a moral person, or a person" (Cf. chap. 5, sec. 2, above). Nor, of course, could the aborted fetuses that seem to overpopulate the fantasies of so many of those in the right-to-life movement. With regard to the future, one can meaningfully say of certain individuals that they might become persons *again*, but only if they have already been persons (and there may well be significant reidentification problems in such cases).

Belief malleability being what it is, it is not at all surprising that personhood has been seriously attributed by some individuals to a wide range of things—generally to living things, but not always just to adult humans. (Frivolous attributions present no special problems, as long as one does not become too serious about humor—itself a higher order intentional manifestation!)[2] By our proposal, of course, vis-à-vis intentional selection, trial attributions of features to things in the world are a part of the process by which reflective equilibrium operates, whether in the development of our moral reflection and of our knowledge of intentional kinds generally, or in the development of our nonmoral reflection and our knowledge of nonintentional or natural kinds. Our argument has been that our interest in human infants and our interest in human rights are both due to our concern with the continued production and maintenance of persons and of moral persons. Since both persons and moral persons come into existence over a relatively long span of time, and not over a short period—as at the time of the fertilization of an egg a new (biological) individual of a species comes into existence—there must always be some element of uncertainty about the timing for the correct attribution of personhood.

Similar observations may appropriately be made about the way in which a person or a moral person might pass out of existence: only here it is possible that there can be an abrupt transition and not a gradual one. In the latter case there may well be an uncertainty about the appropriateness of the continued attribution of personhood or moral personhood. It is not surprising here, either, given the malleability of belief, that there might well be those who would continue to look upon me as a person or as a moral person when I no longer could be such in anything like the sense we have proposed in this essay.

One useful result of our investigations is that it is now possible for me to say, speaking strictly, that *I* could not (logically) have been a John Storar, or an anencephalic individual. My parents certainly could have produced one or more offspring of either of these types, but none of them could have been *me*. Whatever uncertainty might attach to the attribution of "Storar-hood" (a human individual with a chronological age older than the eighteen-month stage of its completed mental development), diminished "Storar-hood" (an individual possessing Storar-hood but who becomes irreversibly comatose, say) or "anencephalous-hood" (a human individual born with a brain stem but no upper brain) to an individual at a certain time in its life would be connected with the uncertainty about attributing personhood or moral personhood to it. However, whatever happens to me in my future, it will remain forever true that I was a person and a moral person for a certain period of my life, and impossible that I could have been a John Storar or an anencephalous.

As to the talk of the possibility of my never having been born, in which I indulged in chapter 1., I think what needs to be said here is that this will not do either as a genuine possibility, and for similar reasons. If it is correct to say that whatever happens to me in the future it will (forever) be true that I was a person, this means that, again speaking strictly, *I had to have been born* (and this, given our best current scientific knowledge, entails such things as that a certain egg was fertilized by a certain sperm during a certain period of time, and that a great many different developmental processes went through in a routine way for many months) *and to have developed in certain ways over a period of years.*

Its being "always true" in the future that I was a person and a moral person for a certain period of my life may be as close to immortality as I am likely to get, aside from artifactual, biological, and memory "immortality." This consideration plays a principal part in my reluctance to grant the possibility of *my* existing in any manner either before the fertilization of a certain egg, or after the time at which I shall cease to be a person or a moral person.

I do need to speak anew to the *moral opinions* I suggested it would be appropriate for me and for others to hold with regard to certain possible future states of myself. Since I am a certain kind of material (i.e., *biophysical*) higher order intentional system—one having a characteristic type of neurophysiology—there are ways in which this neurophysiology can malfunction in a strictly nonintentional sense (as happens because of Alzheimer's and other neurological diseases that have similar effects, and because of certain types of neurological injuries).

No matter what its cause, such malfunctioning can have a direct effect upon my higher order intentional capacities: it can either diminish the functioning of these capacities or it can bring about a complete cessation of this functioning by way of destroying the relevant sort of causal efficacy (cf. chap. 6, sec.1). Since one is, as a person, in a sense equivalent to this functioning, the prospect of the diminishing or cessation of this functioning is logically equivalent to the prospect of loss of personhood. Since, given such future cessation of functioning, *I* would have ceased to exist, *I* can have no personal interest *then*, moral or otherwise, in what happens subsequently to the body (living or dead, but minus the essential neurological-functionality features) that could continue to exist for some indefinite period of time after my demise as a higher order intentional system. I can, of course, have an interest, *before* my death as an intentional system, in the manner of disposal of various objects, including a certain corpse, and can, in my "last will and testament," in the customary legal way, leave a variety of instructions about their disposition.

I can also, in advance of my death (as a higher order intentional system), investigate the question whether a greater or lesser (moral) harm might issue to certain persons from my (living) body's being kept around than from my causing, either directly or indirectly, my death (complete or total, or my death *as a person*). And if I can do this out of concern for the welfare of others, I can do it because it relates to my own welfare. In fact, I may, because of quality of life considerations with regard to my own future, be entitled to take actions to prevent my finding myself in the position of a William Bartling (cf. Preface, n. 2). For I may, as a higher order intentional system, desire not to have the desire that William Bartling presumably had for some time prior to his death: this desire was, of course, that his life not be maintained any longer by the devices to which he was attached at the hospital. There seems little doubt that he no longer (if he, indeed, had ever) desired to maintain the quality of life that he found himself experiencing near the end of his life.

But it also seems clearly to be possible that I might one day, even without being in the straits of a William Bartling, come to the realization that I no longer possessed *the desire to continue to have desires*. Bernard Williams 1973, in his valuable essay on immortality, has proposed that this sort of desire be called a "categorial" desire (as contrasted with a "conditional" desire, i.e., a desire conditional upon my desiring to remain alive), a desire to continue to have desires. The realization of this desire's no longer being present could lead even someone like the fictitious Elena Makropulos depicted in Williams' article, who had experienced a form of immortality by having lived for several centuries at the presumptively optimal age of forty-two, to decide in favor of an unusual form of suicide by way of not quaffing another dose of the elixir of eternal (or prolonged) life. Whatever the facts of the matter might be with regard to the best way of understanding the concept of human immortality, it is clear enough that such a desire would be a *higher order* desire, in the sense in which we have been speaking. For it is only functioning higher order intentional systems of the type we have described which would be capable of having this sort of desire, and of desiring no longer to continue to have this desire—actually a third-order desire.[3]

We can also usefully bring to bear here the proposal of Frankfurt (1971), which we mentioned earlier (chap. 2, sec. 2, *Intentional Systems: Higher Order*) to the effect that the meaning of freedom for persons is definable in terms of the capacity both for having and for bringing about the objects of such higher order desires: so one might successfully will or desire (assuming the absence of akrasia), given the imminent prospect of the destruction of this capacity in oneself, and while one were still able to bring about the object of one's desire, one's own death as a higher order intentional system. In so doing, one would be ruling out a certain possible world and its associated quality of life. For an individual who had permanently lost these higher order capacities would no longer be a person in the sense for which we have argued. Personhood in this sense and Frankfurt-freedom appear to enjoy an equivalence relationship with one another.

Since, as I also suggested in chap. 1, I might find myself in the position of not being able by myself to bring about states of affairs corresponding to my moral desires, the aid of other persons might have to be enlisted. This possibility raises several additional questions, the answers to which we are now in a position to supply: one question has to do with the *morality* of my shifting responsibility to others; another with the *prospects* for receiving aid from others; yet another concerns the *legality* both of my plans and of the assistance of others. I begin with the first of these questions.

Given the malleability of belief of persons, it is possible, of course, that I might be successful in convincing some other persons of the moral appropriateness of my desire to initiate a certain course of action—or it is possible that there might be persons who would be capable of convincing themselves of the appropriateness of my project. The shifting of moral responsibility to them under certain circumstances via my moral rights is implied by our moral person schema, whether or not they would elect to fulfill their correlated duties (cf. Wellman's notion of rights having "dominion if respected").

But it might also be possible that while there are such persons they, due to certain nonintentional matters beyond their control, might be unable to offer the assistance they would feel quite pleased to offer if they could. A depressing, if not a worst-case, possible-world scenario clearly could ensue if the only persons available to assist me could not be persuaded by me, nor could they persuade themselves, to offer the necessary assistance.[4] These are all quite real possibilities, to be weighed together with the rest of my deliberations. Whether any assistance at all would be forthcoming is an ineliminably intentional matter, as is one form of nonassistance, and is subject to the underdetermination of personal action entailed by anomalous monism. The other form of nonassistance, resulting as it does because of nonintentional obstacles, is a nonintentional affair, but no less off-putting because of that.

The business of the legality of my enterprise and of my receiving assistance from others, on the basis of the theory we have developed, is wholly an intentional affair. For the law—of whatever jurisdiction, as we have argued (above, chap. 7)—presupposes the existence of a variety of higher order intentional objects and capacities. My having a legal right (/not having a legal right) to do x (/to refrain from doing x), for example, deals with my expectations about the beliefs (and the expectations, understandings, desires, etc.) of certain classes of other persons with regard to my expectations. If I am fortunate, the applicable laws will have been developed by persons who have arrived at similar conclusions to my own. But there is a possibility that I might not be so fortunate, and that I would not be in a position to work to bring about changes in a law that ran counter to what I considered my best interests to be. And if I were unable to "take the law into my own hands" in some sense, then I would have to reconcile myself as well as I could to whatever prospects were open, none of which might be desirable to me. Such was the plight of William

Bartling, who, realizing that he no longer possessed the categorial desire to live, and hence desiring to die, was unable to bring about that state of affairs by himself; but any assistance by other persons was made impossible by the laws that existed at that time and place. A higher court did finally make it legally possible for his desire to be realized by the assistance of appropriately designated persons, but too late for him. As a consequence, in the future some of those who find themselves in a position like his can have the implementation of their desire to die be a legal one. Our characterization of moral personhood, we submit, can supply a nonarbitrary basis for such legal decisions, by making morally permissible the carrying out of a person's (higher order) desire no longer to have desires, and so contributing to the understanding required for drafting appropriate legislation in this area.

NOTES

Preface

1. I do not wish to imply that *all* philosophers have been unaware of the lack of attention given to the concept of personhood of interest here, and I should mention here some exceptions. John Rawls (1971, 505-510) observes that his theory of justice requires, as those entitled to equal justice, moral persons possessing certain capacities; but he chooses not to discuss all of the complications arising from either lack of, or loss of, the capacities in question, or even how, precisely, one is to determine whether an individual possesses the minimal capacities. A. I. Melden (1977, 216) comments, in the course of his account of rights and persons: "a full discussion of the nature of personhood is impossible within the limits of this work." Douglas Walton (1979, 9-10) gives notice at the outset of his discussion of the concept of death that the question of what constitutes a person is an essential part of the picture, but a part he cannot investigate in that book. Walton undoubtedly had been influenced by the technological changes I have referred to, as these served as one of the motivations leading him to his study of death. I need to mention also E. M. Adams 1989-, J. English 1975, J. Margolis 1978, J. Reiman 1976, M. A. Warren 1977 and 1979,1985, and R. Wasserstrom 1979.

2. The nightmarish case of Mr. William Bartling was reported in the *New York Times*, Sunday, 21 October 1984, page 1. Unfortunately for Mr. Bartling, who was suffering from multiple terminal conditions, and who repeatedly expressed his wish to be allowed to die, the legal process culminating in a decision making it possible for him to be released by the hospital from life-support apparatus did not run its course until after he had died a decidedly unnatural death (a death worthy of an E. A. Poe tale). Mr. Bartling, in a very real sense, was a hostage held by the medico-legal system. The legal references: Bartling v. Superior Court, 163 Cal. App. 3rd 186, 209 Cal. Rptr. 220 (Ct. App. 1984), *later appeal, Bartling v. Glendale Adventist Medical Center*, 184 Ca. App. 3rd 97, 228 Cal. Rptr. 847 (Ct. App.), *later appeal*, 184 Cal. App. 3rd 961, 229 Cal. Rptr. 360 (Ct. App. 1986).

3. It is perhaps unnecessary to comment upon the false hopes for improvement in quality of life raised by the Jarvik heart and other experimental procedures: cf. *The New York Times Magazine*, 28 August 1988.

4. Sunday, 5 April 1981, page 8 of the Editorial Section. Cf. *In re Eichner (In re*

Storar), 52 N. Y. 2d 363, 420 N. E. 2d 64, 438 N. Y. S. 2d 266, *cert. denied*, 454 U.S. 858 (1981).

5. The so-called COBRA [Consolidated Omnibus Budget Reconciliation Act of 1985] Federal legislation has since then been enacted, in part to cope with this problem.
6. 1987, Simon and Schuster.
7. 1988, Oxford University Press.

Chapter 1. Square One

1. Here, to postpone certain problems to be dealt with subsequently, by "I," I understand "my parents' first-born" (it would be possible, of course, to get rid of the "my" in this expression as well, by suitable devices).
2. Again, there are modifications required in order to understand the reference of "I"; instead of "my parents' first-born",it would now have to be something like: "the _____ , which if it had survived to full-term, would have been my parents' first-born", with the'_____' to be filled in by some appropriate biological term such as *fertilized ovum, blastosphere, embryo, fetus*, etc.
3. If some of my readers have not already felt some discomfort at some of my uses of "I" and "my" in these contexts, they should be fairly squirming by now, or most likely will be before I have finished with this section; and the same thing may be true of my uses of "person."
4. There are obscurities here that have continued to bedevil the controversy over abortion.
5. An aside for some philosophers: it is perhaps true, in a Quinean manner, that my parents were experiencing childlessness in a *de dicto* way, but not in a *de re* way that could have had any reference to *me*.
6. Of course, our leaders in Washington might determine that federal funds could usefully be spent to support indefinitely the lives of myself and others in a similar state.
7. As I shall show below, this is in fact a description of what may be called an instance of "intentional causation," using the term *intentional* in a special sense to be explained in chap. 2.
8. I omit, for the time being, consideration of some of the problems arising in connection with the lives of those whose moral personhood is not so much in question —e.g., the problem of akrasia, usually translated "weakness of will," which may afflict otherwise morally normal persons, or that of servility (see below, chap. 5, sec. 2).
9. For example, Dennett 1976, who speaks (metaphorically?) of persons and moral persons being found on the same continuum—see below, chap.2. "Material Persons," 2, *Intentional Systems: Higher Order*.
10. Things are less clear with regard to the conditions to be placed upon the recipient of moral attention, who might be termed the moral *patient*: our practice seems to suggest that almost anything, whether animal, vegetable, mineral, or other, can be a moral patient.

11. As is true of most arenas of philosophical debate, there remain some unresolved issues, some of which might yet make a difference to both our theoretical and our practical deliberations. And some views, like the speculations of David Lewis 1984 with regard to the metaphysical status of the objects to be found in possible worlds, might appear to be so abstruse as not to make that much difference in practical affairs. I shall be describing a way of talking about possible worlds in terms of what I shall term 'intentional states of affairs', since such states of affairs, I shall argue, supply the immediate context for both moral reflection and moral action. (See below, chap. 6, sec. 1)

12. There is the short paper by S.McCall 1980, and that of D. High 1978.

13. The year of "A definition of irreversible coma," by the Ad hoc committee of the Harvard Medical School to examine the definition of brain death. *Journal of the American Medical Association* 205, 337-340. Since the Conroy case (N. J. Supreme Court, 1985), the American Medical Association Committee on Ethics has recommended the removal of feeding tubes in certain cases; it is not clear what proportion of the members of the AMA might in practice concur. The Hastings Center has produced a useful set of guidelines (1987) and an accompanying casebook (1988) for the use of hospital ethics committees and other interested parties in their dealings with terminally ill individuals.

14. An example of this malleability has shown itself already in my discussion, in the case of those who, contrary to my own expressed belief, might insist upon attributing moral features, or personhood (or both) to individuals who never develop past a mental age of eighteen months. And there are those who hold the belief that animals are persons, and those who talk to their plants (and not because they wish only to exhale carbon dioxide upon them!), etc.

15. The locution, intentional object, will be employed as a technical term: see chapter 2, 2. *Intentionality as a Feature of Material Objects.*

16. At one point, I had hoped to be able to include an investigation of moral development as a part of this project. I came to realize, however, that to do so would entail an enormous increase in the size of this essay, and so, with some reluctance, decided to leave it out.

17. Or alternatively, a special way of charting the features of what might be called "counterintentional" statements.

Chapter 2. Material Persons

1. I view myself as the very model of a modern minor materialist, since I am not interested, of course, in all of the labyrinthine moves canvassed in such treatments as those provided by D.M. Armstrong 1968, J. J. C. Smart 1970, or R. Boyd 1980.

2. As Putnam 1975 has suggested.

3. Dennett (Dennett 1984 and some earlier writings) has taken great pains to try to pull the teeth from this particular bogeyman (or as he prefers to say, "bugbear"). Davidson 1970, in a somewhat Kantian manner, thought to make freedom possible by way of his "anomalous monism" version of materialism. Putnam 1975

argued, via a functionalist approach to the mind, that contemporary materialism need not threaten our mental autonomy. One certainly may elect, as E. M. Adams 1989 does with his way of defining materialism as a type of "naturalism," to disagree.

4. "Homunculus," or "little man," has been employed in the literature to refer to an explanation of the nature of certain human features which builds into the explanation the very features supposedly being explained, something on the order of Moliere's fictional doctor's explanation of the sleep-inducing properties of opium as being due to its *virtus dormitiva*. In offering as an explanation of the features that are unique to man (in the generic sense) the suggestion that these features are due to the activities of a little man (or men) inside the main man, one does not make much explanatory headway. One may, however, in espousing "homuncular functionalism" (cf. Lycan 1987), propose that there be counterparts of a functional sort, counterparts that need not be comprised of the same "material" as the (main) man they are being used to construct.

5. Talk of kinds of things in nature, each with its own essential features, has reappeared in philosophical discussion in recent years, after a period when discourse about "essences" had fallen into disrepute in certain quarters, under the aegis of discourse about "natural kinds" in the writings of Hilary Putnam, Saul Kripke, and others: see below (this chapter), sec. 2. Intentionality as a Feature of Material Objects, *Intentional Causation, Intentional Explanation, and Natural Kinds.*

6. One of the most recent and more careful philosophical examinations of the puzzles referred to here may be found in Rosenberg 1983, chap.2.

7. Of course, even the so-called theoretical terms or intervening variables found in physical theories had to have their connections established with the "observational terms" which presumably were the physical vocabulary itself.

8. As in Putnam and P. Oppenheim (1958), "Unity of science as a working hypothesis," *Minnesota Studies in the Philosophy of Science* Vol. II. [H. Feigl, M. Scriven, and G. Maxwell, eds.] Minneapolis, Minnesota: University of Minnesota Press.

9. "Reductionism and the nature of psychology", Putnam 1973a; "Philosophy and our mental life", Putnam 1975 291-303 (Reprinted in Block 1980 135-143.) Talk of "Turing machines" is explained below, in chap. 3.

10. Cf. Fodor, "Special sciences, or the disunity of science as a working hypothesis" (Block 1980 120-133). Also Davidson 1970 (at Block 1980 113) on "definitional reductionism" and its failures; and Boyd 1983 on the permissibility of employing unreduced causal notions in philosophical analysis.

11. One might lose, in Putnam's terms, functional isomorphism, and as well the insight that a functional explanation need not be identical to a physical explanation in order to be in some sense a "good" explanation. Earlier in this century, some attention was given by philosophers (especially G. E. Moore and others following his lead) to certain problems having to do with the nature of philosophical analysis itself as a form of reductionism: one of the foremost of which was that if the analysis was correct, it was not informative, and if was informative it was not correct. The discussion of this so-called "paradox" of analysis was usually couched in the analytic-synthetic vocabulary, a vocabulary enshrined by Quine as one of the

"dogmas of empiricism." I shall make no attempt to trace the history of the discussions of the problem of analysis, but mention it only as another example of a misdirected interest in reductionism of the sort referred to by Davidson 1970.

12. Cf. Lycan 1987, chap. 1, for one such account of behavioristic efforts to cope with consciousness.

13. Following Dennett 1978 and others; unless otherwise indicated, all references in the following section will be to Dennett's (1978) collection of essays, but primarily to Dennett 1976, reprinted in Dennett 1978 as pages 267-285.) Dennett 1987 represents a refinement and summary of his thinking on the intentional stance. In correspondence and conversation, he has informed me that he has not done as much as needs to be done, since his 1976 essay, on the nature of personhood.

14. The terms *intensional* and *extensional* are also to be met with in philosophical writing, especially where matters of the logic of terms are under discussion, and carry with them a rather different meaning (although there are some connections) from that furnished, as here, for 'intentional'. Roughly, the "intension" of a term is supplied by giving the meaning or definition of it, while the "extension" of a term refers to an enumeration of the members of the class of things designated by the term. The history of the logical problems to be encountered here goes back, in modern times, to Frege and Russell, and concerns the things that happen when one tries to employ standard Russell-Whitehead mathematical logic to capture the logical features of the kind of statements expressing what Russell referred to as "propositional attitudes." e.g., statements about beliefs, such as 'Smedley believes that Pynchon is the author of *Gravity's Rainbow*'. Translation of such statements into the notation of quantificational logic may lead to a variety of problems, among them that christened "referential opacity" by Quine, which is a way of saying that the context is not an extensional one, or (among other things) that the quantifiers tend to misbehave in a distinctive way. For example, while it is true that Pynchon is the author of *Gravity's Rainbow*, and true also that the author of *V* is alleged to be a recluse, from which it may be inferred that Pynchon is alleged to be a recluse (given the truth of 'The author of *Gravity's Rainbow* is the author of *V*'), one *cannot* infer, even on the assumptions that it is true both that Smedley believes that Pynchon is the author of *Gravity's Rainbow* and that he believes that the author of *V* is alleged to be a recluse, that he also believes that Pynchon is alleged to be a recluse. The first inference succeeds in a standard extensional context, the second cannot be guaranteed, it is said, because of its intensional context: for Smedley need not, of course, *believe* that the author of *Gravity's Rainbow* is the author of *V*.

15. In his introductory essay, "Semantic engines: an introduction to mind design," p. 33.

16. For a very careful—and very critical—examination of Skinnerian behaviorism, see Dennett 1978, "Skinner skinned" 53-70, which contains a reference to the famous review by N. Chomsky (reprinted in Block 1980, 48-63) of Skinner's *Verbal Behavior* (New York: Appleton-Century-Crofts, 1957).

17. I might add that the circle of intentions has been related in the literature to a concept due to Quine, a concept he referred to as "the indeterminacy of translation" (Quine 1960). This concept reflects the actual difficulties to be encountered in attempts to discover, as a matter of fact, whether those who speak another

language mean what we think they mean by certain words. The notion of the circle of intentionality is itself usually traced to the work of Franz Brentano, to which the attention of analytical philosophers was brought by Roderick Chisholm 1957.

18. As usual in philosophy, there are complications: on differing ways of handling the role of intentional causes in the work of Davidson and von Wright, see F. Stoutland 1982.

19. A "skinnerian creature" is one which, like one of Skinner's favorite animals, the pigeon, is a suitable subject for operant conditioning. Other animals, like one of Dennett's favorites, the ("hardwired") sphex wasp, fail to make the grade even as skinnerian creatures, since their hardwired behavior cannot be altered by operant conditioning, but only, perhaps, by some form of tinkering directly with their genes.

20. Dennett credits P. Grice 1957 and 1969 for this notion of verbal communication.

21. Interestingly enough, Dennett, almost in passing, alludes to a requirement he has not mentioned before, when he says that, in addition to rationality, *trust* also is required for the possibility of verbal communication: we normally trust each other to use language in standard ways. I shall have reason later (in chapters 4 and 5) to point to the claim that another kind of trust appears to play a principal role in moral theory, as argued persuasively by Annette Baier in several articles. Our dog might perhaps be said to possess at best some sort of proto-trust, as do human infants and children, with the infants and children (if normal) having the potential for developing forms of genuine trust. (Jay Garfield 1988 refers to animals lacking the capacity for verbal communication as "infralinguals.")

22. As of this writing (1988), there continues to be no generally accepted way of capturing in a theoretical framework the "felt," or subjective character of consciousness: cf. Nagel 1974, Dennett 1982b, and Lycan 1987.

23. Matters are, alas, even more complicated than they appear so far: see chapter 3, n. 6, and the Davidsonian argument that in order to *understand* someone else's language, one must have some sort of *theory* of that language.

24. Dennett, op.cit. 285.

25. "How to change your mind" (Dennett 1978 300-309) which was written as a response to a piece of Annette Baier's entitled "Change of mind," given at the UNC Philosophy Colloquium in Chapel Hill, North Carolina, 1977. Baier's piece was published under the title of "Mind and change of mind" in her *Postures of the Mind* (Minneapolis, Minnesota: University of Minnesota Press, 1985). (For another approach, cf. G. Harman 1986.)

26. I say more about some of the reasons for this state of affairs in connection with an analogy with levels of programming in computers, in discussing malleability in the following chapter. There is good reason to believe that we presently are unable to do little more than to speculate about the number of neurobiochemical levels required to do something relatively simple like tracking the mechanisms required for human visual perception, much less to deal with such things as consciousness and intentionality. On consciousness, see again Dennett 1978, 1982b, and Lycan 1987.

27. It should be noted, as has been suggested by such writers as Churchland (1984) and Stich (1983), that talk of unreduced intentional causes and explanations has been around for many years in what they refer to as "folk psychology": as when one says that an individual did what he did because he was "driven by desire, lust, greed, etc." This folk psychology, through the accumulation of generalizations, rules of thumb, and principles, might even be said to have its own "theory," on the basis of which it is enabled not only to supply explanations for, but to make predictions about, the behavior of persons. What I am doing here is certainly connected with this folk psychology, just as some of the things that scientists and philosophers of science do is connected with what might be called "folk physics," "folk biology," "folk chemistry," and so on. If the intentional reading I shall presently be placing upon Boyd's (1983) version of moral realism is correct (see below, chapter 4, sec. 3, Moral Theory, Solutions: *Intentional Moral Realism and Homeostatic Consequentialism*), philosophers' talk of intentionality can be viewed as a part of the process of reflective equilibrium brought to bear upon this folk psychology, a process now producing cognitive science, and, if I am right, capable of showing eventually the sorts of constraints to be placed upon what might be called "moral science." I do not share the optimism expressed by S. Stich 1983 in the eventual elimination of folk psychology from refined cognitive science, at least as it is understood today. But that is another story (cf., for others who also lack faith in the jettisoning of folk psychology, Horgan and Woodward 1985, Horgan and Graham 1988, and also, at least by implication, Adams 1989). I shall have more to say below [chap.5, n. 1] also about the prospects in Artificial Intelligence research for simulating what might be termed "moral intelligence," or even "intentional intelligence," in light of such views as those expressed in Dennett 1978, H. Dreyfus 1979, 1982 and J. Fodor 1983.

28. The qualifier "almost" no limit, of course, stems from the logical antinomies that show up, for example, in naïve set theory if one operates with no limits on the manner in which sets may be formed.

29. That *some* mental events or the other are occurring, as revealed by an electroencephalogram, offers little surcease if we are interested, as we often are, in either predicting, explaining, or understanding the intentional activity of persons. "A penny for your thoughts" can suitably have only an intentional response, a response that may have to be hedged in a variety of ways, as we have noticed—to be offered an EEG printout would be hopelessly inappropriate!

30. For a brief story on the history here, see Stoutland 1982.

31. His "How is weakness of the will possible?" (Reprinted in Davidson 1980) is a step in this direction, but as he points out, having an incontinent (akratic) will is not a moral matter alone. I deal with moral akrasia in chap. 5,sec. 2.

Chapter 3. Malleable Persons

1. As with concepts, so with beliefs—for beliefs may be viewed from an epistemological point of view as one way of instantiating concepts or connected sets of con-

cepts: concepts never appear in isolation but only as components of a variety of conceptual frameworks; similarly, it would appear to be impossible that there could be such a thing as *a* belief, or an isolated belief. Beliefs, in order to exist, seem to require the support of a connected set of other beliefs which together make up what I am calling a "belief system." Such belief systems range in complexity and sophistication from those of the "common man" and/or religious believer to those of the theoretical physicist, pure mathematician, theologian and philosopher, and may involve a variety of orders.

2. *Sex and Temperament in Three Primitive Societies*, 1935. Joseph Margolis 1978 has argued for the position that persons should be viewed as cultural artifacts, a position which assumes the sort of malleability under scrutiny here.

3. See below, chapter 7, the section on privacy, for further discussion.

4. The term has a variety of nuances, however: see Block 1980a and 1980b.

5. Unlike Lycan 1987, p. 37, I am not sure that I would be willing to *kill* for functionalism!

6. And, as Davidson (1970a, 116) has suggested, we could not discover even what particular beliefs an individual holds unless we have a (viable) theory of that individual's belief system. *Access* to such a system is ordinarily had by linguistic means, and in this connection Davidson 1973 has argued that this in turn requires a theory of the speaker's language. These points are connected with the notion of the indeterminacy of translation (cf. n. 17 in chapter 2).

7. To say this need not be taken to deny the fact that (some) religious groups have at times performed socially valuable functions, although often the "society" has been limited strictly to the class of members of the religious group.

8. It may be that the connection between being a scientist and being an adherent of a religious belief system is no accident, due to the fact that the belief system of science, if I might call it that, is a system requiring belief in truth of a kind independent of the idiosyncratic belief variations of its individual practioners: the kind of truth, *par excellence*, long desired by the adherents of many religious belief systems.

9. *The* universal Turing machine, is of course, a sort of mathematician's intentional object, the existence of which was established by A. M. Turing in his celebrated 1937 paper on computable functions. One of Turing's main goals in this paper was to arrive at a formulation of the concept of computability, a concept he was to define by describing a certain relatively simple theoretical machine. A group of such machines appropriately hooked together could, in principle, perform any computation—hence the notion of a universal machine. A function for which no such machine(s) could be defined would be a noncomputable function. Thus computers might be looked upon as embodied sets of Turing machines, or particular physical realizations of such machines, machines which can, in fact be realized in other physical forms as well. Turing machines, in a manner analogous to minds, might be said to have the property of malleability, although they might better be described in less restrictive functional terms.

10. The reader would be better advised to look, for example, at Block (1980, 1981), and Haugeland (1981), which together supply an excellent overview of most of the currently recognized philosophic problems to be met with in the area.

11. For the candid confessions of one such programmer, one can do no better than to look at Drew McDermott's "Artificial Intelligence meets natural stupidity" (Haugeland 1981, 143-160) who describes in the course of his confessional such programs as a once-celebrated one by G. W. Ernst and A. Newell, entitled "General Problem Solver," which by only the most extreme stretch of the imagination could ever have been such a thing. For telling evaluations of the limitations upon computer simulation of human intelligence, see Dreyfus 1979, Fodor 1983, and Searle 1980.

12. Cf. Putnam and the development of his own views about the nature of reductionism, chapter 2, n. 9. "Turing machine functionalism" was a view to the effect that the mind is constituted in a fairly literal way of Turing machines; the view seemed more plausible before the development of computer science.

13. Cf. A. Newell and H. Simon, "Computer Science as Empirical Inquiry: Symbols and Search," *Communications of the Association for Computing Machinery* 19 (1976), 113-126. [Reprinted in Haugeland 1981, 35-66.]

14. One might try for an enhanced form of Turing machine functionalism that would include the developments I refer to. But there are other troublesome matters connected with computable functions and the possible applicability of Church's thesis and Gödel's (incompleteness) theorem to minds (cf. J. R. Lucas, "Minds, Machines and Gödel," *Philosophy*, 1961, and the body of literature provoked by the paper).

15. And, if Fodor 1983 is right that the mind has "non-modular" as well as "modular" components, the sort of computational model that seems (at least implicitly) to have guided much research in AI and to have made possible some degree of success in a modular area such as vision, cannot be expected to succeed in the (nonmodular) area of thought itself. As Fodor remarks about efforts so far to capture what goes on in intelligent problem solving, "the result was an account of central processes which failed to capture precisely what is most interesting about them: their wholism, what we have been calling their Quineianism and isotropy. What emerged was a picture of the mind that looked rather embarrassingly like a Sears catalogue." (127) I would be remiss if I failed to point out that, as with many models, there can be a two-way street: it may also become commonplace to say that (suitably programmable) computers may "suffer" from "viral infections" and "worms" (cf. Dewdney 1985).

16. For an inspired account of such matters, one can do no better than to browse Hofstadter 1979.

17. Dennett (1984) 12. The case description appeared in H. Whitaker, "A case of the isolation of brain function", H. Whitaker and H. A. Whitaker, eds., *Studies in Neurolinguistics* Vol. II. New York: Academic Press.

18. Such cases, but especially those involving even more extensive brain damage of the sort found in certain types of comatose individuals and those having advanced stages of Alzheimer's disease, offer evidence more eloquent in its way than that supplied by philosophic reasoning in support of the physical or material nature of persons. (Perhaps a neurology residency of the sort undergone by medical students would be even more effective than philosophical reflection!) In this connec-

tion, it is hardly necessary to mention the effects of drugs of certain types upon mental capacities, effects which, even if only temporary, may lead us to question the personhood of those involved. In Dennett's terms, we might find ourselves, for want of knowledge of their beliefs, simply unable to take an intentional stance toward such individuals in trying to predict their behavior. The case of S. Hawking, the British theoretical physicist who has fallen victim to one of the most frightening sorts of progressively debilitating neurological disorders known, one which leaves the thinking capacity intact as various motor functions (including speech) collapse, certainly has some troublesome features. One of our fears, of course, (and his, too) is that we might too early decide that in some sense *he*, as a person, is no longer there. And there is the wonderful character, Chance Gardner, in Jerzy Kozinski's novel and movie script, *Being There* (Peter Sellers played the part in the movie), who perhaps was never there entirely as a person!

19. A historical aside: Aristotle (*Metaphysics* Gamma) referred to some such situations as involving an individual who is in effect denying the "first principle of metaphysics": s/he both affirms and denies that a certain predicate attaches to a subject.

20. Cf. Boyd 1983 and the notion of "homeostatic cluster concepts" which seem to be required in order to cope with the fact that biological species, unlike chemical elements and compounds, do not always appear in neat and tidy compartments. For more on these concepts, see below, Chap. 4, sec. 3, *Moral Theory, Solutions: Moral Realism and Homeostatic Consequentialism*.

21. It should perhaps be noted that religious belief systems themselves have on occasion incorporated certain mathematical trappings, as in the Jewish kabbalah, probably because of the hope that mathematical certainty vis-à-vis belief sorting might bolster religious certainty.

22. This is not to say that all scientists by any means have arrived at complete unanimity with regard to how it is that particular scientific beliefs should be sorted: witness the rear guard action fought for many years by Albert Einstein and David Bohm in opposition to the so-called Copenhagen interpretation of quantum physics, which was, in spite of their efforts to the contrary, destined to become the ruling interpretation. Nor is it true that there is universal agreement among philosophers of science as to the best way to characterize what goes on in successful science. The notion of "reflective equilibrium," due to Rawls 1971 and modified by Boyd 1983 in the context of an account of the reasoning processes involved in the production, regulation and refinement of beliefs in scientific theory, is perhaps one of the best concepts so far found to capture some of the detail of the mechanisms of what I have called intentional selection. I shall have more to say about it in the following chapter in connection with an attempt to develop a further modification of it in the area of moral theory, in spite of the apparent greater difficulty to be met with in the production and regulation of moral beliefs. In this connection, Geoffrey Sayre-McCord 1988b has made some interesting suggestions on the relevance of *justificatory theories* (higher order theories) to both scientific and moral theory.

23. There are some nonintentional causes here, too, but nothing to compare to what is true when one says that water = H_2O. The employment of a definite descrip-

tion, such as 'the first professional movie actor to become U.S. President', does not serve as a rigid designator in the intended sense.

24. Newell and Simon 1975 have proposed, on the basis of computer science, an empirical hypothesis dealing with the possible structural features of symbol-using physical systems, features sufficient and necessary for characterizing them as intelligent. Their hypothesis (and the revisions of it that will undoubtedly be necessary as our knowledge develops in this area) appears to be closely connected with the (materialist) views being developed here.

Chapter 4. Moral Theory

1. The notion of defeasibility employed here is due, in part, to H. L. A. Hart 1959, and means that there could well be certain conditions which, if present, would excuse A for failing to do what otherwise he/she ought morally to have done. Hart's account is actually framed in the legal language of "defeating pleas" which, like "extenuating circumstances," may be thought, if applicable, to relieve an individual of responsibility for actions performed in specifiable contexts.

2. The assumption throughout this discussion (where it has not been observed explicitly by the use of the term *voluntary*) has been that a thing's being a human *action* entails that it be intentional, in the usual dictionary sense of "intentional"—i.e., that it be something the *individual* (i.e., person) has *chosen* to do, and not just something that the body of the individual has done: a reflex action (or reaction), as a neurologist would call it, is not an intentional action in this sense.

3. Or it might even be taken as an *ontological* proposition, where (following a well-known proposal of Quine's) saying that there are moral rights and that these are equivalent to certain intentional objects commits us to saying that there are such things in reality as a certain sort of intentional objects.

4. While the moral features of moral performances are invisible in the sense suggested, as performances of *material* persons, they must be also in some sense "concrete" (nonintentional) and not "abstract" (intentional). For one presumably (although there may be legal complications here) does nothing immoral by merely *thinking* about committing an act both criminal and immoral. ("If thoughts could kill," etc.) In the law, *Mens rea* could not be said to exist in the absence of overt (i.e., actual concrete) action. (Cf. Morris 1976, "Punishment for Thoughts," who discusses the curious issue of trying to prohibit intentions by law.)

5. The notion of 'informed consent', frequently taken as an excusing factor permitting experimentation of a medical sort on human beings, has been subject to a variety of attacks. The difficulties with the notion are due, I would argue, to the fact that it is, of course, an intentional concept itself, entailing that those supplying it have both suitably developed intentional capacities and the relevant knowledge.

6. Cf. Quine 1960, chapter 2, and the troubles with 'gavagai'. Quine, of course, does not *want* to buy the intentional circle; whether he succeeds in his *intention* to avoid it is a matter of disputation.

7. A categorical imperative, so-called, is an unconditional command—rather than a

hypothetical, or conditional one. Perhaps the best known of Kant's versions of his imperative is one to roughly the following effect: 'So act that you treat everyone, including yourself, as an end, and never as mere means to some end.'

8. At least *so far*, even if one were a diehard Stichean who persisted in expressing the view that intentional talk be expurgated from proper cognitive science. There is, it is to be remembered, another view—cf. Horgan and Woodward 1985.

9. Boyd borrows the notion of a "cluster" concept from work in ordinary language philosophy which suggests that there are concepts whose definitions cannot be pinned down in terms of a simple set of necessary and sufficient conditions. The "homeostatic" feature is an attempt to capture the fact that such concepts have the property that several things working together are required to define them. He supplies as a familiar example of a scientific homeostatic cluster concept that of a biological species; the property, 'x is healthy,' and the relation, 'x is healthier than y' are other examples.

10. There are philosophers who view the prospects for the development of the kind of moral knowledge called for by moral realism as very dim indeed. Bernard Williams 1985 voices such a view in the form of a kind of reasoned skepticism about the possibility of answering the fundamental question of ethics, which he attributes to Socrates, "What kind of life is worth living?" in any way which would have the sort of universality we have alluded to here. Gilbert Harman has also for some years expressed skepticism about the prospects for moral realism, as have J. L. Mackie and a number of others. Sayre-McCord 1988 is the best single place to find discussions, both for and against, of moral realism.

11. "Folk" moral psychology, of course, in employing this language, does make substantive claims in the way of explaining and predicting human behavior. Philosophical investigation of the notion of intentionality may, I think, be viewed as a part of the development of this psychology, some of which has been underway in the field of cognitive psychology. Moral philosophy might be seen as another way of developing this same psychology, if one were to accept both moral realism and the instantiation of it I am proposing here.

12. An approach different from my own has been taken by Carl Wellman: see below, chap. 7, sec. 1.

Chapter 5. Moral Persons: I

1. It has become customary for philosophers to make disclaimers to the effect that their observations are intended to be so comprehensive as to cover all contingencies—in this case all possible beings, nonhuman-terrestrial, extraterrestrial, Supreme, etc.—but I am not that sanguine. Suffice it to say that by speaking of 'schemata', and in line with my stance as a functionalist, I leave it open as to what sorts of objects might exemplify or instantiate a schema (and I think I am not being unduly meretricious in saying this). There seems to be little ground for optimism, for example, about the prospects in AI research for computer program instantiations of either the person schema or the moral person schema I am about to

sketch (there are severe and apparently insurmountable problems connected with the so-called problem of "background" knowledge, at least as argued by Dreyfus 1979, as well as with the matter of capturing the nature of higher order (original) intentionality, as asserted by Haugeland 1981), and so I really have in mind the rather more prosaic purpose of beginning to describe the features of the subclass of human beings who prove to be successful in being able to manifest the characteristics of moral persons. I shall leave it to the theologians to determine whether my asseverations are either applicable to, or illuminating of, the nature of the Deity qua person; to the defenders of animal rights as to whether the nature of nonhuman animals is thereby clarified (since I know they will do this anyway); extraterrestrials will have to fend for themselves.

2. I think it likely that E. O. Wilson's (1975) speculations in regard to sociobiology, if they should turn out to be true in some sense, will require theory of a sort different from any we now possess (Cf. his *Sociobiology: The New Synthesis*, Cambridge, Massachusetts: Harvard University Press. But also, for a criticism of this view, P. Kitcher's (1985) *Vaulting Ambition*, Cambridge, Massachusetts: MIT Press.)

3. Cf. Ronald De Sousa's (1984) remarks, which suggest that the construction of even natural kinds need not be subject to rigid requirements.

4. Cf. Harman 1986 for an approach to the business of sorting out what is logically required in change of belief. He proposes that change of belief be associated with theoretical reason, change of intention with practical reason, using the latter terms in a relatively traditional sense.

5. My proposal is indebted, in part, to some suggestions put forward by Jeffrey Reiman 1976, about which I shall have more to say in the chapter to follow, chap. 7, sec. 2.

6. I understand by 'caring' in this context the (higher order intentional) capacity for a sensitivity to the belief of someone else that his/her intentional capacities are being interfered with in some way—whether or not this belief is justified need make no difference to the effects of the belief upon its holder. While children might more often be in the position of having unjustified beliefs, it is no less true that adults frequently find themselves in this position. Adults, unlike children, have the capacity for higher order beliefs and beliefs about their own intentional capacities; it certainly may happen that without the assistance of a sensitive, caring person, their lives might be thought by them to be not worth the living. S. Ruddick 1985, interestingly enough, defines the notion of moral benefit in such a way that it involves caring in a higher order intentional sense, although she does not use this terminology.

7. Cf. Gilligan 1982. While it might be true that women, for a variety of reasons, have deserved more recognition than they have usually received for having the capacity for caring, which has always been associated with the skills needed for child-rearing, it would appear unlikely that men, while arguably being *culturally* deprived, are *genetically* incapable of the capacity. This surmise could be falsified, of course, by advances in the genetics of intentionality: it is perhaps possible that there is some structure, such as a sex-correlated gene for caring.

8. "Each person has the [second order] right to expect all other persons to treat
   him/her in accordance with the principle that no person should be treated differ-
   ently (morally) from all other persons (unless there is some general and relevant
   reason justifying different treatment)." Wasserstrom 1964. It is interesting to note
   that there is an explicit reference to the *intentional* notion of expectation as a
   feature of the right. Here the expectation is of a second order sort, since if our
   proposed way of describing rights as expectations is accepted, it is an expectation
   about the expectations of others. It must be admitted that a second order right, as
   thus characterized, is subject to the kinds of criticisms raised by Williams 1976,
   1985, and Melden 1977 with regard to its high abstractness. The capacity for
   caring just referred to reflects the sort of thing that is needed to flesh out a more
   concrete feel for the condition of actual persons: as Williams has suggested, one's
   moral decision might appropriately be altered in light of one's position as a care-
   provider—as, say, to a member of one's own family (cf. n. 20).

9. The notion of an open concept is often attributed to Wittgenstein, who argued
   that there are many concepts which cannot be defined by supplying a list of conditions that will be exhaustively sufficient and necessary. The belief that concepts
   must be defined in this way seems to be correct enough in a field like mathematics
   (or in formal logic), but need not hold true in other areas. One of Wittgenstein's
   favorite examples of an open concept was the concept of a game (*Philosophical
   Investigations*, sections 66-71): his claim was that there is no finite list of conditions that would be sufficient and necessary to categorize a thing as a game. One,
   at best, can supply only a "family" (or "cluster" in the sense in which Boyd uses
   this term, see above, chap. 4, sec. 3) of features, which in some way function as
   a definition.

10. Rosenberg 1983 suggests that we think of ourselves—at least in our "received"
    morality—as speaking of human beings in terms of the notion of an "ethical kind,"
    which is to be viewed as a "bestowed kind." This is a way of taking a conven-
    tionalist as opposed to a realist approach, and certainly is capable of reflecting the
    fact that there is a social practice in accordance with which a variety of kinds may
    be bestowed in an oftentimes quite capricious manner: one of Rosenberg's nicer
    examples is that of the Roman emperor, Caligula, who decreed that his horse was
    a Roman citizen. I prefer to think that ethical kinds ought to have *some* basis in
    reality for their bestowal. For more on Rosenberg's views, see below, chap. 6, the
    section, *Moral Persons and Death*.

11. This curious "thick and thin" vocabulary, and the concepts associated with it, are
    found in Williams 1985, where he urges that moral philosophy (as it has been
    articulated by most philosophers) is incapable of dealing with, for example, such
    thick concepts as promises, courage, and brutality (this is part of a theme upon
    which he has been elaborating since at least Williams 1976). Melden (1977 120)
    also refers to the need to have such concrete, as opposed to abstract, knowledge
    of persons.

12. Cf. McCloskey 1979 for a comprehensive yet succinct setting out of the variety of
    things that have been understood to be human rights. He suggests that one of the

most powerful arguments is based upon "man's capacity to be a moral agent, a moral person," a capacity "self-evidently conferring" the right to be such. (At Wasserstrom 1985, 501)

13. David Pears 1984, p. 38, urges, instead, "lack of control," since Aristotle pointed out that weakness of will is only one explanation for such lack of control.

14. Book II, chap. 27, *Essay Concerning Human Understanding*.

15. In symbols, $(x)(y)(F)[(Fx \equiv Fy) \supset (x=y)]$. Translated: *For any individuals x and y and any property F, if x and y have (lack) every property in common, then they are identical.*

16. In symbols, $(x)(y)(F)[(x=y) \supset (Fx \equiv Fy)]$. Translated:*For any individuals x and y and any property F, x and y are identical only if they have (lack) every property in common.* There is also an additional principle, sometimes alluded to as "The Principle of Leibniz," which represents the outcome of accepting *both* the Identity of Indiscernibles and the Indiscernibility of Identicals: $(x)(y)(F)[(x=y) \equiv (Fx \equiv Fy)]$, which may be read, *For any individuals x and y and any property F, x and y are identical if, and only if, they have (lack) every property in common.* This is the strongest requirement one may place on the identity relation, and is generally assumed to hold for the sort of identity that obtains, say, between numbers.

17. Perry 1976, 81.

18. There is perhaps little to prevent immaterial-substance enthusiasts from *trying* to transfer our entire account of the features of a certain class of intentional systems to their account of souls. Souls, it might be argued, are, or are functionally equivalent to, higher order intentional systems. Aside from the problem with identity conditions for disembodied souls posed by Shoemaker and Quinton, there would be problems of an insurmountable sort to be met with because of the role to be played by verbal communication (which requires embodiment) in both identifying and reidentifying moral persons, as I shall shortly argue. Rosenberg 1983 has argued for the impossibility of there being *any* coherent dualistic theory of the sort that would attempt to make sense of souls as ontologically distinct from bodies.

19. Kant's well-known proposal that total success in such attempts (which he said is not possible in the present world) supplies an argument for immortality, is a curious one. We shall have more to say about this sort of proposal in the section on possible worlds below (chap. 6, sec. 1).

20. Cf. Boer and Lycan 1986, who for this reason cite Williams along with others as "personalists." (Cf. also n. 8.)

21. The possibility of a shift, in different situations, from a utilitarian to a nonutilitarian assessment, as we have noted, need not reflect a crucial alteration of beliefs, expectations, etc. Problems would be posed, however, if we were confronted with someone whose beliefs in this regard were vacillating with respect to one and the same situation, for this might raise questions about the rationality of such an individual; or if vacillation were a regular part of the individual's manner of arriving at practical conclusions of a moral sort, about her/his moral character.

22. Hill notes—although he does not use our terminology— that there is a sense in which servility entails a kind of *higher order* disrespect: not only does the servile

individual fail to respect him/herself as a person, but s/he in effect has disrespect for moral law.

Chapter 6. Moral Persons: II

1. By 'complete akrasia' I mean that an individual suffering from this condition *never* would be able to engage in successful practical reasoning (by 'successful practical reasoning' we refer to reasoning resulting in action, whether or not the reasoning itself is correct in some suitable sense) of the sort we would describe by saying that s/he acted in accordance with his/her best judgment.

2. Robert Veatch 1976 deals mainly with death-related issues as they impinge upon our health care, legal, and policy-making systems, and has relatively little to say about the nature of persons, although he is concerned to give attention he thinks long overdue to "the patient's point of view." Douglas Walton 1979, while giving more attention to philosophic matters than Veatch, is still concerned, in large part, with medical ethics, and acknowledges that he has neglected the nature of personhood.

3. 'Syntropic' is a word coined by Rosenberg to refer to the set of characteristics that are commonly taken to distinguish living from nonliving (as he proposes to call them, 'entropic') things; these characteristics include such features as being able, by assimilating materials from the environment, to continue the process of metabolism and so maintain certain structures and a certain identity. 'Entropic' things, in contrast, do not maintain their structures, and are subject to disintegration over time and to loss of identity.

4. It might be recalled that we left the question open as to the matter of "reducing" intentional kinds to natural kinds, in the sense that while there seems no immediate prospect for making such a reduction, there might one day appear a sufficiently sophisticated form of materialism that would make this possible. Such a prospect is perhaps not consistent with the adoption of something like Davidson's (1970) anomalous monism or the view developed in Adams 1989, both of which seem to imply that explanations and predictions of higher order intentional behavior must forever escape assimilation to any standard patterns of scientific prediction.

5. Such withdrawal of status runs afoul, of course, of the claim (made in "our implicit moral theory") that all biological humans are persons (with no restrictions); I do not think that Rosenberg would want to say that such withdrawal occurs only if a (biological) species change takes place!

6. In re Conroy, 98 N.J. 321, 486 A.2d 1209 (1985).

7. In re Quinlan, 70 N.J. 10, 355 A.2d 64t, *cert. denied sub. nom.*, Garger v. New Jersey, 429 U.S. 922 (1976).

8. A committee of the American Medical Association did go on record in the Spring of 1986 in effect endorsing the 1985 New Jersey Supreme Court decision in Conroy, but unanimity of the members of the organization is another thing entirely. In the late Fall of 1986, a public opinion poll indicated that a large percentage of the public also in effect endorsed the decision. And the practice even in some local hospitals seems also to be coming around to the same point.

9. The main so-called indirect arguments against mercy-killing, are I think, more difficult to maintain (so long as it is assumed that mercy-killing is not morally obligatory), with the theory of persons as malleable higher order intentional systems. The argument re the possibility of a mistaken diagnosis of destroyed higher order intentional capacity remains, of course, and there would have to be left open a reasonably wide margin for error. The "slippery-slope" argument according to which the making of mercy-killing morally permissible will shortly and inevitably lead to something like genocide is one I have never found very persuasive, for it assumes somehow that the very persons who have developed a way of making a moral case for the *permissibility* of mercy-killing will, *because of this*, go on to adopt an agenda for political or social action that would itself be immoral by making mercy-killing *obligatory*. I think many of those who have been upset by Callahan 1987, in his controversial *Setting Limits*, have failed to grasp this distinction.

10. This was one of the main considerations motivating Woozley 1977 in relation to the Quinlan case, a consideration which may now be seen as a consequence of our characterization of moral personhood.

11. It perhaps goes almost without saying that there are suicides that are irrational or nonrational, and that the possibility of such suicides is a primary reason for supporting the relevance of a particular form of paternalism. Literal paternalism might be said to be clearly called for in case of the attempted suicide of a nonrational individual, such as a child. Nonliteral paternalism seems equally appropriate in the case of the attempted suicide of an individual having fully developed higher order intentional capacities but who for a variety of reasons suffers from an impairment of belief malleability. There is long historical precedent of suicide for those whose belief malleability is temporarily impaired by a variety of frustrated expectations, as in the classical case of the rejected lover. A more recent phenomenon has made its apppearance in the form of women who as athletes aspiring for perfection have pushed their expectations with regard to their own accomplishments beyond a realistic point. In such cases by "impairment of belief malleability" we understand an inability to entertain alternative beliefs with regard to the future course of one's own life.

12. While we omit here a characterization of the death of individuals who have not developed into full higher order intentional sytems, e.g., children, an account which would go in a similar way to the one given, we might point out that the relevant moral issues would connect with our first class of (enabling) needs (see above, chap. 5, sec. 1).

13. Among other theoretical possibilities, one might include such things as complete akrasia or irreversible servility—see the sections above on akrasia and on servility, and the section on moral persons and possible worlds.

14. For some interesting speculations in this connection, cf. Nagel 1974, "What is it like to be a bat?"

15. And perhaps to nonliving things as well: cf. Regan 1983 and P. Taylor 1986, who speak of the "good" of individuals having "inherent worth," whether or not the individual is a person. Such talk might lead one to talk also of "quality of existence" in addition to quality of life.

16. On 9 September 1988 there was a news item regarding a German animal rights group objecting to the practice of catching fish with hooks and returning them to the water: in their view, the fish do experience distress in the process.

17. I do not qualify 'professional movie actor' with *human*, for the sense in which a nonhuman—dog, chimpanzee, or whatever— deserves to be referred to as a 'professional movie actor' is, I think, at best metaphorical.

18. Cf. Ruth Garrett Millikan (1987), who proposes that one can usefully describe intentional systems as consumers of representations without having to know the details of their construction, encoding, and retrieval.

19. As we noticed above, on Harry Frankfurt's proposal, the essential nature of human freedom seems to be associated with such higher order desiring. As he has suggested, one certainly could characterize the quality of life of those he calls "wantons": animals capable of first order, but not of higher order, desires.

Chapter 7. Moral Persons, Rights, and Law

1. Cf. R. M. Hare 1975, who also inveighed against loose talk about rights, although without much hope that tight talk would be forthcoming.

2. As other exceptions, I should mention also the careful work of McCloskey 1979, 1983 ; Regan 1983; Taylor 1986.

3. *Fundamental Legal Conceptions*. New Haven: Yale University Press, 1919.

4. Unless otherwise indicated, all references to Wellman are to Wellman 1985.

5. Wellman recognizes that there is, in ordinary usage, an employment of 'right' in this way; but his primary aim is to develop a more carefully refined way of employing 'right' in connection with talk of legal, institutional, and moral rights.

6. He argued for the moral objectivity thesis in an earlier book: cf. Wellman 1971.

7. For an articulate defense of an opposing thesis, see Mackie 1977.

8. It should be clear enough that I share Wellman's belief that the norms of what he calls "morals" would not be so subject to change, but would remain invariant over newly discovered ways of acting in a morally good or morally evil fashion.

9. Cf., for example, Hare 1975, who speaks of "Level I" and "Level II" moral thinking, to the same effect.

10. Here we might note in passing that Wellman has recourse to a particular application of the notion of *intentional causation* reasons, as intentional things, may be said under certain circumstances to be causes of actions.

11. While I shall make more of this shortly, I do think it useful to point out here that the "intention" referred to in this quotation, whether actual or imputed, is, of course, a *higher order intention*.

12. Picnics, incidentally, are one of the curious ways persons have developed for subjecting themselves to the possibility of a range of uncivilized physical discomforts; they are intentional performances having no counterpart in the behavior of nonhuman animals!

13. These features, it should be noticed, are both (higher order) intentional in nature, as is the notion of a norm itself. To propose that an individual's actions can be

explained by saying that he/she was acting in accordance with a norm is to give an intentional explanation of those actions.

14. It is possible, of course, and this cannot be denied, that *beliefs* about such norms might have not only intentional effects, but nonintentional (i.e., physical) effects, too, via the biofeedback produced by the ubiquitous "power of suggestion." Voodoo and witchcraft survive for this reason. And, of course, the U. S. Constitutional protection (via the First Amendment) afforded religious beliefs and practices has been interpreted to allow adult individuals, on religious grounds, legally to do things that would even result in their own deaths under certain conditions.

15. My view is in agreement with that of Paul Taylor 1986 vis-à-vis the attribution of moral rights to nonhuman animals. Taylor argues that only *legal* rights may be attributed to nonhumans (whether living or not). In my opinion, if one is referring to law in the normative sense discussed below (appendix), there is here, too, a metaphorical use of 'legal rights.'

16. One of the best single sources, with its included bibliographies, is Schoeman (1984a).

17. The word *privacy* is by no means limited to legal and moral contexts: anthropologists and sociologists also make use of it, along with other terms, such as *social distance* (or *psychological distance*): cf. Murphy 1964 and Westin 1967. Whether, and in what sense, there might be a "cross-cultural" form of privacy (or whether the meaning of privacy is strictly relative to a culture) is subject to the disputes familiar in these fields.

18. Fried 1968, Reiman 1976, Wasserstrom 1979b.

19. Prosser's views were incorporated in the *Restatement (Second) of Torts* section 652A (1976), American Law Institute. Privacy as an *explicit* constitutionally protected right, as Richard Wasserstrom observes (at Wasserstrom 1979b, 392), did not make its appearance until *Griswold v. State of Connecticut* 381 U. S. 479, 85 S.Ct. 1678 (1965).

20. Prosser argued for four distinct torts as basic: intrusion upon seclusion or solitude, public disclosure, "false light" in the public eye, and appropriation of name or likeness, which as species of invasion constituted the "law of privacy" (at Schoeman 1984, 107).

21. In which Thomson argued that the right to privacy is parasitical upon the right to property and the rights a person has over his own person (she did not say here precisely what constitutes a person, as she did not in her very widely read piece on abortion (Thomson 1971), where she assumed for the sake of argument that the human fetus, even at its earliest stages, was a person. This assumption, of course, she made clear in the last sentence of the article, was made only for the sake of the argument at hand).

22. Op.cit. at Schoeman 1984, especially pp. 373 ff., the section of her paper III.A. "The poverty of reductionism."

23. Schoeman 1984, pp. 26 ff., argues that those who hold that there is no such thing as a distinctive moral category of privacy should also be described as "skeptics," and includes not only the views expressed in Thomson 1975, but those in Posner 1978a, 1978b, and some of those in Wasserstrom 1979b. Apparently what Schoe-

man is trying to allude to by using the term in this context is the view that there could be in some possible world a kind of person for whose existence privacy (in some form) is not either a sufficient or a necessary condition. Such a view seems to be supported in part by the fact that in our world there are forms of privacy that turn out to be thought reprehensible: e.g., the exercise—by the presumptively guilty—of the privilege granted by the Fifth Amendment; or the privacy required by criminals generally to insure the successful outcome of their plans; or the condition of individuals who suffer from various forms of mental illness because they are keeping certain matters entirely to themselves.

24. I should mention also the article by Stanley Benn 1971, which deals with the concept of privacy and connects it with what he calls "the principle of respect for persons." As Benn says, "to *respect* someone as a person is to concede that one ought to take account of the way in which his enterprise might be affected by one's own decisions. By the principle of respect for persons, then, I mean the principle that every human being, insofar as he is qualified as a person, is entitled to this minimal degree of consideration." (at Schoeman 1984, 229). Benn does not say, however, what it is that he means by the expression, "insofar as he is *qualified as a person*" (emphasis mine). This, in my opinion, is a major defect in a discussion that is otherwise quite nicely put together; we surely need to know *which* human beings are to be qualified as persons, in order to know how we are to apply Benn's principle of respect for persons. Benn seems to imply, at any rate, that it is possible that not all human beings are persons.

25. Wasserstrom 1979, 387.

26. Ibid., 388.

27. "On the characteristics of total institutions," *Asylum.* New York.

28. Wasserstrom 1979, 391. Reiman's paper was, as a matter of fact, written in response to Thomson 1975, and he felt he was entitled, in rebuttal to Thomson, to conclude that the right to privacy, defined as he proposed it, was itself the basis for the rights to person and property Thomson had argued were the basis for the right to privacy (see n. 21). Thus, in his opinion, Thomson's reductionist thesis was refuted.

29. Wasserstrom 1979, 397.

30. Wasserstrom 1979, 398.

31. Wasserstrom, in speculating about possible ways of altering the process of socialization, joins an enterprise going back at least as far as Plato's *Republic* (which did, incidentally, have some theoretical foundation, at least in Plato's own mind) and is still going strong—as in Skinner's *Walden II* (also supplied with a theoretical basis in Skinner's own form of behaviorism). And there certainly have been those who have not been satisfied with mere speculation, but who have tried to alter, in actual societies, the process of socialization, e.g., via such programs as the Russian state nursery, the Hitler Youth, the Boy Scouts of America, etc. But Wasserstrom presumably means that we do not have the sort of theory that we need in order to evaluate such programs.

32. By "intrusively coercive circumstances" I understand the use of drugs (i.e., "truth

serum"), lie detectors, or torture; proceedings involving the Fifth Amendment are certainly coercive from an intentional point view, but they are not intrusively so.

33. One of the sources of our uneasiness with the Fifth Amendment is due, surely, to the fact that the context in which it is likely to play a rôle will be one involving a conflict of the rights and interests of at least two and possibly several persons. One would not, presumably, even be in the position where one might find it appropriate to exercise the Fifth Amendment privilege unless the rights of some other person(s) were also at stake, and part of the very rationale for having the machinery of the law is precisely to effect a compromise between such conflicting rights, a compromise which frequently requires that all of the parties involved give up certain rights. Thus I, in order to prevent someone else from being falsely accused (so I believe), might choose to give testimony which I believe to be damaging to my intentional capacities and/or my role in a society of like individuals. Another facet of the problem is that the law itself may be usefully construed as a kind of intentional object, an intentional object connected with a framework of concepts many of them of the open sort, which makes the sorting of legal beliefs especially troublesome. But I shall have more to say about this in the appendix, *Some Possible Connections between Law and Morality*.

34. And as to the difficulty involved in figuring out how this might best be done even in theory, one need only think of the efforts of Robert Nozick 1974.

Chapter 7 Appendix

1. Unfortunately, there seems to be no noncircumlocutory way in standard English of conveying the distinction between idealized and actual concepts. Cf. the section *Legal Rights and Moral Rights: Wellman's Theory of Rights*. Wellman by stipulation employs the term *morals* to refer to the idealized, noninstitutional, objective notion; similarly he uses *moralities* to refer to the local, conventional, positive, or received notion found in a particular historical society; but this stipulation is by no means shared by all moral philosophers.

2. To those familiar with mathematical logic, the propositions in I-III would, properly notated, be the "universal closures" of the expressions actually given. For example, IIIA. would be *For all x, x is . . . from a moral right*.

3. It should be noted that how one comes in practice to know that an individual action (/inaction) actually is of a certain (legal) type requires the operation of a good bit of legal machinery: for example, whether Smedley, in doing what he did to bring about Snarf's death, *murdered* him, need not be at all a clear-cut or an easily determined matter, depending as it does upon various types of evidence, including evidence of Smedley's intent and/or his state of mind at the relevant time, as well as whether Snarf was, at the time of his death, a *legal person*. Cf. in this connection especially, a series of precedent-setting decisions by the New Jersey Supreme Court: Quinlan 1976, Conroy 1985, and three handed down in June, 1987. All deal with what is legally allowable in the case of individuals about whom there appear to be significant doubts as to the (legal) grounds for supposing that

they should continue to be entitled to be treated as legal persons in the fullest sense. The latest rulings affirm in strong terms the right of the individual in regard to the refusal of medical treatment designed to maintain a life of severely diminished quality for the one who has it—or who may no longer be surviving as a person to have it (cf. chap. 6, the sections *Moral Persons and Death* and *Moral Persons and Quality of Life*).

4. Cf. the theoretical efforts to characterize what constitutes an injury under law, Harrison 1970; or alternately, a harm, Woozley 1977.

5. Cf. Vlastos 1962, who proposes to simplify talk of human rights by reducing all such rights to just two: the rights to well-being (physical and psychological) and freedom.

6. An account of what it is, in any detail, that goes into making a law a just law, is clearly beyond the scope of this essay. The contemporary standard for a place to start is, of course, Rawls 1971; but for the apparent inevitability of structural injustice (as opposed to Rawls' procedural injustice) in the actual formulation of law (even of constitutional law), cf. Harrison 1971. The hope is, naturally, that Rawlsian reflective equilibrium will insure that defective jurisprudential conceptualization will be constantly displaced over time by improved formulations.

7. This is true, I submit, whatever particular account of rights one chooses: Wellman's story on rights, which requires their construction out of Hohfeldian elements, is, as we have urged, no exception.

8. Cf. H. L. A. Hart's comments (*The Listener*, 30 July 1959) upon the lecture by Devlin that eventually appeared as Devlin 1965. Hart calls attention, in the manner of a moral philosopher, to the importance of being sure that what the "public" find "morally outrageous" *really is* morally outrageous.

9. Individuals who are not deterred by the threat of the enforcement of law might plausibly be viewed as not capable of performing as malleable higher order intentional systems, either temporarily or permanently. Cf. also the next note.

10. In terms of our characterization of personhood, there presumably would be some sort of *failure* of intentional selection on the part of the individual who is in actuality undeterred by the threat of punishment. Since punishment is itself an ineliminably intentional thing, such a failure would most likely be connected with at least a temporary lapse in higher order intentional capacity. (Is it this sort of lapse that led Dennett 1976 to conclude that in such a circumstance one has a legitimate doubt as to whether such an individual is indeed a person?) Much more needs to be said, of course, than there is space for here, about the nature of punishment. There seems to be merit, for example, in the opinion of Wasserstrom 1980 that attempts, such as those of Morris 1968, to show that punishment is best thought of as a mechanism for restoring benefits unfairly usurped by the individual being punished, do not succeed in capturing the fact that there are cases where this is simply not true. Wasserstrom's own view is that in all cases of punishment there is a kind of deprivation, and that deprivations are, almost by definition, a kind of evil. Again, I think more needs to be done with the notion of the *threat* of deprivation, which is an intentional thing. The curious notion of Morris's that punishment might also be thought of as a right has something going for it, I think,

especially when one is discussing punishment as an alternative to "treatment": here, even on Wasserstrom's terms, the deprivation produced by treatment could be much more serious than that produced by punishment.

11. Cf. Feinberg 1984, vol. 4.

Chapter 8. Not Quite Back to Square One: Reconsiderations

1. I recognize the peculiarity involved in saying that "I might arrange nonintentional things." I think there need be no difficulty here so long as one acknowledges that there will be of necessity two different kinds of explanation for why those particular nonintentional things occur *when* they do. For example, there is an explanatory difference between Smedley's death by accidental drowning and his death by my holding his head under water for the purpose of killing him. The morally troublesome issues revolving around 'killing' vs. 'allowing to die' (as discussed by J. Rachels and many others) are intentional issues, or as we earlier characterized them, issues that are ineliminably intentional.

2. Aristotle's reference to 'risibility' as a distinguishing feature of the rational featherless biped was, we can be sure, a reference to a higher order feature. Other animals are apparently incapable of cracking jokes: the hyena's laughter is incommensurable with the human's.

3. Being in this condition need not entail that one is servile.

4. These persons might, of course, suffer from akrasia.

BIBLIOGRAPHY

Adams, E. M. (1982). "Persons and morality," *Philosophy and Phenomenological Research* 42, 384-390.

Adams, E. M. (1985). "The *Concept* of a Person," *The Southern Journal of Philosophy* XXII, no. 4, 403-412.

Adams, E. M. (1989). *Persons and the Social World*. MS. (Forthcoming: Temple University Press.

Armstrong, D. M. (1968). *A Materialist Theory of Mind*. London: Routledge and Kegan Paul.

Baier, Annette (1982). "Caring about caring: a reply to Frankfurt." *Synthese* 53, 273-290.

Baier, Annette (1984a). "What do women want in a moral theory?" *Nous* , 53-63 (with a missing section supplied in typescript by the author).

Baier, Annette (1984b), "Trust," University of North Carolina Philosophy Colloquium, Chapel Hill.

Baier, Annette (1985a). *Postures of the Mind*. Minneapolis: University of Minnesota Press.

Baier, Annette (1985b). "Hume, the women's moral theorist?." typescript.

Beauchamp, Tom, and LeRoy Walters (1982). *Contemporary Issues in Bioethics*, 2nd ed. Belmont, California: Wadsworth.

Benn, Stanley (1971). "Privacy, freedom, and respect for persons." Schoeman 1984, 223-244.

Berger, Fred (1977). "Pornography, sex, and censorship.," *Social Theory and Practice* 4. (Wasserstrom 1979, 337-358)

Block, Ned (1980). *Readings in Philosophy of Psychology*, vol.I. Cambridge, Massachusetts: Harvard University Press.

Block, Ned (1980a). "Introduction: What is functionalism?" Block 1980, 171-184.

Block, Ned (1980b). "Troubles with functionalism." Block 1980, 268-305.

Block, Ned (1981). *Readings in Philosophy of Psychology*, vol. II. Cambridge, Massachusetts: Harvard University Press.

Bloustein, Edward (1964). "Privacy as an aspect of human dignity: an answer to Dean Prosser." *New York University Law Review* 39, 962-1007. (Reprinted in Schoeman 1984, 156-202).

Boer, Steven E., and William G. Lycan (1986). *Knowing Who*. Cambridge, Massachusetts: MIT Press.

Boyd, Richard (1980). "Materialism without reductionism: What physicalism does not entail." Block 1980, 67-106.

Boyd, Richard (1983). "How to be a moral realist." University of North Carolina, Chapel Hill, Philosophy Colloquium, October. Published in Sayre-McCord 1988a.

Boyd, Richard (1984). "The current status of scientific realism." Leplin 1984, 41-82.

Brandt, Richard (1983). "The concept of a moral right and its function." *Journal of Philosophy*, 29-45.

Callahan, Daniel (1987). *Setting Limits*. New York: Simon and Schuster.

Carey, Susan (1985). *Conceptual Change in Childhood*. Cambridge, Massachusetts: MIT/Bradford Press.

Childress, James F.(1982). *Who Should Decide: Paternalism in Health Care*. New York: Oxford University Press.

Chisholm, Roderick (1957). *Perceiving*. Ithaca: Cornell University Press.

Chisholm, Roderick (1976). *Person and Object*. La Salle, Illinois: Open Court Publishing Co.

Chisholm, Roderick (1977). "Coming into being and passing away: can the metaphysician help?" Spicker and Engelhardt (1977), 169-182.

Chomsky, N. (1959). Review of B.F.Skinner's *Verbal Behavior. Language* 35, no.1, 26-58. (Reprinted in Block 1980, 48-63).

Chomsky, N. (1975). "On cognitive capacity." Chapter 1 of *Reflections on Language.* New York: Pantheon Books. (Reprinted in Block 1981, 305-323).

Churchland, Paul (1984). *Matter and Consciousness.* Cambridge, Massachusetts: Bradford/MIT Press.

Daniels, Norman (1987). "Justice and health care." Chapter 8 in *Health Care Ethics: An Introduction,* ed. Donald VanDe Veer and Tom Regan. Philadelphia: Temple University Press.

Daniels, Norman (1988). *Am I My Parents' Keeper?: An Essay on Justice Between the Young and the Old.* New York: Oxford University Press.

Davidson, Donald (1970a). "Mental events." Foster and Swanson 1970, 79-101. (Reprinted in Block 1980, 107-119).

Davidson, Donald (1970b). "How is weakness of will possible?" In Davidson 1980.

Davidson, Donald (1973). "The material mind." *Logic, Methodology and Philosophy of Science IV,* ed. Patrick Suppes, et al. (Reprinted in Haugeland 1981, 339-354.)

Davidson, Donald (1980). *Essays on Actions and Events.* New York: Oxford University Press.

Davidson, Donald (1984). *Inquiries into Truth and Interpretation.* New York: Oxford University Press.

Dennett, Daniel (1976). "Conditions of Personhood." Rorty 1976, 175-196. (Reprinted in Dennett 1978, 267-285.)

Dennett, Daniel (1978). *Brainstorms.* Cambridge, Massachusetts: Bradford/ MIT Press.

Dennett, Daniel (1982a). "Beyond belief." Andrew Woodfield, ed., *Thought and Object.* Oxford: Clarendon Press.

Dennett, Daniel (1982b). "How to study consciousness empirically: or nothing comes to mind." *Synthese* 53, 159-180.

Dennett, Daniel (1984). *Elbow Room: The Varieties of Freedom Worth Having*. Cambridge, Massachusetts: Bradford/MIT Press.

Dennett, Daniel (1987). *The Intentional Stance*. Cambridge, Massachusetts: Bradford/ MIT Press.

De Sousa, Ronald (1984). "Teleology and the great shift." *Journal of Philosophy* 81, 647-653.

Devlin, Lord Patrick (1965). *The Enforcement of Morals*. Oxford: Oxford University Press.

Dewdney, A. K. (1985). Computer Recreations, *Scientific American*, March 14-23.

Dreyfus, H. (1979). *What Computers Can't Do: The Limits of Artificial Intelligence*, revised edition. New York: Harper & Row.

Dreyfus, H., ed., in collaboration with Harrison Hall (1982). *Husserl, Intentionality and Cognitive Science*. Cambridge, Massachusetts: Bradford/ MIT Press.

Engelbretsen, George (1984). *Speaking of Persons*. Toronto: The Canadian Association for Publishing in Philosophy.

Engelhardt, Tristram (1982). "Medicine and the concept of a person." Beauchamp and Walters 1982, 93-101.

English, Jane (1975). "Abortion and the concept of a person." *Canadian Journal of Philosophy* V, 233-243.

Feinberg, Joel (1982). "The problem of personhood." Beauchamp and Walters 1982, 108-115.

Feinberg, Joel (1984-88). Four Volumes: (I) *Harm to Others*; (II) *Offense to Others*; (III) *Harm to Self*; (IV) *Harmless Wrongdoing*. New York Oxford: Oxford University Press.

Feldman, Fred (1983). "Obligations—absolute, conditioned, and conditional." *Philosophia* 12, 257-272.

Feldman, Fred (1985). "Foundations of Utilitarianism," chapters 1 and 2, Book MS.

Fine, Arthur (1984). "The natural ontological attitude." Leplin 1984, 83-107.

Floistad, G., ed.(1982), (1983). *Contemporary Philosophy: A New Survey*, vols. 3 and 4. The Hague: Nijhoff.

Fodor, Jerry (1980). "Methodological solipsism considered as a research strategy in cognitive psychology." *The Behaviorial and Brain Sciences* 3, 63-73. Cambridge: Cambridge University Press.

Fodor, Jerry (1983). *Modularity of Mind*. Cambridge, Massachusetts: Bradford/ MIT Press.

Fodor, Jerry (1985), "Fodor's guide to mental representation: the intelligent auntie's Vade-mecum." *Mind* XCIV, 76-100.

Fodor, Jerry (1987). *Psychosemantics: The Problem of Meaning in the Philosophy of Mind*. Cambridge, Massachusetts: MIT Press.

Foster, Lawrence, and J. W. Swanson, eds. (1970). *Experience and Theory*. Amherst: University of Massachusetts Press.

Frankfurt, Harry (1971). "Freedom of the will and the concept of a person." *Journal of Philosophy* LXVIII, 5-20.

Frankfurt, Harry (1982). "The importance of what we care about." *Synthese* 53, 257-272.

Fried, Charles (1968). "Privacy." *Yale Law Journal* 77, 475-493. (Reprinted in Schoeman 1984, 203-222).

Fried, Charles (1970). An Anatomy of Values: *Problems of Personal and Social Choice*. Cambridge: Harvard University Press.

Garfield, Jay (1987). *Belief in Psychology*. Cambridge, Massachusetts: MIT Press.

Gavison, Ruth (1980). "Privacy and the limits of law." *Yale Law Journal* 89, 421-471. (Schoeman 1984, 346-402).

Gerstein, Robert (1978). "Intimacy and privacy." *Ethics* 89, 76-81. (Schoeman 1984, 265-271).

Gilligan, Carol (1982). *In A Different Voice: Psychological Theory and Women's Development*. Cambridge, Massachusetts: Harvard University Press.

Graham, G., and T. Horgan (1988). How to be realistic about folk psychology, *Philosophical Psychology* 1, 69-81.

Grice, P. (1957). "Meaning." *Philosophical Review*, 66.

Grice, P. (1969). "Utterer's meaning and intentions." *Philosophical Review*, 78.

Grünfeld, Joseph (1980). "Possible worlds and human freedom." *Logique et Analyse* 23, 431-436.

Gustafson, James (1973). "Mongolism, parental desires, and the right to life." *Perspectives in Biology and Medicine* 16.

Hanson, N. R. (1958). *Patterns of Discovery*. Cambridge: Cambridge University Press.

Hare, R. M. (1975), "Abortion and the Golden Rule." *Philosophy and Public Affairs* 4.

Harman, Gilbert (1977). *The Nature of Morality*. New York: Oxford University Press.

Harman, Gilbert (1986). *Change in View: Principles of Reasoning*. Cambridge, Massachusetts: MIT Press.

Harrison, Bernard (1970). "Violence and the Rule of Law," J. Shaffer, ed. *Violence*. New York: David McKay.

Hart, H. L. A. (1959). "The ascription of responsibility and rights," A. G. N. Flew, ed. *Essays on Logic and Language*, First Series. New York: Barnes and Noble.

Hart, H. L. A. (1961). *The Concept of Law*. Oxford: At the Clarendon Press.

Hart, H. L. A. (1973). "Bentham on Legal Rights," A. W. B. Simpson, ed., *Oxford Essays in Jurisprudence*, 2nd Series. Oxford: The Clarendon Press. 171-201.

Hart, H.L.A. (1979). "Between utility and rights," *The Idea of Freedom: Essays in Honor of Isaiah Berlin*, ed. Alan Ryan. Oxford; Oxford University Press.

The Hastings Center (1987). *Guidelines on the Termination of Life-Sustaining Treatment and the Care of the Dying*. Bloomington, Indiana: Indiana University Press.

The Hastings Center (1988). *Casebook on the Termination of Life-Sustaining Treatment and the Care of the Dying*, ed. Cynthia B. Cohen. Bloomington, Indiana: Indiana University Press.

Haugeland, John (1981). *Mind Design.* Cambridge, Massachusetts: Bradford/MIT Press.

Herrnstein, R., and J. Wilson (1985). *Crime and Human Nature.* New York: Simon & Schuster.

High, Dallas (1978). "Quality of life and the care of the dying person," Michael D. Bayles and Dallas M. High, eds. *Medical Treatment of the Dying: Moral Issues.* Cambridge, Massachusetts: Schenkman Publishing Co., 85-104.

Hill, Thomas (1973). "Servility and self-respect." *The Monist* 57, 87-104. (Reprinted in Wasserstrom 1979, 133-147).

Hofstadter, Douglas (1979). *Gödel, Escher, Bach: An Eternal Golden Braid.* New York: Basic Books.

Honderich, Ted, ed. (1985). *Morality and Objectivity.* London: Routledge and Kegan Paul.

Horgan, T., and J. Woodward (1985). "Folk psychlogy is here to stay." *Philosophical Review* 94, pp. 197-226.

Kitcher, Patricia (1979). "Natural kinds and unnatural persons." *Philosophy* 54, 541-547.

Kohlberg, Lawrence (1981). *The Philosophy of Moral Development.* San Francisco, California: Harper and Row.

Kohlberg, L., C. Levine, and A. Hewer (1983). *Moral Stages: A Current Formulation and a Response to Critics.* Basel: Karger.

Kohlberg, L., *et. al.* (1987). *Child Psychology and Childhood Education: A Cognitive-Developmental View.* New York and London: Longman.

Kripke, Saul (1980). *Naming and Necessity.* Cambridge,Massachusetts: Harvard University Press.

Kuhn, T. (1970). *The Structure of Scientific Revolutions,* 2nd edition. Chicago: University of Chicago Press.

Langford, Glenn (1978). "Persons as necessarily social." *Journal for the Theory of Social Behavior* 8, 263-283.

Leplin, Jarrett, ed. (1984). *Scientific Realism.* Berkeley: University of California Press.

Levin, Michael (1984). "What kind of explanation is truth?" Leplin 1984, 124-138.

Lewis, David (1984). "Possibilities: concrete worlds or abstract simples?." presented at Chapel Hill Philosophy Colloquium, October. (An extract from *On the Plurality of Worlds*, Blackwell.)

Loux, Michael (1979). *The Possible and the Actual*. Ithaca: Cornell University Press.

Lycan, W. G. (1969). "On intentionality and the psychological." *American Philosophical Quarterly*, October.

Lycan, W. G. (1987). *Consciousness*. Cambridge, Massachusetts: MIT/Bradford Press.

Lyons, David(1984). *Ethics and the Rule of Law*. New York: Cambridge U. Press.

Mackie, John (1977). *Ethics—Inventing Right and Wrong*. New York: Penguin.

Mappes,T., and J. Zembaty, eds. (1981). *Biomedical Ethics*. New York: Mc-Graw-Hill.

Margolis, Joseph (1978). *Persons and Minds: The Prospects of Nonreductive Materialism*. Dordrecht, Holland: D. Reidel.

Martin, Rex (1982). "On the justification of rights." Floistad 1982, 153-186.

Matthews, Gareth (1985). "The idea of a psychological organism." *Behaviorism* 13, 37-51.

Matthews, Gareth (1987). "Concept formation and Moral Development." Chapter 8 in James Russell, ed., *Philosophical Perspectives on Developmental Psychology*. Oxford: Blackwell's.

McCall, Storrs (1980). "What is quality of life?" *Philosophica* 25, 5-13.

McCloskey, H. J. (1979). "Moral rights and animals." *Inquiry* 22, 23-54. [Reprinted in Wasserstrom 1985, 479-505].

McCloskey, H. J. (1983). *Ecological Ethics and Politics*. Totowa, New Jersey: Rowman and Littlefield.

Melden, A. I.(1977). *Rights and Persons*. Berkeley and Los Angeles, California: University of California Press.

Mele, Alfred R. (1987). *Irrationality: An Essay on Akrasia, Self-Deception, and Self-Control*. New York: Oxford University Press.

Millikan, Ruth Garrett (1987). "Biosemantics." University of North Carolina, Chapel Hill, Philosophy Colloquium, October.

Montefiori, A., ed. (1973). *Philosophy and Personal Relations*. London: Routledge and Kegan Paul.

Morris, Herbert (1968). "Persons and punishment." *The Monist* 52. (Reprinted in Morris 1976.)

Morris, Herbert (1976). *On Guilt and Innocence: Essays in Legal Philosophy and Moral Psychology*. Berkeley and Los Angeles: University of California Press.

Murphy, Robert (1964). "Social distance and the veil." *American Anthropologist* 66, 1257-1274. (Reprinted in Schoeman 1984, 34-55).

Nagel, Thomas (1970a). *The Possibility of Altruism*. Oxford: Oxford University Press.

Nagel, Thomas (1970b). "Death." *Nous* IV, 73-80. (Reprinted, Rachels 1979.)

Nagel, Thomas (1974). "What is it like to be a bat?" *Philosophical Review* 83, 435-450. (Reprinted in Block 1980, 159-168.)

Newell, A., and H. Simon (1976), "Computer science as empirical inquiry: symbols and search," *Communications of the Association for Computing Machinery* 19, 113-126. (Reprinted in Haugeland 1981, 35-66.)

Nozick, Robert. (1974). *Anarchy, State, and Utopia*. New York: Basic Books.

Parfit, Derek (1973). "Later selves and moral principles." Montefiori 1973.

Parfit, Derek (1976). "Lewis, Perry, and what matters." In A. Rorty 1976, 91-107.

Parfit, Derek (1984). *Reasons and Persons*. Oxford: Clarendon Press.

Pears, David (1984). *Motivated Irrationality*. New York: Oxford University Press.

Penelhum, Terence (1971). "The importance of self-identity." *Journal of Philosophy* 68, 667-678.

Perry, John (1975). *Personal Identity*. Berkeley: University of California Press.

Perry, John (1976). "The importance of being identical." In A. Rorty 1976, 67-90.

Perry, John (1983). "Personal identity and the concept of a person." Floistad 1983, 11-43.

Posner, Richard (1978a). "An economic theory of privacy." *Regulation* (May/ June), 19-26. (Reprinted in Schoeman 1984, 333-345).

Posner, Richard (1978b). "The right of privacy." *Georgia Law Review* 12, 393-422.

Prosser, William (1960). "Privacy." *California Law Review* 48, 383-423. (Reprinted in Schoeman 1984, 104-155).

Puccetti, Roland (1968). *Persons: A Study of Possible Moral Agents in the Universe*. London: Macmillan.

Puccetti, Roland (1982). "The life of a person." Beauchamp and Walters 1982, 101-107.

Putnam, Hilary (1970). "Is semantics possible?" *Metaphilosophy* 3, 187-201.

Putnam, Hilary (1973a). "Reductionism and the nature of psychology." *Cognition* 2, 131-146. (Reprinted in Haugeland 1981, 205-219.)

Putnam, Hilary (1973b). "Meaning and reference." *Journal of Philosophy* 70, 699-711.

Putnam, Hilary (1975). *Mind, Language, and Reality, Philosophical Papers*, vl. 2. London: Cambridge University Press.

Putnam, Hilary (1978). "What is realism?" *Meaning and the Moral Sciences*. London: Routledge and Kegan Paul. (Reprinted in Leplin 1984, 140-153.)

Quine, W. V. O. (1960). *Word and Object*. Cambridge, Massachusetts: Harvard University Press.

Rachels, James, ed. (1979). *Moral Problems*, 3rd edition. New York: Harper and Row.

Rawls, John (1971). *A Theory of Justice*. Cambridge, Massachusetts: Harvard University Press.

Raz, J. (1982). "The problem about the nature of law." Floistad 1982, 107-125.

Regan, Tom (1980). *Matters of Life and Death*. Philadelphia: Temple University Press.

Regan, Tom (1983). *The Case for Animal Rights*. Berkeley and Los Angeles: University of California Press.

Reiman, Jeffrey (1976). "Privacy, intimacy, and personhood." *Philosophy and Public Affairs* 6, 26-44. (Wasserstrom 1979, 377-391).

Robertson, John (1975). "Involuntary euthanasia of defective newborns." *Stanford Law Review* 27, 251-261.

Rolston, Holmes (1982). "The irreversibly comatose: respect for the subhuman in human life." *Journal of Medicine and Philosophy* 7, 337-354.

Rorty, Amélie, ed. (1976). *The Identities of Persons*. Berkeley and Los Angeles: The University of California Press.

Rorty, R. (1979). *Philosophy and the Mirror of Nature*. Princeton, New Jersey: Princeton University Press.

Rosenberg, Jay (1983). *Thinking Clearly About Death*. Englewood Cliffs: Prentice-Hall, Inc.

Ruddick, Sara (1985), "Better sex." Wasserstrom 1979, 1985.

Sayre-McCord, Geoffrey, ed. (1988a). *Essays on Moral Realism*. Ithaca, New York: Cornell University Press.

Sayre-McCord, Geoffrey (1988b). "Moral Theory and Explanatory Impotence." In Sayre-McCord 1988a.

Schoeman, Ferdinand, ed.(1984). *Philosophical Dimensions of Privacy: An Anthology*. New York: Cambridge University Press.

Schoeman, Ferdinand (1984a). "Privacy: philosophical dimensions of the literature." Schoeman 1984, 1-33.

Schoeman, Ferdinand (1984b). "Privacy and intimate information." Schoeman 1984, 403-418.

Searle, John (1980). "Minds, brains, and programs." *Behaviorial and Brain Sciences* 3, 417-457. (Reprinted in Haugeland 1981).

Searle, John (1982). "What is an intentional state?" Dreyfus 1982, 259-276.

Searle, John (1983). *Intentionality*. Cambridge: Cambridge University Press.

Shoemaker, Sydney (1963). *Self-knowledge and Self-identity*. Ithaca, New York: Cornell University Press.

Shoemaker, Sydney (1976). "Embodiment and behavior." In Rorty 1976, 109-137.

Smart, J. J. C. (1970). "Sensations and brain processes." C. V. Borst, ed., *The Mind/Brain Identity Theory*. London: Macmillan.

Spicker, S., and T. Engelhardt, Jr. (eds.) (1977). *Philosophical Medical Ethics: Its Nature and Significance*. Dordrecht, Holland: D. Reidel.

Stevenson, Ian (1975). *Cases of the Reincarnation Type*. Vol. I, *Ten Cases in India*. Charlottesville: University of Virginia Press.

Stich, S. (1983). *From Folk Psychology to Cognitive Science*. Cambridge, Massachusetts: Bradford/MIT Press.

Stoutland, Frederick (1982). "Philosophy of action: Davidson, von Wright, and the debate over causation." Floistad 1982, 45-72.

Taylor, Gabriele (1985). *Pride, Shame, and Guilt: Emotions of Self-Assessment*. Oxford: Clarendon Press.

Taylor, Paul (1986). *Respect for Nature: A Theory of Environmental Ethics*. Princeton, New Jersey: Princeton University Press.

Taylor, Richard (1969). "How to bury the mind-body problem." *American Philosophical Quarterly* 6, 136-143.

Thomson, Judith (1971). "A defense of abortion." *Philosophy and Public Affairs* 1, 47-66.

Thomson, Judith (1975). "The right to privacy." *Philosophy and Public Affairs* 4, 295-314. (Schoeman 1984, 272-289).

Veatch, Robert (1976). *Death, Dying, and the Biological Revolution: Our Last Quest for Responsibility*. New Haven: Yale University Press.

Vlastos, G. (1962). "Justice and Equality." *Social Justice*, ed. R.B. Brandt. Englewood Cliffs, N.J.: Prentice-Hall.

Wagner, Paul (1983). "The idea of a moral person." *J. Thought* 18, 85-96.

Walton, Douglas N.(1979). *On Defining Death: An Analytic Study of the Concept of Death in Philosophy and Medical Ethics.* Montreal: McGill-Queen's University Press.

Warren, Mary (1973), "On the moral and legal status of abortion." *The Monist* 57, 43-61.

Warren, Mary (1977). "Do potential people have moral rights?" *Canadian Journal of Philosophy* VII, 275-289.

Warren, Mary (1979, 1985). "On the moral and legal status of abortion." Wasserstrom 1979, 1985.

Warren, Samuel, and Louis Brandeis (1890). "The right to privacy." *Harvard Law Review* 4, 193-220. (Reprinted in Schoeman 1984, 75-103).

Wasserstrom, Richard (1964). "Rights, human rights, and racial discrimination." *Journal of Philosophy* 61. (Reprinted in Rachels 1979.)

Wasserstrom, Richard (1979a, 1985). *Today's Moral Problems*, 2nd & 3rd ed. New York: Macmillan.

Wasserstrom, Richard (1979b). "Privacy." Wasserstrom 1979a, 392-408.

Wasserstrom, Richard (1980). "Punishment." In his *Philosophy and Social Issues: Five Studies.* Notre Dame: University of Notre Dame Press, 112-151.

Wellman, Carl (1971). *Challenge and Response: Justification in Ethics.* Carbondale: Southern Illnois University Press.

Wellman, Carl (1985). *A Theory of Rights: Persons Under Laws, Institutions, and Morals.* Totowa, New Jersey: Rowman and Allanheld.

Wellman, H. (1985). "The Child's Theory of Mind: The Development of Conceptions of Cognition." In Yessen, S. ed., *The Growth of Reflection.* San Diego: Academic Press.

Werner, Richard (1979). "Abortion: the ontological and moral status of the unborn." Wasserstrom 1979, 51-73.

Westin, Alan (1967). "The origin of modern claims to privacy." From *Privacy and Freedom.* New York: Atheneum Press. (Reprinted in Schoeman 1984, 56-74.)

Wiggins, David (1967). *Identity and Spatio-temporal Continuity*. Oxford: Blackwell.

Wiggins, David (1976). "Locke, Butler and the stream of consciousness: and men as natural kind." A. Rorty 1976, 139-173.

Williams, Bernard (1973). "The Makropulos case: reflections on the tedium of immortality." In his *Problems of the Self*. Cambridge: Cambridge University Press.

Williams, Bernard (1976). "Persons, character and morality." Rorty 1976, 197-216.

Williams, Bernard (1985). *Ethics and the Limits of Philosophy*. Cambridge: Harvard University Press.

Winch, Peter (1965). "The universalizability of moral judgments." *Monist* 49.

Woozley, A.D. (1977). "Euthanasia and the principle of harm." *Philosophy and Public Policy*, ed. D. Self. Old Dominion Research Foundation, 1977. (Reprinted in Rachels 1979).

Young, Fredric (1979). "On Dennett's conditions of personhood." *Auslegung* 6, 161-177.

INDEX

197